TAKING OR MAKING WEALTH?

TAKING OR MAKING WEALTH?

EDITED BY
ANTHONY HALL

BREAKOUT EDUCATIONAL NETWORK
IN ASSOCIATION WITH
DUNDURN PRESS
TORONTO · OXFORD

Publisher: Inta D. Erwin
Copy-editor: Amanda Stewart, First Folio Resource Group
Designer: Bruna Brunelli, Brunelli Designs
Printer: Webcom

National Library of Canada Cataloguing in Publication Data

Taking or making wealth?/edited by Anthony Hall.

One of the 16 vols. and 14 hours of video which make up the
    underground royal commission report
Includes bibliographical references and index.
ISBN 1-55002-420-5

    1. Fiscal policy — Canada. 2. Regionalism — Canada. 3. Canada —
Economic conditions — Regional disparities. I. Hall, Anthony
II. Title: underground royal commission report.

HC115.t28 2003   336.3'0971   C2003-902300-9

1   2   3   4   5   07   06   05   04   03

Printed and bound in Canada.
Printed on recycled paper. ♻
www.dundurn.com

Exclusive Canadian broadcast rights for the *underground royal commission* report

intelligent television

Check your cable or satellite listings for telecast times

Visit the *urc* Web site link at:
www.ichanneltv.com

About the *underground royal commission* Report

Since September 11, 2001, there has been an uneasy dialogue among Canadians as we ponder our position in the world, especially vis à vis the United States. Critically and painfully, we are re-examining ourselves and our government. We are even questioning our nation's ability to retain its sovereignty.

The questions we are asking ourselves are not new. Over the last 30 years, and especially in the dreadful period of the early 1990s, leading up to the Quebec referendum of 1995, inquiries and Royal commissions, one after another, studied the state of the country. What *is* new is that eight years ago, a group of citizens looked at this parade of inquiries and commissions and said, "These don't deal with the real issues." They wondered how it was possible for a nation that was so promising and prosperous in the early 60s to end up so confused, divided, and troubled. And they decided that what was needed was a different kind of investigation — driven from the grassroots 'bottom,' and not from the top. Almost as a provocation, this group of people, most of whom were affiliated with the award winning documentary-maker, Stornoway Productions, decided to do it themselves — and so was born the *underground royal commission*!

What began as a television documentary soon evolved into much more. Seven young, novice researchers, hired right out of university, along with a television crew and producer, conducted interviews with people in government, business, the military and in all walks of life, across the country. What they discovered went beyond anything they had expected. The more they learned, the larger the implications grew. The project continued to evolve and has expanded to include a total of 23 researchers over the last several years. The results are the 14 hours of video and 16 books that make up the first interim report of the *underground royal commission*.

So what *are* the issues? The report of the *underground royal commission* clearly shows us that regardless of region, level of government, or political party, we are operating under a wasteful system ubiquitously lacking in accountability. An ever-weakening connection between the electors and the elected means that we are slowly and irrevocably losing our right to know our government. The researchers' experiences demonstrate that it is almost impossible for a member of the public, or in most cases, even for a member of Parliament, to actually trace how our tax dollars are spent. Most disturbing is the fact that our young people have been stuck with a crippling IOU that has effectively hamstrung their future. No wonder, then, that Canada is not poised for reaching its potential in the 21st century.

The *underground royal commission* report, prepared in large part by and for the youth of Canada, provides the hard evidence of the problems you and I may long have suspected. Some of that evidence makes it clear that, as ordinary Canadians, we are every bit as culpable as our politicians — for our failure to demand accountability, for our easy acceptance of government subsidies and services established without proper funding in place, and for the disservice we have done to our young people through the debt we have so blithely passed on to them. But the real purpose of the *underground royal commission* is to ensure that we better understand how government processes work and what role we play in them. Public policy issues must be understandable and accessible to the public if they are ever to be truly addressed and resolved. The *underground royal commission* intends to continue pointing the way for bringing about constructive change in Canada.

— Stornoway Productions

14 hours of videos also available with the *underground royal commission* report.
Visit Stornoway Productions at www.stornoway.com for a list of titles.

TABLE OF CONTENTS

VIEWS FROM CENTRAL CANADA

CLOSING THOUGHTS
— TAXATION AND THE UNDERGROUND ECONOMY

INTRODUCTION

Canadians from every region of the country have a long experience with government policies, programs and structures designed to further economic goals. Our history provides an exhausting list of examples particularly, though not exclusively, designed by the federal government and meant to achieve economic benefits. *Taking or Making Wealth?* examines this history in a collection of edited interviews that provides a survey of the results of such intervention in Canada's regions, from east to west.

The contributors to this volume generally share similar views about what this economic participation, funded by the taxpayer, has brought about. It should not surprise most Canadians who are familiar with one misguided government program or another that the contributors' judgments are hardly favourable. We should attach much weight to the views expressed in these conversations since, as the reader will discover, they are insights from "expert witnesses."

The edited conversations that comprise this volume trace their origins to a documentary television series, *Days of Reckoning*, which was produced by the Breakout Educational Network and Stornoway Productions. In that series seven young Canadians travelled across the country to uncover the truth behind 30 years of out-of-control public spending and the devastating disregard for its long-term consequences. In essence, a compelling brief for the prosecution was assembled. On trial were the elected politicians and the voters who had allowed spend-thrift policies to mortgage the futures of succeeding generations of young Canadians. Viewers of that series would be hard-pressed not to return a guilty verdict. The researchers compiled hundreds of hours of "expert evidence" for the television project, but time constraints permitted only brief extracts to be included in the completed project.

Taking or Making Wealth? offers a "user-friendly" exposition of insights from a unique assembly of knowledgeable speakers. As a colleague has reminded me, readers should be encouraged to listen to, rather than simply look at, the text. The various contributions, after all, started out as dialogues in which leading figures from the field under examination addressed their opinions to a panel of young Canadians. It will become evident to the reader that the panel feels a deep sense of moral indignation about government practices that blur the lines of accountability and obscure the real effects of misguided programs.

The title of this collection of interviews, *Taking or Making Wealth?*, describes the difference between the actual consequences of federal government intervention into certain economic sectors and the original aim of such initiatives. In short, the reader will discover the coast-to-coast history of failure of programs such as the Atlantic Canada Opportunities Agency or instruments like the Canadian Wheat Board, in terms of actually achieving the ends they were intended to bring about. Moreover, this analysis comes from people who have direct and comprehensive knowledge of this history.

Readers of *Taking or Making Wealth?* may further examine the consequences of misguided government economic and administrative policies in a companion volume, *Guardians on Trial*, a collection of edited conversations providing a broad analysis of government with an Ottawa-centred focus.

Anthony Hall
Barrie, Ontario
March 29, 2002

BRIAN CROWLEY

An Overview: Making or Taking?

The most fundamental force driving the economy is innovation. It's change. It's when people see new ways of doing things, new ways of using the resources they have at their disposal, and they change their traditional activities to produce new goods, new services and new value.

The decline in economic growth rates and the growth in unemployment, even in times of strong economic growth, come from some very fundamental causes. They come from the shifts in the way we have run the economy in Canada over the last 30 or 40 years. We have progressively moved to a system in Canada where innovation is harder and harder to achieve. One of the reasons for that is that government has begun to take a larger and larger place in the economy. Government is an agency that almost has to be involved in any kind of investment that private companies make these days. Many of them want government approval or government involvement before they will make any decisions. Many of them want government approval before they lay off workers, before they close plants. Government is involved in almost every economic decision that is made.

The reason that this has contributed to a sort of seizing up of the economy is because government has created an expectation in many people's minds that it can remove everything that is unpleasant in their lives, everything that is difficult, everything that might affect their jobs and everything that might affect their health. In fact, over the last 30 years we have seen government take control of something like 40 percent of the gross domestic product. In other words, 40 percent of the value of the goods and services that we produce in Canada passes through the hands of government. They've become a huge redistributive machine.

When you think about how the economy works, you know that the economy is made up of people who want to make themselves better off. They want to get more. They want to live better. They want to have nicer homes. They want to have better cars, etc. There are basically two ways that people can make themselves better off. They can either make wealth or they can take wealth.

Look, for example, at anybody who is involved in the production of a good or service that they sell in the marketplace, in other words, that people buy voluntarily. You offer your service and somebody comes along and says, "I want that, here's some money for it," and they take it. Everybody is made better off by that transaction. You're made better off because you prefer to have the money instead of the product or service. The buyer would rather have the service you provide than the money that he or she had. That transaction has made everybody better off. That's what I call making. That's making productivity. That's making economic wealth. Taking, on the other hand, involves some agency stepping in and saying, "You have something that this other person over here should have, so I'm taking it from you and giving it to them. OK?" That's taking.

Now, as I said earlier, government plays a huge redistributive role in society. They are the principal agency of taking as opposed to making. What's happened is that as the size of government has grown, more and more of us — and believe me, every one of us is involved in some way — have become part of the taking activity. We all receive some kind of good or service from government that is subsidized by the general taxpayers. And that includes people who are at university. It includes people who watch the CBC. It includes people who buy goods and services that have some kind of government subsidy in them. We're all involved. As the size of government has grown, more and more people have developed an interest in the activity of taking rather than the activity of making.

Almost everything that the government does involves some element of redistribution. For example, unemployment insurance is a system in which employees who are rarely laid off, who rarely need unemployment insurance, transfer part of their wealth to workers who are frequently laid off or who are perhaps seasonal workers. It's not just workers that are making that transfer, but also employers. Employers are subsidizing other employers whose labour costs would otherwise be higher.

There are all sorts of subsidies that are paid to businesses to invest in places like Atlantic Canada because there are economic disparities between regions of the country. There are things like tariffs. On goods that you and I might like to buy abroad, the price is raised by the government through tariffs so that people in Canada are forced to buy from domestic producers who can't produce as cheaply as foreigners. Milk marketing boards that allow farmers to restrict the supply of milk and therefore drive up the cost — that is a cost to you and me. That's a taking from you and me as consumers that goes straight into the pocket of the milk producers.

Most people know that governments in Atlantic Canada have been very active in promoting industrial development in this region, partly because of the tremendous economic disparities which separate Atlantic Canada from, say, places like Ontario, Alberta and British Columbia. Essentially governments try to identify employers who are going to perhaps hire new people and they give them a subsidy. Well, not everybody is qualified for the subsidy. Successful businesses by and large don't qualify for subsidies from government. However, successful businesses pay taxes. So we have a system in which successful businesses can't get support from government because they're too successful, but they are taxed so that the tax money that comes from them goes to subsidize their competitors who are less successful.

We therefore have a system in Atlantic Canada in which weaker companies are rewarded and supported by government through a taking, through a transfer at the expense of those companies that are more successful at making things, more successful at getting in the market and supplying goods and services that people actually want. So there's a perverse kind of incentive at work here.

Another example is the unemployment insurance system. It's a system that pays people an important percentage of their wages after they've lost their job, but on certain conditions. For instance, you can't be a full-time student and get unemployment insurance. We all know that in the modern world people who aren't able to upgrade their education become less and less employable. So you've got a perverse incentive in the system against people on unemployment getting the kind of education they need in order to get off unemployment. You can't make more than 25 percent of your benefit through part-time work before you start losing every dollar that you earn through losses in benefits. So again we've got an incentive against people being productive, even on a part-time basis, while they're on unemployment insurance. Far better that you do nothing or work in the black market than have a regular part-time job and be part of the above-ground economy.

I think these are both examples of government creating a system of transfers from people who are making wealth to people who for various reasons are unable to produce wealth. The problem with this system, and this is the really key element, is that it creates huge, powerful vested interests that are in favour of the system as it exists. The more money that is transferred to people through government, the more people there will be within society who have an interest in keeping government large and active, with its fingers in various parts of the economy. Back when government only handled 20 or 25 percent of the gross domestic product, people didn't spent a lot of time thinking about government and thinking about how they could get extra benefits out of government. They had to put their efforts into the private economy, into finding goods and services that people actually wanted to buy. What's happened, now that government has almost reached the point where half of the value of the economy is passing through government's hands, is that people see that it's in their interest to spend a lot more time putting their energies into taking than into making. And that's getting worse and worse all the time.

I think the crucial feature of the inertia that seems to have struck the economy in all parts of the country is the kind of asymmetry in this system, where it's very easy to get benefits out of government. It's very easy for groups to organize and ask for a specific benefit, whether it's a tariff or a wage subsidy or a subsidy for investment, whatever it is. It's very hard for government to stop paying a benefit once they've started because paying a benefit creates a group which has an interest in keeping that benefit, and they will lobby till the cows come home in order to defend that interest.

One of our most fundamental problems is that we've created a government structure or system whose size is growing all the time, and as its size grows the momentum toward further growth continues and it becomes more difficult to rein in government. It becomes more difficult to orient people toward making rather than taking. On the contrary, everybody's interest becomes more and more in taking and less and less in making. And when you consider that economic growth flows, in the vast majority of cases, from innovation, from change and from transferring resources from one use to another where they're more productive, that is a huge drag on the economy and one that we have not begun to come to terms with.

The role of government is a question that many people ask themselves because a lot of people have come to understand that government is trying to do too much. We were talking about inertia and about innovation, and perhaps innovation is the opposite of inertia. I think people have lost sight of what it is that really drives economic growth. Many people have come to assume that economic growth happens because government identifies a growth sector, then entices companies to move into it and pays subsidies, and that's the way a new sector of the economy emerges. In fact, if you look at the studies, it seems to me crystal clear that government is very poor at picking the growth sectors of the future.

One example of inappropriate investment decisions by government in Atlantic Canada is the heavy-water plant in Port Hawkesbury on Cape Breton Island, which was built in order to supply heavy water to the Canadian nuclear reactor industry. At the time the plant was built everybody thought it was going to be a huge export industry for Canada. In fact it has turned out to be a minor, reasonably successful industry, but certainly not big enough to support a heavy-water plant of that size. We could look at Clairtone, which received a huge government subsidy in order to make consumer electronic equipment. We could look at the famous greenhouse that the government in Newfoundland built on the island in order to grow cucumbers. The list just goes on and on and on.

I don't have a dollar figure for any individual project but certainly we know that, for instance, literally billions of dollars have been poured into the Sydney steel plant. Of course, the people who worked in those plants benefited from the money. But all the studies that I've seen have shown that the benefits that went to the workers in those plants were bought at a huge cost to the taxpayer, often a cost of $100,000 a year and more per job. So clearly those jobs would not be sustainable in the private sector. They are jobs that are created and sustained solely because taxpayers in other parts of the country are prepared to send a part of their wealth to keep them going.

Accountability is an interesting concept. Accountability for politicians is not at all the same thing as accountability for someone in private industry. And let me explain what I think the difference is.

In private industry accountability flows to the bottom line. If you make a profit and you can pay a dividend to your shareholders, you're regarded as successful. Now, what is profit? Profit is a signal from consumers that they find you're producing something useful. So if you make a profit, you are doing something good in the economy. That's not at all the signal that indicates success for politicians. Politicians aren't interested in making money. Indeed, they can tax us. They can have as much money as they wish. A signal of success for a politician is finding a job for a constituent who is then going to vote for that politician. Politicians need to win elections; they don't need to satisfy shareholders. And indeed, if you look at the way many of these projects work, the benefits are all up front.

Let's say you build some sort of industrial plant in Cape Breton, New Brunswick, Newfoundland, northern Alberta or northern British Columbia. Let's say you put a $100-million subsidy into it and it hires 4,000 workers and those people work for five years. Well, you can be darned sure that between the time that subsidy is paid and the time the subsidy runs out an election will fall. The guy who paid the subsidy will get some votes out of it, and by the time the subsidy has dried up and the business has failed, some other politician is in office and he's got to deal with the problem.

It's very important that people understand that the incentive system for politicians is radically different, and so is their time horizon, if it comes to that. What's important to a politician is the next election and the next election is two, three, four — at the very most five — years away. But in private business your time horizon may be 20 years away. If you are in the insurance business and you take my life insurance premium, you are promising me that in 25 years you will be able to pay me back some agreed sum of money. You've got to take a very long view of what's going to happen with that money in order to do that kind of business successfully. When you consider that many kinds of business need to take that long view in order to be successful, you understand why it is that when politicians begin to get involved in these kinds of economic decisions, they often don't do a good job of it.

Let me give you a couple of concrete examples of how innovation works and why politicians or people in government are put at a distinct disadvantage by the nature of innovation.

I play the bagpipes. A fellow I know makes Highland paraphernalia: he makes skeans, those little daggers you put in the top of your socks, and he makes sporrans and bagpipe fittings. One day as he was reading the newspaper his eye just happened to fall on an advertisement, a call for tenders from an aircraft company. They were looking for subcontractors to make aircraft parts. He looked at the ad and realized that with the equipment he had for making Highland paraphernalia, he could make the aircraft parts that were being described in the ad. As a result he put in a tender. He won the contract and now employs 12 people making aircraft parts as well as maintaining his original business making Highland paraphernalia. Now, if you were somebody in government trying to identify people to whom you can give a grant to make aircraft parts, this guy would never have applied because he wasn't an aircraft-parts maker. He was a bagpipe-parts maker. It was because he stumbled across an extra bit of information that made him think of himself and his equipment and his workers in a new way. He was able to create new value for people. He was able to put things into the economy that other people valued enough to pay for.

There's another example from the town of Springhill, Nova Scotia, up near the New Brunswick border. If you ask many people what the town of Springhill was, for many years they would have said to you, "It's a clapped-out coal-mining town." Back at the turn of the century it was still an active coal-mining town, but the coal mines got worked out and the place went into what most people thought was a long, terminal decline. Then one day in the middle of winter a man was out walking his dog in Springhill. It was a snowy day and he saw a little patch of ground where there was steam rising and the snow had melted. He says, "What's going on here?" He went away and asked a few questions, did a little digging, and he discovered that water had been leaking into the old mineshaft under the town and had been heating geothermally. A whole new industrial park has been built in Springhill, exploiting that cheap energy source that nobody knew existed until that man went out and walked his dog.

If government were the agent of economic development, how would government know these things? It couldn't. It's only through innovation, through people putting together disparate bits of information and knowledge and coming up with something new that economic value is created. You can't do that sitting around a table in Ottawa, or indeed in the ACOA headquarters in Moncton, because it's only people on the ground who have an intimate knowledge of the time and the circumstances, and who understand consumers and what they want. Even the people who come up with these innovations often don't understand the nature of what they have discovered. When Coca-Cola was first put on the market it was marketed as a mouthwash. Consumers came around and said, "Hey, this is a lousy mouthwash, but I like to drink it." And it became the most successful consumer product in the history of the human race.

There are lots of other examples. When the motor car was invented, the people who invented it thought that the number of motor cars in the world would forever be limited by one factor, and that was the number of members of the working class intelligent enough to be trained as chauffeurs. They completely misunderstood what they had created. It was only when they put the idea out in the marketplace of a self-propelled vehicle with an internal combustion engine that other people said, "I can add value to that." Henry Ford came along and created mass production and other people created a whole series of other innovations, all of which were piled onto that original idea, creating an industry that now employs millions of people throughout the world, and none of which could have been foreseen by the political authorities. At the time the motor car was first being introduced, government authorities everywhere tried to discourage it. Why? Take the horse industry in North America. At that time there were 20 million horses and a huge industry for saddle makers, nail makers and blacksmiths, and hay was a major cash crop. All that has been swept away. It doesn't exist anymore. You can't go to a community college and become a blacksmith.

You can, however, go to a community college and take courses in 100 different professions that did not exist before the automobile was invented. If we had allowed politicians to do what politicians do so well, which is to stop innovation because innovation threatens established interests, we would still be riding horses and we would still be growing hay and we would still be making horseshoes. And we would be much less well off than we are today.

When you think about what makes business successful, it is all about managing risk. Business is all about managing risk. And governments can do things that increase risk and governments can do things that decrease risk. One of the most important things they can do to decrease risk is guarantee people the value of their currency. In other words, if I'm going to invest a dollar in a car plant or in a fish plant or in railway infrastructure today, I want to have a pretty good idea of what my dollar is going be worth in 10 years, 15 years, 20 years or 25 years because that's going to influence how much I can pay in interest and a whole series of other things. Government controls the value of money. That may be a good thing, or it may be a bad thing. It's just a fact. And if government doesn't guarantee us a stable value to our currency, they increase the risk that businesspeople undertake in every aspect of their work.

Government can also increase risk for business by all of a sudden coming up with new regulations, new taxes, new obstacles to doing business. Remember that businesses are not in a stable environment. Every day in the marketplace they have to meet competitors who are constantly striving to do a job better than they are. If government is constantly throwing obstacles in their path, such as obstacles to innovation and obstacles to change, and if they can't change the way they deal with the environment, then they're putting these businesspeople in Canada at a competitive disadvantage with their competitors all around the world who don't face those obstacles.

Government has a tendency to change things like taxes and regulations from year to year. If they said to business, "Look, you're going to pay this tax rate and we know it's fairly high but we're going to guarantee you that tax rate for 10 years or 15 years or 20 years," most businesspeople would say, "OK, it's a high tax but I can organize my work around it if I know that that's what I have to deal with." But if they're going to come back next year and say, "Well, actually we need to raise it, and maybe next year it's going to be up again," they're creating additional risk over and above those ones that are created for business-people by competition. Competition is what keeps businesspeople honest. Competition is what keeps them improving productivity. It keeps them improving investment. It keeps them improving employment all the time. But the kind of obstacles that government puts in their path don't contribute to that healthy regulation which competition imposes on them. They merely increase the risks that businesspeople have to face, and therefore have difficulty managing because they can't predict.

One final role for government which I think is absolutely essential is that of investing in certain kinds of infrastructure or common services that it wouldn't pay private business to provide. I have no objection to government taxing us or indeed borrowing money if it is to invest it in the economy in a way that will make the economy more productive. Government is no good at doing that if it's trying to choose businesses that are going to be winners. On the other hand, it's actually quite good at investing in things like highways, railways, education and improving our human capital. Private business, in the current climate anyway, has difficulty doing that and making a profit at it, and there are all sorts of reasons why that is. That's a role that government needs to play and indeed, if they are investing in a productive future for Canada, there can be no objection to their spending or borrowing to do that. So that's quite important to establish.

When we come to the question of government debt, let me say a couple of preliminary things. We talked a lot about the way in which there's a shift going on in Canada away from being productive in the economic sense, from making to taking. In other words getting benefits from government that government takes from other people.

One of the forces that is driving the growth of government borrowing and the debt is that we have probably reached the limit of what taxpayers are willing to take out of their pocket. I mean money they'll take out to transfer to other people in the form of subsidies to industries, such as unemployment insurance and welfare. The debt represents a way of making people who aren't even alive yet pay those costs today. That's what the debt is. The debt is a transfer to future generations of the cost of things we are consuming now. That's when government borrows in order to subsidize taking and not to invest in those things that make the economy more productive, like infrastructure. That's a very important distinction to make.

We have reached a point, if I am not mistaken, where over 40 percent of the value of goods and services produced in the economy is taken by the government in the form of taxation. That's huge. I'm absolutely convinced that one of the factors behind the growth of the underground economy, for instance, is the fact that the tax burden has reached a stage where people prefer to deal in cash and go underground than to pass through the tax system and have so much of the fruits of their effort taken by government. I don't think people have any objection to government taking a legitimate share of their income in order to provide services. We all agree they are needed by people who are less well off in our society, in order to fund medicare, in order to provide a world-class education system, in order to provide infrastructure that is necessary to make the economy work. But we've gone far beyond that. We have created a system in which there are huge transfers of money going from productive people in the economy who are making goods and services to people who find it's more profitable to get benefits from government than to get out and work in the marketplace.

Many of the programs that were put in place with the best of intentions have turned out not to be the social safety net that we all hoped for. We thought they would be a temporary helping hand along the way for people who had fallen sick or gotten on unemployment insurance or whatever.

If we take people on unemployment insurance as an example, the trend has been upward even during the boom years of the 1980s. After the recession at the beginning of the 1980s we enjoyed six or seven years of really stellar economic growth, but the number of unemployment beneficiaries continued to go up. It seems to me that we have created a system in which it is easy for people to drop out of the productive economy. I'm not saying, by the way, that those people are lazy or they're welfare bums or anything else. Those people are responding entirely rationally to a set of incentives that we have put into place. If you are a fish plant worker in Newfoundland and you know there are hundreds of people in your village but there are only 40 or 50 jobs in the local fish plant, it makes perfect sense for the community to get together and parcel out those jobs in 10-week slices, because once you work for 10 weeks, your income is then guaranteed for the rest of the year. "We don't have to worry about you. Bring on the next person." These are ways in which we have created an incentive system for communities to look after themselves at the expense of other workers in other kinds of industries, and I don't blame those people for doing that.

I think the systems were put into place with the best of intentions, but they were bad systems. The incentives need to be changed fundamentally so that people cannot look on these systems as a way of life. I think it's entirely appropriate that we put in place systems that help people across some of life's crises. It's entirely appropriate that we put in place programs that help people who cannot, for physical or other reasons, be a part of the productive economy. But as a society we cannot afford to pay people who are able to be part of that productive economy not to participate in it. The only way that we have been able to do so over the last few years is by passing on the cost to future generations, and they will find that the public services they'll get will be infinitely inferior to those we're able to get now. Yet their cost, in terms of taxes and so on, will be just as high, if not higher, because of the miracle of compound interest. We've borrowed all kinds of money and we're paying interest on it every year.

The hard fact is that there is not an infinite amount of money in the world. We're talking about the government borrowing $39 billion this year, and getting it down after what they want us to believe are huge exertions. That means that if the federal government is out there borrowing — let's use a round figure of $40 billion a year — not counting the provincial governments or municipal governments, that's $40 billion that is going on consumption today, that is going out in terms of all kinds of benefit cheques or salaries to civil servants, whatever it is. That's money that is not available for private industry to invest in productive capacity in order to build the economy in the future. We have to be investing now if we want to be more productive in the future. So if there isn't an infinite quantity of money in the world and governments are borrowing $40 billion a year, they are in competition with people who want to make more productive uses of that money.

The thing is that because government can afford to pay whatever it needs to pay in order to borrow that money, it will often price capital out of the area that private business can pay. By driving up the cost of borrowing, government is therefore reducing our ability to be productive in the future. That's problem number one with the debt. Problem number two is that the size of the debt has now reached the point where it's roughly equal to one year's entire gross domestic product of Canada, and that's only the most visible kind of debt. There are all kinds of other debt that send it through the stratosphere.

What happens when you ask someone to lend you money? Well, most people are actually fond of their money. They don't want to lose it. So if I'm going to give you $100, first I'm going ask myself, "What are the chances this guy's going to be able to pay me back?" We have reached the point in Canada where investors are asking themselves that question about the Government of Canada. "If I give the Government of Canada money, how likely is it that they are going to be able to pay me back?" For years nobody would have even thought about asking that question because Canada has traditionally been such a good credit risk. We've got such a big, productive economy that it didn't seem to be a question worth asking. We have now borrowed so much money that it's a question very much worth asking.

What happens when people begin to have doubts about whether or not you'll be able to pay back? They begin to say, "Well, if I'm going to lend you my money, you're really going to have to make it worth my while because I'm taking a bigger risk with you." The cost of borrowing is going up all the time. That borrowing is added on to the debt and so on and it becomes a vicious circle. The more we borrow, the more we have to pay. The more we have to pay, the less able we are to pay it back. The next time we have to borrow, the price goes up. And so on.

We have reached the point where I don't believe there's room to raise taxes any further. We are rapidly coming to the point where either people won't lend to us at all or they will lend to us at rates of interest so high that even the Government of Canada won't be able to pay them. To my mind that leaves only one alternative, which is to begin to examine the way in which we have let government grow over the last 30 years and ask ourselves if there aren't some hard choices we have to make.

One of the problems with making cuts in government is that everything that government does, does something good for somebody. You have to be prepared to say, "We know that this government program does something good for you, but we cannot do all good things for all people." And there are some good things that are more important than others, and those are the things we have to do first. We have been unwilling to establish priorities, unwilling to ask ourselves the hard questions about what really needs to be done. We have allowed the system to grow in a way where it's infinitely easier to create a new benefit, to give a new kind of cheque, a new kind of program to people, than it is to shut down an existing program. The pressures are always to increase expenditures of government, the programs and the borrowing. But this cannot go on forever. I think we are rapidly running out of capacity to continue the way we have been.

Let me give you a good example from Atlantic Canada, with respect to this system where it's much easier to give benefits than it is to reduce them or end programs. There's nothing unique about this in Atlantic Canada. This goes on in every corner of the country. Suppose that you have a steel plant, as we do in Sydney, and in order to keep that steel plant operating you need a $1-million subsidy. You go to government and you ask for the $1 million. There are about one million people in Nova Scotia, so that's about $1 apiece. A dollar apiece, no big deal. So the government taxes everybody and gives the money to the steel plant.

Let's say there are 100 people working in that steel plant. I, as a taxpayer, pay $1. You, as a steel plant worker, get a benefit of $10,000. You're going to fight like the devil to keep that subsidy. On the other hand, I'm only paying $1. The interest that I have in organizing to end that subsidy is tiny. The incentive that you have to fight to keep it is huge. Of course, the ordinary MLA in Nova Scotia who represents the ordinary Nova Scotia taxpayer doesn't get very much pressure from his or her constituents to cut a program like that; it's only costing each person $1 every year. The people who represent the town where the steel plant is located get huge pressure from a very concentrated, well-identified group in their community who want that subsidy continued because they realize huge benefits from it. Indeed, if you think about it, if you were getting, say, a $10,000 subsidy every year from the taxpayer, it would be worth your while to pay $9,000 a year to defend it because you'd still be $1,000 a year better off. If I'm paying, through my taxes, $1 a year to pay that subsidy, it's not worth any time on my part to get out there and fight to have it ended. So there's a huge imbalance in the forces between those who get benefits and those who pay for them because the benefits are so concentrated and the costs are so widely spread out. The problem is that if there are 10,000 people like the steel plant workers, or 10,000 groups and every member of those groups is getting $1 a year, that starts to add up to something very serious.

28

Where does the taxpayer, or indeed the taxpayer's representative, begin to reduce those costs? If you attack one group that's getting a subsidy, they will fight back with all the resources at their disposal, including most of the subsidy that they're getting. If you try and attack them all at once, you can imagine the sort of resources that those people will be willing to throw into that fight. So it's always an unequal struggle, and the more government spreads benefits around, the greater the difficulty in reducing the size of government.

There's no doubt that when we prevent the economy from evolving and growing naturally over the course of the years, and we make people believe that they can continue to do what they have always done, all we end up doing is putting off the day of reckoning. When we pay subsidies to industries that are not economical, that don't make a profit, that have lost their markets, we just put off the day when we all have to recognize that people cannot be protected from the changes that are going on in the world every day. When the industrial revolution started, 90 percent of the people who worked, worked on the land. They were agricultural workers. Had we stopped those people from making the move from the land to the cities and industrial occupations, we no doubt would have prevented a lot of suffering in one generation of people. There's no doubt, as Dickens novels and a whole series of other sources illustrate majestically, that a lot of people were hurt. The transition was very costly to a lot of people.

Would we, their descendants, thank them for having stopped the creation of a world in which we are infinitely better off than we would have been had we all been locked into the land and continued to plow it with horses and primitive iron implements? One of the benefits that we as a generation confer to the rising generations is our willingness to bear the costs of change that will make the world better. We cannot make the world better without change. So to bring that all back to Atlantic Canada, there is no doubt that we have slowed down through all kinds of transfers both to provincial governments and to individual industries and workers. We have slowed down the transition away from certain kinds of traditional industries, the fishery, forestry, mining and agriculture. We slowed the move out of those industries and into other, more modern productive industries.

We have no choice but to begin to make it clear to people that government cannot forever shield them from the changes that are sweeping the world. There are economic changes that are affecting every corner of the world that make old, traditional industries uneconomic but that make new industries emerge and employ many thousands of people. By striving to protect the traditional industries, all we do is prevent the shift into new industries that would give people here a brighter future. But there can be no denying that the shift will be a painful one. It's made more painful by the fact that we have put it off longer than we needed to. I'm sure that there are all sorts of ways in which government can be helpful in managing that transition, but the transition cannot be avoided.

Remember that economic development flows from innovation. The more we strive to protect our established way of doing things, our established industries, the more we freeze out innovation and, therefore, the very source of economic growth. With the best of intentions we have created a situation in Atlantic Canada in which economic growth is far from being encouraged; rather it is hobbled by many of the activities that government claims and undertakes in order to promote economic development. There can be no doubt that once you have created a system in which people can ask for subsidies and get them, everyone will ask for them. I mean, just think about it. If you are in business and you see your competitor get some kind of competitive advantage, you are going to seek the same advantage. It doesn't matter whether the competitive advantage is access to cheaper capital, whether it's access to better-trained workers or whether it's access to government grants. If your competitors have it, you can't afford not to pursue it. If you are a successful business and you see your competitors getting grants, you will ask for those grants. Indeed you should ask. It's a perfectly rational thing to do. I'm not blaming successful companies that say, "My competitors are getting grants, I have to do the same thing." If I were in business I would do that.

But we have to take a step back and look at the system we've been creating, a system in which we allow individual people to take individually rational decisions which, when you add them all up, make something that is irrational for us as a society.

VIEWS FROM THE EAST

TOM MCMILLAN

Atlantic Regional Development

At the time I was minister of state for tourism, the ministry was a part of a troika. The Department of Regional Industrial Expansion (DRIE) was the senior department and it had the two smaller ministries, Small Business and Tourism, underneath. Along with André Bissonnette, the minister of state for small business, and Sinclair Stevens, who was the senior minister for DRIE, I had a lot to do with tourism and with regional development granting.

The current generation of bureaucracy for regional development is ACOA, the Atlantic Canada Opportunities Agency. Before that it was called the Department of Regional Industrial Expansion, DRIE, and before that it was the Department of Regional Economic Expansion, DREE. It was established in 1969 by the Trudeau government and its rationale was supposed to be to help eliminate, or at least alleviate, regional disparities across the country, to narrow the gap in income and job opportunities between "have" and "have-not" areas. The truth of the matter is, while it began with that rationale, over the years — and it didn't take very long — it became a honey pot for practically every part of the country, notwithstanding its job levels or its per capita income. The honey pot doled out millions of dollars in the name of regional development and job creation to entrepreneurs and enterprises — small, medium, large, right across the country, from one end of the continent to another — such that, certainly in my time as minister, we were party to decisions that were granting millions of dollars to wealthy parts of the country just as much as we were doing so for small areas and poor areas.

Regional development policy did not act in a way that helped the disadvantaged or have-not provinces because it was fundamentally flawed. It was based on the premise that bureaucrats and politicians could pick winners and losers, could identify enterprises that had the potential to create wealth without government. A further premise was that these enterprises could not get under way or be expanded without government assistance. But the truth of the matter, is those companies that did receive such money and succeeded would have succeeded anyway, in which case the money was a windfall at the taxpayers' expense. And those companies or entrepreneurs that received money of this kind and didn't succeed couldn't have succeeded anyway, with or without government money. For the most part, the program and the policy and the approach were fundamentally flawed and doomed to failure.

There are some examples of companies and entrepreneurs that did receive money from DRIE or DREE or ACOA, in the name of regional development, and probably couldn't have succeeded without government money and went on to create the jobs that were intended. But those examples are rare; so rare that if they were birds or animals, they'd be on the endangered species list.

The history of DRIE and DREE and ACOA is really one of accumulating a steadily longer list of failed enterprises that ended up wasting millions, in total, billions, of taxpayers' money. In my own province of Prince Edward Island, where I was the federal Cabinet minister, I think one of the classic examples which involved hundreds of thousands, even millions, of dollars of taxpayers' money, both provincial and federal, was Benner Skis. It was established under DREE in the era of the Alex Campbell government, which really began the process of trying to force-feed these enterprises with federal and provincial government money, largely based in the West Royalty Industrial Mall.

Benner Skis was a branch plant of a European-based multinational company. It was based in Germany and it was going to create a ski for the world market. You have to keep in mind that there aren't many hills in Prince Edward Island. The highest hill anywhere in the province would not qualify as a bunny slope at most self-respecting ski resorts in Quebec, Ontario or anywhere else. In other words, P.E.I. was not exactly an ideal candidate for an enterprise of this kind. But that didn't prevent the bureaucrats and the politicians from thinking it was a wonderful idea to build a manufacturing plant to create skis. Predictably the company fell flat on its face.

The main problem was that there was a built-in bias toward enterprises on which the government and the politicians, and by association the bureaucrats, could put a great big plaque saying, "Built by the Government of Canada." This meant that projects that involved building a plant with bricks and mortar were favoured over ones that didn't involve bricks and mortar. In P.E.I. there was lots of space already but the relevant grant went toward building a plant. They didn't address some fundamental problems.

First of all, there were all kinds of companies around that were producing skis. Secondly, there was no domestic market. Very few people in Prince Edward Island are going to buy skis, let alone ski in the province, or in the Atlantic region for that matter. More fundamentally, the input costs were exorbitantly high to produce these skis. Electricity rates, for example, were twice the national average. They were appreciably higher than even in the neighbouring province of New Brunswick. Transportation costs were very, very high because the plant was on an island; the island was far from the central markets, central Canada or abroad. It ended up costing more per unit to produce these skis than they could sell them for. And of course there were all kinds of plants around, including the parent plant in Europe, that were producing skis of the same type more cheaply. So after the federal government money and the provincial government money dried up, so did the plant and so did the skis. It ended up costing the P.E.I. government alone about $2 million. When you say "the P.E.I. government," almost all the money spent by the P.E.I. government comes in one form or another from the federal treasury. Of course, there were some substantial direct federal government subventions for the same project.

There are all kinds of other examples. More recently, under ACOA the federal government spent quite a few thousands of dollars to help build a brewery for Red Rock Beer in Milton, just outside of

Charlottetown. There had not been a brewery in Prince Edward Island at that point for something like a century. If common sense had anything to do with it, there wouldn't be another brewery in P.E.I. for at least a further century, if not two or three. But they put it there because the federal government and the bureaucrats and even the politicians, myself included (I was the Cabinet minister at the time), got sold on the idea. While I must confess I was a reluctant convert to this particular project, we got sold on the idea that it would create jobs. It would also complement an existing company called Charlottetown Metal Products, which, by the way, was very prosperous without any government money. The people associated with Charlottetown Metal Products saw the brewery as an opportunity to get sales for that company because Charlottetown Metal Products could have produced the equipment for the brewery.

Anyway, a few investors, mostly people like teachers and small-time entrepreneurs, put in about $20,000 each. The master investor, who I don't think put in much more than that, ended up buying all the others out, having convinced the federal government to put in a substantial amount of money to build the brewery in the first place. To boot, he put up his own business, Charlottetown Metal Products, as collateral for his own involvement. So the brewery floundered like so many of these other projects, and not only did the brewery go down the drain, but it also brought Charlottetown Metal Products to the same fate.

There were various reasons for this. How do you sell beer in such a small market, even allowing for the fact that we Islanders do have a taste for the Bud? Labatt and Molson were already well entrenched in the same market. There was no natural competitive advantage for this particular product. It wasn't necessarily better. It couldn't be sold more cheaply. I mean, what was the edge that would give this particular brewery a competitive advantage? Now, that's the sort of question that government should have asked before approving funding of this magnitude. It was only after it proved a colossal failure that people asked, "Why did we get into this in the first place?" Of course, the problem was compounded by the fact that at one stage the Red Rock Brewery produced what was called a skunky beer. It was just a bad batch of beer, which intimidated the market. Those people who had a taste for Red Rock Beer were soon put off it and were never to buy another bottle. What was probably ill conceived and ill fated from the beginning had its fate sealed by that final turn of events.

I don't think the Cabinet ministers wanted their faces emblazoned on the side of the Red Rock bottle. I intervened on behalf of that company with DRIE, and with the minister in particular, and with my Cabinet colleagues to get the funding. It was, after all, within my riding and it was in the province that I represented in the federal Cabinet. But I had no particular interest in having my visage on the label, let alone on the bottles that were described as skunky. The government's thinking on this was not totally irrational, even though the consequences would lead one to think that the whole thing was ill conceived. I think we have to accept that most of the people making these decisions are well intentioned, even if misguided. And there is the premise or the principle that public people such as politicians and bureaucrats can identify potential winners and losers in the marketplace.

Well, we're finding out from experience that only the marketplace can do that. You can't dictate that from on high. Nevertheless, departments like DRIE and DREE and ACOA, by whatever name, have these elaborate structures and very expensive and confusing processes involved in showering entrepreneurs and enterprises with money, on the grounds that somehow the public interest will be advanced in this way because employment will be created. People who otherwise are drawing unemployment insurance or welfare will be taken off the dole and gainfully employed and end up paying taxes. The problem with all of this is that we're not talking tens or hundreds of thousands of dollars, not even tens of millions. Over time we're talking billions of dollars of taxpayers' money, much of which does not serve the very purpose for which it was spent in the first place. We are blowing fortunes on enterprises that have in most cases very little chance of success. Often the enterprises themselves are required to present start-up capital of their own, but as often as not it represents a very small portion of the total investment. It's most often government, and therefore the taxpayer, that's taking the risk. In some cases the contribution from the entrepreneur was "in kind," an expression that's often used in Ottawa: the person's brains, experience, labour, effort, ingenuity, whatever. And there may be some minimal contribution of cash along with that, but too often it's the government that's putting the cold hard cash on the barrel head. And that is of course the taxpayer. So that if the business fails, it's not the investor or the entrepreneur who takes the hit, it's John and Mary Q. Taxpayer. Us. You and I.

And, look, it's not a conspiracy. It is not a conspiracy at all. It's a form of incompetence. I think the programs are, as I said before, well intentioned. I think government is trying to do the right thing. But more often than not it's the wrong thing because it doesn't work and it can't work. And the very approach is fundamentally flawed. If the government is going to get involved in regional development, force-feeding enterprises that otherwise couldn't succeed without that help, it's going to have to be much more targeted. It's going to have to be much less generous. It's going to have to be much more careful, for example, to make sure that the marketing is done, to ensure that there is actually a consumer out there who will buy the product, to ensure that the product is not already being created in the marketplace by somebody else, by private sector interest without government help. And to ensure that federal government money isn't going toward enterprises that artificially create competition for entrepreneurs who are already in the marketplace using their own risk capital. But a lot of this thinking is just not done.

My ministry was ensconced in the very department whose activities I have just described, the Department of Regional Industrial Expansion. Even after I left Tourism I was still involved in these decisions at the Cabinet table, either directly or indirectly, in connection with projects that had to do with my own riding or province or more generally with Cabinet responsibilities. When I first began I was like so many other naive and callow politicians. I thought, "We're going to do all sorts of wonderful things by approving grants to industries and to entrepreneurs and we're going to help the unemployed, we're going to help disadvantaged areas." That was my mindset.

Gradually, as I sat at Cabinet, and sat in particular on a board that approved all projects of this kind over $1 million, I started asking myself some questions. Why, for example, are we approving millions of dollars in grants to enterprises based in communities like Newmarket, Ontario, where the per capita income is among the highest in the world, forget in Canada? We were approving millions of dollars of beneficence for companies like Magna International, for auto parts companies that were making zillions of dollars internationally and certainly didn't need the help of the little taxpayer. I think the government was doing it because sometimes these companies were seduced by politicians, and maybe by their bureaucratic first cousins, into investing in places like Cape Breton. Now, it wasn't always in places like Cape

Breton. As I say, some of these grants went to activities in the heartland of wealthy Canada.

I don't think anybody sat back and said, "OK, how are we going to screw the taxpayers to the wall?" If we had done that, if we had sat down as a Cabinet and asked, "How are we going to do it," we could not have come up with a more brilliant way of achieving that end. But we didn't do it.

It was more incremental during the Trudeau era. When DREE was first established it was a fairly modest effort. And it grew like ragweed to the point where successive governments, successive ministers, successive Cabinets just larded onto already too-bloated bureaucracies yet another layer of decision making and yet another pocketful of federal taxpayers' money for this purpose. They did this to the point where every region of the country had its own bureaucracy for this purpose.

Originally it was one department for the entire country trying to identify the disadvantaged parts of each province in each region to help out, create jobs and stimulate economic activity by helping entrepreneurs and individual businesses. Later DRIE was broken up and individual bureaucracies were created for each of the regions. For example, Western Economic Diversification was established from the remnants of DRIE to help Western Canada. And ACOA was the counterpart in Atlantic Canada, and so forth and so on.

It had its own momentum, and at times it even had its own inertia. But there was no whistle blower. There was no one to sound the gong, if you will, and say, "Does this make sense and where is it leading? Have the billions of dollars that we've already spent actually created the jobs and the wealth that were contemplated? And if not, then why are we continuing on this conveyor belt?" It was a gamble. But the gamble and the risks far outweighed the proven advantages from this approach. And the risk and the gambles were, more often than not, not being taken by entrepreneurs who were so advantaged, but ultimately by the taxpayer. It is a flawed approach that I think cannot work, but if it can be made to work at all, it has to be on a much more targeted and much more modest basis. And it cannot be one that showers federal government largesse from sea to sea, irrespective of the unemployment rates in the communities concerned or the per capita income of the people residing in those communities.

The Atlantic Canada Opportunities Agency was supposed to make the granting process more regionally sensitive. It was supposed to root it within the region. Both the personnel and the decisions were to be based here. And what is more, the decisions were to be informed. The bureaucrats and the politicians were to be assisted by entrepreneurs with real on-the-ground experience in the private sector through an advisory board. That's the way it operated initially, at least ostensibly. The truth is before long you had more or less the same types of people, if not the same people themselves, making the decisions. A lot of the decision making that had been for a time rooted within the region, all of that was moved back, sometimes by stealth, to Ottawa.

It was supposed to be an entirely different approach to regional development for Atlantic Canada. Instead of having bureaucrats ensconced in Ottawa making decisions by remote control for the bene-fit of Atlantic Canada, the idea was that it was to be rooted right within the region. The headquarters, for example, was to be in Moncton and the bureaucrats were to be resident there. Preferably the minister responsible for ACOA was to be an Atlantic Canadian himself or herself, but this wasn't always the case. The bureaucrats and politicians were to be advised by real, live, warm-blooded entrepreneurs from within the region, with real, on-the-ground experience in the private sector. There was to be a board for that purpose, and so on and so forth. In other words, it was to be a revolution, a completely different way of creating wealth through federal government expenditures for regional develop-ment purposes. One respect in which ACOA was to be different was that instead of having rigid criteria that were fairly specific, any idea that was worthy of support, even if it didn't fit into a particular pigeonhole, was to be fast-tracked, at least in theory. There would be no delay. There would be a minimum of red tape. All the bureaucracy and the red tape were to be stripped away. A good idea and a good idea maker were to be supported. Money was not to be used for bricks and mortar so much as ideas and an entrepreneurial spirit. It was part of a vision and a new way of doing things.

At first it looked as though there was hope, at least for a more regionally sensitive process. But before long the things that I've just described got watered down. Some of them didn't work anyway. Still others were sort of window-dressing. I think Brian Mulroney, largely because of his own Atlantic Canadian roots (he graduated from St. Francis Xavier University) saw the folly of past ways and really did want to change it. But, my God, it's hard to change mindsets, even if you are the prime minister, if you don't change the personnel, if you don't change the bureaucrats. There wasn't a wholesale firing of bureaucrats; it was kind of a shuffling of the chairs on the deck, and too many enterprises and too many entrepreneurs who didn't have a ghost of a chance of succeeding were still being assisted with generous funding.

I honestly do not see a substantial change in my experience at the Cabinet table under the old system and under the new. I don't think we've gotten around the fundamental problem that government is not very good at picking winners and losers. There is no doubt that these millions have generated some activity. You can't spend as much as the federal government has spent in Atlantic Canada in the name of regional development without having some benefits, some short-term temporary job creation, some purchases of supplies. Too often those supplies are acquired from outside the region. But that's another story.

I guess in a number of cases some significant political advantage accrues to the politicians who are photographed in their local newspapers cutting ribbons in front of the enterprises that are so favoured. And it's great. As a member of Parliament myself, I loved to be photographed with the local mayor, the local members of the legislature, with the local businesspeople. It was good politics to be associated for a change with a good news story, and the opening of a plant or the expansion of something or other was good news. But with the advantage of hindsight, now that I'm out of politics looking back, I can see that a lot of those things of which I was so proud at the time were a great cost to the taxpayers. As far as those cases are concerned, where the plants or projects failed, it was more than a disappointment: it was probably a scandal because they ought not to have been funded in the first place.

If I were still in politics, I think I would be thinking the same things, though I'm not sure I would be quite as outspoken. I can honestly say, as a politician who was in Parliament for 10 years, half of that in Cabinet, that we politicians or former politicians greatly overestimate in our own minds the political advantages that attach to things like this. Ribbon-cutting ceremonies and basking in the success of something opening thanks to the federal government probably don't bring as many votes to the politicians involved as the politicians think.

These regional development policies have cost the Canadian taxpayer a bundle. We are probably the most heavily taxed jurisdiction in the world. If you consider the proportion of the individual taxpayer's income that is taken for income taxes and the approximately 18 percent of it paid out in sales taxes and the further amount to municipal property taxes, most Canadians are paying over half their income in taxes. Canadians would be better off if we were allowed to have a little bit more money left over at the end of the day from our paycheque, instead of having the federal government, like some divinely inspired heavenly influence, make these decisions for us, usually very badly. I think the federal and provincial governments using taxpayers' money should be much more careful than they have been. I think they should spend much less money than they have done. Many fewer entrepreneurs and industries ought to benefit from taxpayers' money because too often the money doesn't create the jobs that were contemplated. If jobs were created, they would have been created anyway without that money.

And look, the federal government has been in this racket since 1969 and even before that under a different form. Yet the disparity in incomes between Atlantic Canadians and other Canadians has not budged even 10 percent. The level of poverty, the level of disparity between Atlantic Canada and the rest of Canada, all of those indices which are measurements of whether this program has succeeded or not demonstrate that the approach is a failure and probably couldn't be otherwise because it's inherently flawed. It presupposes that politicians and bureaucrats can create wealth, that they can choose winners and back them and make them winners when they'd otherwise be losers. But the losers are going to be losers with or without government money, and by the same token, the winners are going to be winners with or without government money. That's not to say there isn't a legitimate role for government to play in the stimulation of wealth in Atlantic Canada. But it is not through ACOA-type approaches. I'm not saying that the federal government should withdraw from Atlantic Canada. My God, if it did the place would most certainly fold. But all these billions of dollars that have been spent through the federal treasury for job creation have been wasted. It would have made more sense to have taken those billions of dollars, put them in a trust account and taken the interest earned to fund the people directly than to do so through entrepreneurs and through enterprises that fail after the money dries up. Given the fact that the federal government doesn't have this money anyway, it has to go out in the international marketplace and borrow it in this era of debt-ridden governance, even that approach doesn't make sense.

I think what does make sense is investments in infrastructure, things that underpin or strengthen or buttress the fundamentals of the economy, rather than showering money on individual projects, except in rare cases where that's absolutely necessary and where such an investment will actually produce a winner. For example, the fixed link between Prince Edward Island and the mainland of New Brunswick. It's largely private sector but with a big involvement by the federal government. But the business of willy-nilly, right across the board from one end of the country to another, playing like Santa Claus, doling out huge dollops of money that the federal government doesn't have to create wealth that usually isn't created and jobs that are usually not created, I think we can safely abandon that approach, to the benefit of not only Atlantic Canadians but also all Canadians across the country.

Now, we have to distinguish between federal government direct grants to individual entrepreneurs and enterprises on the one hand and transfer payments on the other. Transfer payments ensure, for example, that Atlantic Canadians have a standard of education and health and other services akin to those in the rest of the country. There's a big difference between the two. If we're going to have a country, we need transfer payments for Atlantic Canada and for other parts of the country. You can support transfer payments to and through government to individuals for that purpose without embracing this ludicrous notion that bureaucrats and politicians are ideally positioned to pick entrepreneurs and enterprises. Some of these bad investments have made Atlantic Canadians more dependent because we've become hooked on short-term fixes and on white knights that are going to come from Europe or from the States or from God knows where into our communities and overnight create automobile plants, like Bricklin, or breweries, like Red Rock, or ski companies, like Benner.

For a long, long time we Atlantic Canadians thought that the answer to our economic problems resided with others who were going to come in and do wonderful things for us, if only we could convince Ottawa to loosen up the purse strings to help those saviours. Well, we're gradually realizing that those saviours don't exist, and that a lot of the people who came in with federal government money to save us ended up raping us economically.

I think we have had a form of inferiority complex. We've been so poor for so long relative to the rest of Canada, certainly Ontario, Alberta and British Columbia, that we've tended to look to those other jurisdictions and ones outside the country for the answers to our problems. In terms of government Atlantic Canadians have been fairly open in embracing fast-buck operators, shysters who come in and sell us the latest snake oil. We have found out the hard way that these people too often aren't in it to benefit us or our region; they're in it to benefit themselves at our expense. I think there is a growing appreciation that the palliatives, the short-term answers, the quick fixes, haven't worked and can't work, whether it's in the form of unemployment insurance or grants to businesses through ACOA-type bureaucratic structures. I think we're gaining confidence, at least in the notion that somebody else isn't going to come in and save us from ourselves, that it's largely within us to pick ourselves up by the bootstraps and make ourselves more self-reliant and self-sufficient, at a time when Ontario and Alberta and British Columbia, in particular, are much less sympathetic to our plight than they once were.

When I was at the Cabinet table, and certainly well before my time, not much consideration was given to the implications of amassing huge federal government deficits. Deficits that one after another added to the accumulated debt — to the point where it now equals the gross national product of the country. What we were doing was mortgaging the future of our children and their children and children yet unborn. But as politicians all we were concerned about was the next election.

There's no conspiracy here. It's not some kind of plot brewed in a cauldron by politicians in Ottawa. The public is as much to blame as the politicians and the bureaucrats because they condone it. They even demand it. Until we as a society as a whole say, "This is nuts. This is nuts! We're paying the highest taxes in the world to support enterprises that don't work." They just drain the taxpayer dry. It'd be much better for government to spend money more wisely: to spend less of it and to demand less of it from the taxpayer than the sort of drunken-sailor approach to federal government expenditures that we've engaged in, in the past. Vision for a politician is the next election. Eternity is the election after that. And beyond such a scope I don't think politicians have the capacity to give much thought to decisions that are being made.

I think everyone should be responsible for cleaning up the mess, but I don't think the accountability leadership will come from politicians. Nor will it come from the bureaucrats. I think it'll come from the public.

There has to be a widespread recognition from one end of the country to the other that the federal government is costing much, much more than it ought to, given the benefits the taxpayers are getting from their own money. Unless we have sort of a revolution at the ballot box and people actually demand accountability and start questioning how their money is being spent and whether money for regional development purposes actually does develop regions, you're going to have a continuation of the same policies and the same programs and the same politicians that have gotten us into this mess in the first place.

MILLER AYRE

Newfoundland: Development

There are 1,300 villages and towns in the province of Newfoundland, spread around a 7,000-mile coast and 150,000 square miles. They were located there because of the traditional fishing industry, which is the reason why the province was populated in the first place. To find a diversification program that satisfies those needs, to find a way to service all those communities with schools and doctors and so on, produces a lot of pressure on a government. There's more difficulty to administer the process of government in Newfoundland than, I would think, any other province.

There's something in the area of $3 billion, at least $2 billion of which is transfer payments from the rest of Canada, that's come into this province each year. If someone can tell me where we would find those in the absence of being part of Canada, I might listen to the argument that Newfoundland shouldn't have joined Confederation in 1949.

On the other hand I am prepared to say that the Canadian industrial policy of the last 80 years has probably worked against Atlantic Canada and maybe some of the Western provinces. To the extent you can argue that Canada has an industrial policy, or had one, the notion is clear-cut in my view that central Canada, Quebec and Ontario, would be the engines of growth, and that the extremities, the areas not so well populated, would be the areas that would be called the regions.

There would be no great effort made to develop economies in the regions. The idea was to develop the economy in the centre of the country. The regions would get the spinoff effect and be looked after through other government programs, one way or another. So it's not enough when I hear someone in Ontario, for example, arguing, "We've got a strong economy. Now we'll cut Newfoundland loose or we'll cut Nova Scotia loose, every province for themselves." There are only three "have" provinces in this country, so there are seven provinces that can be described as "have-nots." I'm not sure how self-righteous the others like to be. I notice Ontario's less self-righteous in this matter than it used to be. But it's not entirely clear that this is a uniquely Newfoundland issue.

These policies of developing central Canada and leaving the regions to look after themselves are now being turned around and regions are told to get on with it themselves. They were told, "Don't you try to develop an economic centre where you are, we're going to do it in central Canada where the population base is and you'll get the spinoff effects." Now we're going to be told, "Try and do it on your own. How come you don't have your own economic base? Why don't you have your economic centre?" Frankly we might have been better off here now had there never been such a policy in the first instance.

Now, there's always the assumption somewhere along the line that there's a solution to the problems that Newfoundland faces. I doubt that Smallwood knew what the answer was and steadfastly refused to put it into effect. Or that when he handed the reins over to Frank Moores he said, "By the way, Frank, I know what the answer is and it's in the bottom drawer, but just don't ever look at it, and for heaven's sakes don't apply it" — and then Moores said it to Peckford and Peckford said it to Wells. It's not as though somebody in government knows the answers to the problems of Newfoundland's economy, period. It's as simple as that. Newfoundland has been a kind of experimentation centre for a lot of regional government policies. Obviously that's the way the Canadian economic system has tended to work.

We've had a policy in this country which has steadfastly maintained a growth program for the centre of the country that was not actively working for the hinterland, and was known not to work and was agreed on that way. So consequently, any province not part of that central mentality in the policy making has been the beneficiary, if you like, of a form of regional development, or lack thereof. Now, regional development has never worked and no one can really find answers as to what a federal government should be doing to develop the economy of Newfoundland or anywhere else. We've had lots of examples of things that have been tried, some by our own government and some by the federal government. They go all the way from chocolate bar factories and rubber boot factories to shoe factories and glove factories and everything else. Some work. Some don't.

We've had megaprojects. We've had projects like the Upper Churchill, which is very successful as a hydroelectric program. It generates a lot of electricity. But in this country, for reasons that aren't entirely clear to me, you can flow oil freely through pipelines but you can't flow electricity freely through wires and grid systems. When this electricity goes to Quebec, Quebec ends up being the main beneficiary of the dollars that come out of it. It was the nature of the contract as well, but it started with the premise that we couldn't use their grid system. However, you can flow oil from Alberta through a pipeline. That doesn't create the same kind of problem. So we have lots of reasons to complain that, somehow or another, policies alone have acted against us, quite apart from anything else that's happened.

One thing that the Economic Recovery Commission has made clear, and I think ACOA and governments have learned, is that economic development is a long-run problem. It depends clearly not on one or two things, like saying how many jobs you created last month or this year. You've got to recognize that you have to deal with initiative, with entrepreneurship. You have to get into schools; you have to talk about attitudes and about way of life. You have to talk about expanding horizons and opportunities, providing information and networking. There's a whole bunch of things that simply take time, and I'm absolutely certain that proper regional economic development rests on that kind of a base, not on simply sitting down and trying to dream up three very good things, like huge factories, that you can simply bounce into place.

I think we've started down the road we have to go down, which is the longer-run approach. I think people who run around saying there are short-term solutions or ask how many jobs ACOA produced last year, or the ERC, are asking the wrong questions. They've got to ask, "Is there an approach to a long-run solution that fits Newfoundland into the new global economy?" The answer is that there are a lot of things happening here that suggest that we're going in the right direction.

There are a lot of Newfoundlanders who will now argue that when we came into Confederation in 1949 we controlled the fish resource, and we gave the management of the resource, by and large, to the federal government. On the other hand, if you look at what's happened, we expanded the coastal zone from three miles to 12 to 200. There's been a problem of science in managing the stock, a problem of technology for catching and overcoming technologies of control.

The world at large has ruined the biomass, not just Canada or Newfoundland. So can you argue that if Newfoundland was in charge of managing the northern cod and the codfish biomass that we'd have done a better job? You can argue it if you want, but I think there's a lot of evidence that wouldn't stand up. We have a unique problem. Our traditional industry has nothing to do with government policies. You can argue that scientists might have got something wrong about how many fish could be caught. Well, they got it wrong all over the world if that's the case. So our fish are depleted. Now, this is the main part of our industry. It's like no auto industry in Ontario, no wheat in Saskatchewan, no oil in Alberta, no Asia–Pacific for B.C. This is a devastating reality for this province and it makes for a big problem. But you can't lay this at the feet of the government in the context of general policy making on issues such as regional development or how they manage the debt or issues of that kind. That's a separate issue.

There are a number of problems here that you have to recognize. First of all the fishing industry is not completely dead. There's $500 million worth of fishing occurring here, which is probably half of what it was. That may have a greater effect in terms of the employment issue, but that's on a volume basis. So there are fishing opportunities in certain species that are not affected by the moratorium because they're not at risk. This is a worldwide problem and it's now become clear that the biomass problem of the northern cod is not just the northern cod. In every single ocean there's depletion of major stocks that have provided commercial activity in the past. So we're part of a global problem. But we're well situated in terms of growing industries here, if we can find the right ones. If we work hard to find them, we may get lucky.

I don't think that Newfoundlanders spend much time feeling sorry for themselves; they feel sorry for the fact they don't have opportunities that were there. They feel annoyed that a fishing industry which looked like it was going to allow them to advance and diversify and still keep itself there as a base has disappeared.

I think the view that Newfoundland cannot sustain the number of people who live here, that there should be an out-migration to make it sustainable, is academic and simplistic. It doesn't address all sorts of people who live in homes scattered around all over the island. It doesn't address issues of who remains, of what age group remains, of whether you're going to say, "OK, put everybody in Corner Brook and St. John's and let's not have the hinterland or all the small communities." The more people who move out, the less economically viable become the things that remain, and there's a downward spiralling effect that has to be factored into it. You know, it's a neat solution, and there's some wild assumption they'll get jobs elsewhere. But what happens then? Do they go from a province with 20 percent unemployment to one that has 12? I mean, is that a big net gain for Canada that I'm somehow missing?

You may opt to go after something which is not a traditional fishing activity but remain a fisherman or fisherwoman or whatever the case may be. Do you move out of Newfoundland? Well, you're more likely to move if you're a young adult because you have no reason to stay here in the context of capital, for example. If you're a young adult, your parents undoubtedly own their own house. They're 45 or 50 years old and they have a house, a boat, a car, they have everything here. If they tried to move from a small village, they're going to sell the house for next to nothing and they're going to end up in Toronto trying to find somewhere to live, a basement apartment or who knows what, trying to start their life over again. That option, I suggest, is not really on. So the horrible part is, the only significant number of people to out-migrate is going to be the young people, and that creates serious potential problems in terms of developing the economy over time. Yes, that is a serious problem.

But I don't think it's a simple matter of saying, "Moving out of here is your best option." If you're a 25-year-old with the right mindset you have a lot of opportunities here for high-tech industry involvement or for computer-based industries or telecommunications industries, certainly in certain forms of science on the marine side. It's also a community in which people are trying to find answers and grow industries, so you're in the right kind of atmosphere to stay here. I have two children, both of them in that age group. One is here, one is not.

In terms of the older generations being out of work, I think you can argue that these people have a good solid base. They're housed; they grow their own vegetables and have their own communities to live in. In that respect you're talking about people who may take what would be called early pensions if they were part of some big industrial complex that was closing down in Toronto or they would be given early retirement. So maybe something of that order is the only thing government can do.

It's very hard to know what to train people for and this is a problem right across Canada. When Lloyd Axworthy suggests that there be training in part of the unemployment package, everyone says, "Yeah, but where are the jobs?" That is a problem. We have to assume there'll be some general economic recovery and growth in the future. Training makes sense because you're better off having a trained workforce when the economy picks up than one that's not. That's the only context in which you can put it. No one can say that there's any advantage in having a well-trained unemployed workforce, but I can tell you it's still better than having an untrained mass of people in this country.

We're in as good a position as any other province in terms of high-tech and knowledge-based industries. I would suggest that the fishermen can do more things in the context of how he's had to live, cutting wood or whatever the case may be, growing his own vegetables, building his own boat, doing his own carpentry work. There's a whole bunch of activities that fishermen have to engage in. But whether you can argue that he's going to make a good computer operator or a high-tech employee, that's another matter. But that still doesn't mean that a fisherman who gets up at four o'clock every morning to look after his nets because that's the kind of thing he's done can't easily learn another skill. He probably started doing that at a really young age, so he doesn't have a great education relative to somebody who has been stuck in a city environment. There may be arguments that they're harder to retrain but I think a bit of ingenuity is going to find things that people of that kind can do.

Let me say that any company that wants to put a manufacturing plant here is going to discover that the productivity is high, that it's a stable workforce environment, that you're in a community in which you have low crime and low turnover. These are all the things that a factory or a small manufacturer would be dying to find. We have it here. If you have a good idea, a really good idea, and you want to live in Newfoundland, are you going to get it funded? The answer is yes. It's as simple as that.

There's room in this province for a major project that provides taxes and revenues that can be used to grow other industries. There are a number of opportunities for Hibernia. When people discuss it purely in terms of the employment issue, they miss the point that there are royalties involved, there's a reversal of transfer payments. The real issue is, will Hibernia be the springboard for a new oil frontier? Will it be the size of another North Sea? I don't know. There is a good chance that this will be a legitimate frontier oil development and that Newfoundland will have the awful problem in the future — wouldn't it be awful to be faced with trying to deal with prosperity instead of problems? And being a have province instead of a have-not? That would really be something! I hope we don't all move before that happens.

Some people argue that we've lost our initiative because the unemployment insurance payments have been so high. Well, the UI payments here are seasonal and this is a fishing industry. Any seasonal industry is going to have a component part of the year when people don't work. If you want certain foodstuffs, it's almost natural that you work during a harvesting season, and during the other part of the season things are slower. That's the way it is. That's why they had a good curling team out West, at least that's what they used to tell me.

This is an economy of people who, when they take UI, are taking UI in the context of a rural economy. They may be cutting wood, they may be building their homes, they may be building boats. There's a whole industry of a home-based kind of activity — things you do for yourself. After all, this province has the highest saving rate and the highest rate of home ownership of any province in Canada. So what is happening here is very different from what people outside imagine. Yes, there's been some robbing on initiative — obviously. There's a program now where people are getting money while there's no fish. That money has got to be carefully spent and carefully programmed. You can argue that over the last 10 or 15 years there's been too much UI, you can argue about all those things. But my belief is that you don't ruin 500 years of history.

Newfoundland is an area that has a rich cultural heritage. It does things that other provinces don't. It provides a lifestyle that other provinces don't have. We've been a hard-working people. You can't live here without being hard-working. It's as simple as that. You know, there aren't soup kitchens in little towns and villages. You've got to make your own soup.

We have created a huge burden on the country and everyone should be concerned about the debt issue. We spent ourselves into a very nasty problem and I don't think, no matter how hard Wilson tried or Martin is trying now, that they're going to find the answer to that issue. It's only when the debt holders in Canada and around the world simply say, "We've had enough" that the government will have to deal with it whether they like it or not. And whatever comes crashing down around our heads, whether you're 25 or 55 or 95, it's going to happen to you. When it's all said and done, the financial market will deliver the message and then we've got a real problem on our hands. That's the only time we're going to realize we can't afford all the programs we now have, period.

But the younger generation is no worse off. I would sooner see you faced with the problems you've got now than be your age sitting around in 1915, about to be shot at in the First World War. Ten years of good times, another 10 years of the worst depression ever, then shot at again for another few years. I'd say that group had a lot worse time ahead of them than you're going to have. I think you've got a helluva good chance of making it.

PARZIVAL COPES

Newfoundland: Diversification

The problems I see with the Newfoundland economy and fishery are in terms of two conventional wisdoms that have been held for far too long in Newfoundland. John Kenneth Galbraith describes conventional wisdom as a general understanding the public has of a particular issue or problem. He says the enemy of conventional wisdom is the march of time. That is, over time the world changes and conventional wisdom no longer applies. I'd say it's a general understanding that the two conventional wisdoms that have created the present economy in Newfoundland are based in something that historically probably was true, that was realistic at one time, but not today.

First of all, Newfoundlanders have considered it a matter of birthright that anyone who wants to become a fisherman should be able to go into the fishery. Also, that it was the obligation of government to see to it that they can make a decent living in the fishery. And at one time, of course, that was precisely how Newfoundland operated. The one big industry was the fishing industry and the population was small enough and the resource was large enough in relation to the population that you could employ people in the fishery, and there was no reason at that time to keep people out of the fishery.

It was considered, particularly by the politicians in Newfoundland, and this is where the second conventional wisdom comes in, that the greatest asset of the province was the people of the province. "Our greatest assets are our people," Joey Smallwood said. The conclusion of that was that we should discourage emigration from Newfoundland. That's meant that in Newfoundland, where there are so few employment opportunities, where unemployment levels were reaching 16 to 20 percent, you were still discouraging people from emigrating.

Joey Smallwood negotiated with the federal government for all kinds of support for the Newfoundland economy, but the one thing he was adamant about was not giving any money to move people out of Newfoundland. He would take the unemployed or underemployed people from the outports and move them to larger places, but it was just a reshuffling of the unemployed. Many ended up in welfare ghettos where there was no work available at all. Not a penny was spent on moving people to places where there were jobs. They had to stay.

I'm talking about 30 years ago. At that time there were plenty of jobs in the mainland. The opportunity was missed. The greatest asset to the province, its people, was going to waste. These people were unemployed. They were on welfare. That is not a productive asset. The problem is that politicians, in particular, measure their prestige in terms of the size of the jurisdiction over which they preside, so a populous province gives you more prestige than one with few people. And politicians like to keep the people at home.

Actually, what I wrote in 1961 was not considered that controversial at the time, largely because people didn't read it in detail. What was published in 1961 was a report I did for the Newfoundland board of trade. A follow-up to that was far more controversial, and that was a report on the resettlement program in Newfoundland that looked at the whole question of the fishery. So you have to really look at my work in terms of a combination and a progression from one report to the next. The board of trade was interested in what could be done to improve the economy of Newfoundland. I got the assignment to work on this just after I had arrived in Newfoundland, when I was very interested in the problems of Newfoundland.

Obviously unemployment was a major problem, and therefore it was a question of more productive use of the labour force in Newfoundland, putting people to work. So I explored in detail the structure of the Newfoundland economy and the prospects there were of increasing employment in the province and increasing production in the province. I came up with a large number of ideas but they were all fairly small. I did conclude that, even with the best efforts that were going to be made with the growing population, the prospects were that they would never mop up all of the unemployment.

I emphasized in that report that you had to work from two sides. You had to find all of the available jobs that could be effectively utilized, but you also had to promote labour mobility. I emphasized there was no reason why people who were adventurously inclined and would like to see more of the world should not go and look for jobs elsewhere and relieve the pressure on the unemployment situation in Newfoundland. Most of the people concentrated on the positive recommendations that I made for exploring additional opportunities for employment. It was not all that controversial. As a matter of fact, the report was well received and I was asked to do extension programs where a lot of people came in just to take a special course on the development of the Newfoundland economy.

However, what it had done for me was to give me an extensive insight into the problems of the Newfoundland economy and in partic-ular the problems of the fishing industry. What I noticed was that the fishing industry had a unique historical role in Newfoundland, where it had been the main employer for many centuries. Eventually, of course, the economy was diversified. But when we faced the situation of high unemployment in Newfoundland that was developing in the 1960s and 1970s, what would you do with the surplus labour?

The solution in Newfoundland was to look at that conventional wisdom that people should be able to work in the fishery if they want-ed to. The federal government was persuaded by Joey Smallwood to make unemployment insurance available in the fishing industry on such a basis that fishermen could automatically get unemployment insurance for the winter if they had been fishing in the summer. What this meant was that it was no longer an insurance scheme against an unlikely and unfortunate contingency; it was a payout that you were certain to receive during the winter. So it really became a massive subsidy to the fishing industry. You could support far more people in the fishing industry if you paid their way for the winter and they had to fish during the summer. And the result was that an enormous amount of government funding went into the fishing industry.

My second report looked at the fishing industry in the context of the resettlement program that the Newfoundland government was promoting. With the resettlement program they took people out of small communities and put them in the larger ones where it would be easier to give them access to hospitals and schools and so on. That would affect mostly small fishing communities. So what they were doing in that context was concentrating them in certain parts of the province, removing them from some of the fishing sites that they were otherwise accustomed to using, but they could still have access to those sites.

The problem was that in the process they were still trying to put more and more people into the fishing industry because it was the only place where they could accommodate people in the economy. And the reason you can do that in the case of the fishing industry is because it has been, historically, an open-access resource. That is, nobody in particular owns the fish resource, so everybody can go and get a small boat and start dipping into the pool of fish. The result was that the fishing industry essentially became an employer of last resort. If you couldn't get a job elsewhere, go and work in the fishing industry because in the winter you're going to automatically get unemployment insurance. The result was that the fishing industry was overloaded with people.

If you make a comparison to other more productive fishing economies, like Iceland, you find that the Icelanders, with 4,000 to 5,000 fishermen, will catch more than twice as much as the Newfoundlanders will with up to 30,000 fishermen. It's a great deal less right now with the closure of the fishery. But essentially the catch per fisherman in Iceland was five or six times as high as the catch per fisherman in Newfoundland. It really was a scandalous waste of public resources to overexploit the fishing industry. Even with the limitations and conservation measures that were being taken to save the stocks, you couldn't help but have excessive pressure on the fish stocks with that number of people of trying to wrest a living from the fishery.

My study looked at the amount of income they made, which was not great but they could get by on it. It showed that if you put together all of the subsidies and payments made by the provincial and federal government on the fishery, there were years in which the amount of money they spent was in excess of the value of the catch, and far in excess of the incomes earned by fishermen. That's subsidizing an industry to more than 100 percent. That is not sustainable. It means that we're throwing good money after bad. It means that we're building up a public debt and look where we've ended up now.

My specific recommendations at that time were to rationalize the fishing industry, reduce the labour force to at least half of what it was, and reduce the number of vessels because they were using far too many for what was needed. That would save money too, in terms of the net amount that could go to the fishing industry. Far too much was being spent on gear and equipment that was not needed. You could have a far more productive fishery if it were a great deal smaller because you could still catch the same amount of fish but you could do it with fewer people and with fewer boats, and the catch per fisher and per boat would be greatly increased. So you could get a viable fishing industry that would not have to be subsidized that way. That was a major recommendation.

However, I had to face that the major problem in Newfoundland was high unemployment. Even with all of those excessive numbers in the fishing industry, you still had up to 20 percent unemployment. So what are you going to do? If you're going to reduce the fishing industry, which is your major employer, you're going to reduce the number of people in there at least by half and ideally down to one-third. Where are those people going to go when you have so much unemployment already? The logical consequence that could not be avoided was you have to do something about mopping up the unemployment in Newfoundland. Because of my previous work for the Newfoundland board of trade, I knew that the employment prospects were not good in Newfoundland. There is no way that you're going to employ all of those people. So you had to work at it from the other end as well, and that is labour mobility. You had to help people get jobs where there were jobs. In those days there were jobs on the mainland of Canada. Economically Canada was in a good condition in those days. Unfortunately, now that people have come to realize that I was right in my predictions of what was going on in the Newfoundland economy and the fishery in the long run, the solution is no longer so easy because you've got 10 percent unemployment in Canada. Where are you going to employ those people?

There are still some jobs coming up; to a small extent you can still move people to jobs. The problem with the Newfoundland government at the time was that they wanted to create more jobs in Newfoundland. In other words bring jobs to people, which is fine if you can find viable jobs that can be brought to people. Joey Smallwood started up a dozen new industries with subsidies from Ottawa, manufacturing batteries, rubber boots and so on, which could not be done efficiently in Newfoundland. Their market is much too small and you're too far away from the main markets to maintain industries like that. And they all failed.

You have to face the reality that a lot of the jobs that have to be found for Newfoundlanders will be off the island. Of course, on the one hand the Newfoundlanders say, "You know, there are more Newfoundlanders in New York than there are in Newfoundland, there are more in Boston, there are more in Toronto." But when it comes to saying, "We should encourage out-migration," the reaction is fierce against that.

The conventional wisdom that people are our greatest asset and we should keep them in the province held until very recently. Now it is being recognized that the prospects in Newfoundland for full employment are so dim, people are not getting the assistance they might have had. A lot of people are packing up and looking for jobs elsewhere. Even though jobs are scarce everywhere. So it's a solution that is not easy to follow now, but people are realizing that it's the only solution.

I would say that the reaction to the idea of resettlement was so adverse in part because of the timing with which it came. Joey Smallwood had generated a lot of enthusiasm for resettlement as such, for moving people from small outports, where they had very few facilities, to larger towns. In fact that was a very popular move at one time and had strong public support.

The public support started to disappear when it was found that the people who were moved were moved to welfare ghettos where there were no jobs. In other words, they were moved to the wrong places. They were not moved to jobs. Jobs were only to be found on the mainland — not in Newfoundland. The conclusion I drew is that resettlement had to be resettlement to wherever there were jobs, not just reshuffling the unemployed within Newfoundland as was being done. But by the time my second report came out, there was a reaction against the resettlement program because it had failed. Of course, resettlement had become a bad word and so simply saying that you should go further with resettlement was not going over well at that time.

I think that there are opportunities for creating jobs within the province using modern technology. I don't think they're so great that it's going to solve the unemployment problem in Newfoundland. But I've always believed in working from both ends. Work at it from the end of bringing jobs to people and also of taking people to jobs, whatever works the best in the circumstances. In Newfoundland far more still needs to be done to improve labour mobility and to help people to get jobs outside the province if necessary, and that is going to be necessary for quite some time to come. Now, it's unrealistic to think that you can take an unemployed fisherman who has very low levels of skills and put him in a skilled job somewhere else. So when I'm talking about labour mobility, I'm talking about people who have that mobility basically in terms of their skill training. I'm not suggesting that it is a solution for every unemployed person in Newfoundland that they should be sent to the mainland to work there.

Those people who have got the training and social mobility and desire to see some other part of the country, who are prepared with some assistance to take a job on the mainland, will create vacancies for people who are not socially mobile, who do not have the necessary skills. You don't take the unemployed fisherman and put him in an office job in Toronto, but you have him fill in a job for someone else who is moving to the mainland, who has got the skills and the mobility to make the move.

Now, there's an interesting thing with people who for generations have worked in the fishing industry and who can think of no other way of life. But if you have lived in Newfoundland and you have seen the moods that people go through, these moods swing considerably. There was a time at the end of World War II when there were so many good jobs available on the American bases that had been established in Newfoundland, the conventional wisdom for a while was that you shouldn't work in the fishing industry. "It's a poor man's industry, look for the jobs that are available in the new industries that are being developed." Joey Smallwood encouraged that. He said, "Burn your boats," because he was going to create all of those industries.

Of course most of the industries that he created were failures. In fact virtually every one of them was a failure, so it was a misguided judgment. But one has to be careful in assuming that people are terribly enthusiastic about just living in the fishing industry and doing nothing else. The moods swing quite considerably. When all of these small industries were failing, a lot of people went back and said, "Well, the fishery is our salvation. At least we have a job in the fishery. Let's go back to the fishery." But you find many a Newfoundland fisherman who said to his sons, "Don't ever go into the fishery. It's a poor man's job," and would encourage them to do something else. A lot of the young people are in fact adventurers and do want to do something else.

So there is a problem with the conventional wisdom. You cannot accommodate everybody in the fishing industry, except with enormous subsidies, with building fleets that are far, far too large for the amount of fish that is available, putting pressure on the stocks. This ends in disaster in terms of public financing with enormous debts that are being created and not being mopped up, and that hamstring governments now because they have such enormous public debts.

I think that we've had one failure in the fishery too many. There have been fishery failures and repeated crises all along, but the latest one is so severe that I think people realize they cannot accommodate unlimited numbers of people in the fishing industry. This is something that Galbraith predicted in his explanation of the conventional wisdom. He says the conventional wisdom continues to be accepted by the population until there begins a crisis where it is so palpably unrealistic that people's eyes are opened. They say, "We cannot believe in that perception of the fishery." I think that point has come now. They know they cannot accommodate the same number of people in the fishery again, if it is ever restored.

The fishing industry is in a particular position that makes it inevitable for governments to get involved in regulation. I think the new individual transferable quota system is an ineffective way for the government to be involved in the regulation of the fishing industry — one where you're dealing with a common property or a common-use resource. No one in particular owns it and therefore no one in particular will husband the resource and make sure we get the best out of it. Are you going to say to the fisher who catches small fish, "Look, if you throw those fish back, they're going to be much larger fish in a couple years' time. We're going to get a much more profitable fishery by not fishing the small fish, so throw them back?" There's no one willing to manage the resource because they're not going to personally benefit from it. Under those circumstances, it is necessary for the government to step in and to make sure that the resource is not being abused. In other words, you have to exercise the collective interest, and the government is the only one in a good position to do that. You have to come in with some form of regulation of the fishery in order to get the best out of the fishery.

You might think of the problem in terms of comparing it to the agricultural industry, imagining it were run in the same way, that is, as a common-access resource, which would mean that every farmer could go onto his neighbour's land and reap his crops and slaughter his cattle at will. How much of an agricultural industry would we have under those circumstances?

This is why, in the case of the fishing industry, we have to do something that we don't do elsewhere. Elsewhere the government does not have to have its fingers in the pie and regulate everything the farmer does. The farmer is perfectly capable of doing that for himself. The fisherman is not capable of doing it for himself. Not because he has inferior skills or inferior knowledge; it is simply the nature of the industry where he is dipping into a common pool and where he's not given the incentive to look after his resource. So somebody else has to do it collectively for the fishing industry, and that is government. This is where increasingly we have found that, with pressure on the fish stocks, governments have to step in and conserve the stock one way or another.

As I've mentioned, one of the systems invented recently is the individual transferable quota. It was thought up by some theoreticians with little knowledge of the real problems in the fishing industry. This is my complaint about the system: it assumes away all the problems that can be encountered. What you have to do as a fisheries manager is to believe in Murphy's Law. If anything can go wrong in implementing a new fisheries management scheme, it will. This is a lesson that we're learning, to our cost, in many parts of the world by bringing in the individual quota system, which had disastrous results in some cases.

There are cases where the individual quota system will work tolerably well and may be the best system available for a particular situation. But there are two major shortcomings in the system. You say to a fisherman, "This is the total amount of fish that you're allowed to catch this year, no more." The theory is the fisherman will go out and catch that fish in the most efficient manner. So you've got an efficient fishing industry because the individual fisherman has the incentive to catch the amount of fish that he's allowed in the most efficient manner. What you forget is the problem of implementing this. There's the question of how you know how much fish to give to each fisherman. In our current management system we sort of play that by ear during the year, and we open and close the fishery according to the state of the fish stocks. You have to assume that you've got a good knowledge of the fish stocks, that you can say at the beginning of the year, yes, this is the amount of fish that you can take and this is how much each individual fisherman gets. So it only works in the case of fisheries with fairly stable stocks where you can tell ahead of time how much fish can be taken and where you don't do your management on a day-to-day basis. This, for instance, is necessary in the case of the salmon fishery in British Columbia. The salmon fishery is utterly unsuited to an individual quota system.

A second problem is enforcement. If you have 5,000 small boats along a coastline of 10,000 kilometres and you say each fisherman is allowed to take 10,000 pounds this year, how are you going to make sure they don't take 20,000 pounds? Particularly if it's a fish that you can sell over the side of the dock. You've got a 10,000-kilometre coastline. Look at the coastline of British Columbia. How are you going to make sure they stick to their quota? In Europe, where they've tried the quota system, they know that catches taken are 40 or 60 percent more than what is allowed. There's no way of checking on it.

In the case of the large enterprises, the trawler fishery, the quota system may work tolerably well because you can't hide a trawler load of fish. So if you set quotas for the trawler fishery, yes, you need a couple of inspectors at a few plants, where the fish land and they know how much is coming in. But there's another problem, and that is the so-called "discard" problem in the quota fishery. If you say to a company or to an individual fisherman, "You're allowed to have X amount of fish, that's your quota, no more," well, the only way for that company or individual fisher to make more money is to make sure that they get the best price for the fish they get. Which means they don't want to have anything of a lesser quality. They don't want to have anything of the size group that gets a smaller price per pound.

So what happens is that they just keep the very best fish. They throw anything else overboard. This is the discard problem. On the East Coast of Canada we've had an enormous discard problem. We don't know how enormous it is because we're not there watching every fisherman. We have put ship riders on the bigger vessels to make sure that they don't abuse the system by discarding too much fish, but you can't do that on every small vessel. You can't have an enormous police force to keep an eye on this. So there are some terribly wrong incentives in the individual quota system. The enforcement and discard problems are not big problems in some fisheries because of the nature of those fisheries. But if you look worldwide at fisheries, I would be surprised if 20 percent of the world's fisheries are suitable for individual quota management.

The seasonal nature of the industry is a problem. But the problem is exacerbated by the fact that we have supported a higher proportion of our fishing industry in seasonal operations than in year-round operations. A lot of the fishing industry can be conducted on the year-round operation, and the offshore trawler fisheries are in fact year-round fisheries. They draw very little unemployment insurance. In the East Coast the inshore fishery has taken up 90 percent of the labour force in the fishing industry, and yes, it is highly seasonal. But that is the part of the fishing industry that is widely overgrown. There are areas in the Atlantic provinces where the winter fishery is quite possible and is being conducted, so the problem is not as large as it might appear to be.

The question of subsidies, I think, is an interesting one. There can be quite legitimate uses for subsidies where indirect benefits to society are obvious and are considerable, and they make it worth the government's while to put in the subsidy. For instance, if you're opening up the West of Canada, you're not going to do it unless you have a railway system and public facilities of various kinds. Without that, simply nothing is going to happen. But if you did get an infrastructure for the railway, all kinds of things happen. There are pervasive benefits throughout society and all kinds of people make good money as a result of a new area being opened up.

In those circumstances, yes, you pay money to the railways to establish a railway because they cannot recover all of the benefits that they create indirectly. They can only charge for the actual goods they're moving. They can't go around and say, "Hey, you pay your share of the indirect benefits that we have created for you." So this is where a subsidy comes in very usefully. It creates benefits, and of course the governments can recover this because they're putting more people to work and there's a bigger tax base. So you can get your money back.

The problem in the fishing industry in Newfoundland is a misuse of subsidies for a wrong purpose. In creating a dependency you're creating a very large labour force in a fishery that cannot sustain the incomes that are necessary to keep those people employed and keep them in decent incomes. By putting more people in the fishing industry, you create an inefficient industry that cannot by itself create sufficient income. So it simply means that in the future you're always going to have to subsidize the incomes of the Newfoundland fishermen so that they can make a decent living of it. This is exactly what has happened. The unemployment insurance scheme was used as a way of subsidizing the fishing industry by picking up half of the income that is needed for fishermen to stay in the fishing industry. You have to analyze, subsidy by subsidy, whether they have created efficient workforces and had a positive influence; whether the subsidies were put to a good purpose and are creating all kinds of indirect benefits; or whether they were simply creating a greater dependency on more subsidies in the future. Unfortunately, too often it's been in the second category. The problem is that individuals very often don't recognize that they're being subsidized. A fisherman who goes out there and does a day's work thinks that he is doing a day's work and he's earning his keep. Therefore he does not consider that he is sponging off the system because he's got a dangerous job and a hard job and he deserves, as he sees it, what fairly modest income he gets from the fishery.

The problem really is that we have used the subsidies to lure people into jobs that are economically not viable. Most of the hidden subsidies now have disappeared. At one time fishermen were given money to build a boat or one thing or another. Now it has boiled down to mostly subsidization through unemployment insurance. That's the big one now. Most of the other subsidies have disappeared, so in terms of current problems they're not so important.

My research in the early 1970s showed that the total amounts spent by federal and provincial governments on the fishery in some years exceeded the value of the fishery. That gives you some idea of the extent of subsidization. These are public debts that are still hanging around, hanging around our necks now. What it has done is reduced the flexibility the government has to spend money. Now we're having to spend so much money on interest on paying the public debt that we don't have money for very essential public expenditures in the health and education field, where we're beginning to suffer cutbacks that normally we should not have to suffer.

If the government helps to spur the growth of an infant industry, that's a form of subsidy. Historically the Germans and the Japanese have made great use of the infant industry argument. That is, you have to help new industries get established because it is very expensive, if they haven't done the necessary research, to establish an industry. But once they have established a firm base from which to operate, they can operate without subsidies. Japan and Germany are excellent examples of very successful applications of that.

The problem is to identify the industries where that is going to be a successful strategy. In Canada we too often have been backing losers rather than winners, the fishing industry being an example. It's a question of the misapplication of subsidies to some industries which don't have a chance of making it in the long run. There are a host of small industries in Newfoundland which have been utter failures. With a little insight that could have been perceived ahead of time. So little wisdom in the application of these subsidies is the major problem.

I don't know if the tax burden in Newfoundland is too high for new industries to be developed there. I wouldn't want to comment on that now. It would require a new survey of the Newfoundland economy. I'm somewhat skeptical that there are many opportunities, just given the general nature of the geographical disadvantages of Newfoundland and the fairly slender resource base. My guess is that we have to put the balance right, largely by out-migration, but we should be working it from both ends. I've always emphasized that you should look for all the opportunities to create viable jobs within the province but you should not neglect moving people toward jobs elsewhere.

In terms of the have provinces supporting the have-nots, there are always some groups that take care of the problems of other groups. It's a question of what your sense of family is. I mean, do you consider your province your country or do you consider Canada your country? If you consider Canada your country, the mutual support we give each other is across provincial boundaries. We have to bear in mind that historically some provinces that are now very wealthy and can afford to help other provinces at one time needed a great deal of assistance.

Alberta in the Great Depression, when it was largely an agricultural province, required a great deal of assistance, paid for by the rest of the country. When it was struggling to get its oil industry going the Canadian government required the province of Ontario to buy its oil in Alberta at a higher price than it could get for buying it overseas. Of course at a later stage we decided to tax the Alberta oil industry for the benefit of the country as a whole. We had an oil crisis and then a great deal of complaint that "they're taking away our benefits from the oil," forgetting that it was money from elsewhere in the country that got that oil industry going in the first place.

If you take a wider view of the national interest, you have to look at the country as being a family. The support that you give is not confined to one province, but goes to wherever the need is greatest. Another province gets their turn some other time. When Newfoundlanders thought the oil industry was going to come on very big there because of the Hibernia project and they thought they were going to start extracting great amounts of money, there were Newfoundlanders who said, "Let's pull out of Canada. We're going to be wealthy."

This attitude that some people have had in Alberta, the attitude of "Let's keep the wealth for ourselves," is what I call the Katanga syndrome. Katanga was a province in Zaire, Africa, and they wanted to pull out of the country because they happened to be wealthy at that time. You can make your own judgment as to the value of that kind of attitude, but if you have any sense of family for a country, you support those that need it when they need it. In turn you can count on support from elsewhere when you need it.

ROBERT GREENWOOD

Newfoundland: Diversification

For a long time we have had a good quality of life and a good standard of living in Newfoundland. This is thanks largely to transfer payments from mainland Canada. If Newfoundland had not entered Confederation, we would not have the standard of living we have today. We would not have the infrastructure we have today. For a long time we haven't had a prosperous economy that supported itself. And for years we have been losing our best and brightest. Our young people have been going away to Toronto and Vancouver and Alberta for years. I think the pressures we're under now, with the crisis in the fishery and cutbacks in transfer payments, are forcing us to confront the weakness in the economy but also to realize some of the real strengths that are there.

Newfoundland people have survived because they have a lot of ingenuity. They are survivors. And there are examples all over the province of small firms that are succeeding in tapping global markets. Government is being forced to change the way it does business so that there is now, for the first time, a provincial strategic economic plan which has assessed strengths, weaknesses, opportunities and threats. It's gotten government departments, both within the province and at the federal level, to talk to each other for the first time. They actually share information and determine what they can do to enhance the changes of economic development and diversification in the province. I'm quite optimistic about the future of Newfoundland.

I wouldn't want to say that cutting transfer payments might be a good thing in the long run. It's not that simplistic. There is a real need to maintain a level of support for people until there is sufficient economic activity to maintain the standard of living. But we need to be more strategic in our use of government supports than we have been in the past. The unemployment insurance system is by far the best example of a bad program in Newfoundland because it has focused on individuals and seen economic development as a secondary issue to income support. Newfoundland has had the "10/42 syndrome." That was always the term used. It meant that people would work for 10 weeks and then qualify for unemployment insurance for 42. As government goes through fiscal restraint, that's now tightened up to 12/32, and the current reforms that Minister Axworthy is introducing will further restrict the level of support available.

But it's not enough just to cut, in simplistic terms, the money available. What we have to do is change the way support is provided so that we reward entrepreneurship. We reward people for getting an education. We make sure that people have incentives to work additional weeks if the work is available, instead of subtracting it from the amount of money government will give them.

The government agency I work for, the Economic Recovery Commission (ERC), developed an income security program that integrates education reform, income security reform and economic development. We can see opportunities in areas around Newfoundland that the province traditionally has not developed. The way the economy was structured previously didn't favour areas with dispersed populations and isolated small communities. All you could do was catch fish and send them out unprocessed, cut down trees and send them out unprocessed, and the same with minerals. Now that economies are changing worldwide, there's a lot more outsourcing, emphasis on flexibility and small-scale production. A lot can be done in small communities throughout places like Newfoundland as well as they can be done, or in fact better than they can be done, in southern Ontario.

In Buchans in central Newfoundland there's a company in a former mine site. The town council, the rural development association and the union pulled together and formed a development corporation that took over the mine and started to market the facilities they had, like a machine shop, an electrical shop, office space. They now have a company that does defence subcontracting for GE Aerospace in New York and Short Brothers in Belfast. They have another company that's about to set up cutting marble and granite into slabs of dimension stone for the lobbies of fancy buildings. So they're not just extracting raw materials, they're adding value to products. But they have competitive advantages in a place like that, using state-of-the-art equipment and laser-cutting beams for the granite.

There are a lot of downsides to the new economy because a lot of this subcontracting is vulnerable. But in rural Newfoundland you can absorb vulnerability better than you can in large urban centres. That's largely because of home ownership. We have the highest rate of home ownership in North America. People are able to build their own homes with locally cut lumber, and these are well-built, well-insulated modern homes. If you own your own home, you can afford to be unemployed for a couple of months. There are similar regions in Italy, the Jutland region of Denmark and in Norway, where they're competing internationally because the strengths of a rural community can absorb vulnerability but still be competitive.

The origins of the Newfoundland economy and the origins of the settlement of Newfoundland were based on a dependency relationship. Newfoundland was originally not supposed to be settled. The original fishing merchants from the West Country of England didn't want a land-based fishery that would compete with their fishery. Newfoundlanders had to settle here despite the law. Initially the British Parliament passed laws outlawing settlement. They went out to the bays and coves and burnt down houses. So it wasn't an environment that really inspired people to become assertive and develop local forms of responsibility. They were hiding out from the state. In fact, as the province developed and as those laws were rescinded, you still had a fishery that was controlled by merchants outside the local level.

You had fisherman in dispersed communities who caught fish in the summer and sent it in to the merchants in the larger centres, who then supplied them with the wholesale and retail goods that they needed to survive for the year. They never quite managed to pay off the merchants, surprisingly. So there was very little local capital within the community in Newfoundland. It was all going back to Britain. Gradually a merchant class developed in Newfoundland that maintained some of the wealth in St. John's, in Harbour Grace and some of the other larger centres. But very little of it resided at the community level where there were fishermen who could reinvest it in new technology and develop market activities that would promote the industry as a competitive contributor to economic development. It became more a survival mechanism.

When we entered Confederation, what had been largely a cashless economy — except during the war when military intervention contributed a lot of cash to the economy, but only in terms of employment in building the bases and the like — was suddenly an economy in which people had all the benefits of the welfare state. In fact, that was one of the main ways Joey Smallwood sold Confederation to Newfoundlanders. In rural Newfoundland, where people had survived on very little for a long time, getting the baby bonus and the Canada Pension Plan, and later on, unemployment insurance, people thought Smallwood himself was personally responsible for delivering the cheque. They would have been fools to turn it down.

I think what really screwed things up, to be honest, was when the unemployment insurance system was extended to the fishery. At that time the number of fishermen involved in the fishery greatly increased because then people could fish for a part of the year and collect unemployment insurance for the rest of the year. And while they were only operating as economic men or women optimizing their circumstances based on the available incentives, from the government's perspective it was the wrong thing to do because it contributed to a decline in productivity in the fishery. It led to fish plant workers and fisheries workers working less than they actually could have. Once you had your stamps and qualified for unemployment insurance, you were better to quit while you were ahead because if you worked and made less money, you would collect less money later on.

We're trying to reform the income security system with the ERC. It's developed an integrated program that would maintain income support for people who need it, but would provide incentives for people to work those extra weeks if work were available, and to enhance entrepreneurial skills and education too. One of the big problems in the fishery is that people didn't need to finish high school to make a very good living and have a good quality of life. Now that the fishery has declined and there are few other opportunities unless you have basic education, that's really one of the big adjustment problems we have.

What's happening now for the first time is that educational institutes and educators are getting involved in the process. So when they develop a strategic plan to determine what opportunities exist outside the fishery, or what opportunities exist to diversify the fishery or add value, they're going to gear the educational institutions to adapt to the needs of those industries. But there are still a lot of examples of someone choosing the fishery over furthering an education.

A principal of a community college commented that he had a student who was almost finished a technical degree that was in an area where he likely would have found employment, and this guy quit. He's 19 years old, two months from finishing or so, and the principal said, "You're nuts, what are you doing? There's opportunity for you to have options and make good money." And the kid said to him, "Look, I'm going into the shrimp fishery. I'm going to make more in the next two months than you're going to make all year." What do you say to an 18- or 19-year-old who has those kinds of options?

The incentive is not there to stay in school. I think for a young person, clearly if he has that opportunity to work two months with big money and then collect unemployment insurance, he'd be a fool not to do it. If you change the system so that people who do need unemployment insurance qualify, that's fine. But if you can make $40,000 or $50,000 in a couple of months, I don't think the federal government or the provincial government should be supporting you to do nothing the rest of the year.

You need consensus between the federal and provincial governments in order to change the system. But one of my fears is that, while the national government is rightly looking for ways to reform the system, they're going to look for a uniform approach across the country. One of the real examples we see from the private sector is the need to adapt and make flexible arrangements tailored to the needs of different regions. More companies are outsourcing and subcontracting so that they can respond to that kind of flexibility.

I think the national government needs to look at downloading in ways that are constructive, not just as a way of saving money. So they need to work in co-operation with the provincial governments and with the regional and municipal governments so that we adapt policy to the needs of the regions. I don't think the ERC should be applied across the country. It's not appropriate. It's geared to the needs of Newfoundland and Labrador. And I think if the Canadian government ignores those kinds of approaches that are tailored to local needs, we're missing an opportunity to save money and to do it in a way that will enhance effectiveness.

In terms of diversification what we need to do is harness the communities and the workers and the leadership at the local level so they can identify for themselves some alternative uses for things like fish processing plants that no longer process fish. They need to look at what the external opportunities are. In terms of food processing there are skilled workforces who are used to high standards in terms of quality control and who are used to the routine of working in a fish plant. That can be adapted to other uses by, for example, taking agricultural products, taking existing fish products and underutilized species and adding value in ways that we haven't done in the past. To do that we need to work with them to adapt local capital and marketing skills — because they haven't needed to have those kinds of expertise in the past. I think there is a role for government and educational institutes in working with local entrepreneurs and community development groups to adapt appropriately to the opportunities that are there.

There is a future for the North Atlantic Rim, Scandinavia, Iceland, and certainly for Newfoundland. I know Memorial University is focusing on our European connections, just as on the West Coast of Canada it makes sense that they're emphasizing the Pacific Rim. For us Newfoundland has always had very close ties with the eastern seaboard of the United States. My grandparents, one from Carbonear and one from Old Perlican in Conception Bay, met in Boston, married and moved back to Newfoundland. The Boston States, as they were called for years, had a close connection with Newfoundlanders. We can trade on that connection, as well as on our role in the Canadian confederation, but also play on our links in the Scandinavian countries, Iceland and the European countries, Britain and France, Portugal, Spain. Through the fishery we have strong historic ties and geographic proximity, which for some types of production still matters. So those are some of the opportunities that we can identify in linking underutilized resources, workforces and facilities in Newfoundland into the global economy.

One of the projects I'm involved in is comparing island economies across the North Atlantic. One of the most telling examples was comparing Newfoundland to Iceland, which has half our resources, fewer people, and yet has four times the gross domestic product per capita. This is because they use their fishery to full effect. When there was foreign overfishing, especially by Britain, they brought out the gunboats and little tiny Iceland chased off Britain. Ottawa would never do that for Newfoundland because they might insult our European trading partners who buy from southern Ontario. Well, we should want to market southern Ontario's goods, but not at the expense of the economic lifeblood of Newfoundland and Labrador.

There is a political dynamic to economic development that we have to factor in when we understand what our opportunities are. I don't think that means Newfoundland should try to go it alone, but I do think within the Canadian confederation there are opportunities to devolve more authority and decision making to the level appropriate to the function. Some of that may be local government. Some of it may be regional government. Some of it may be the province. But we can't leave it all centralized and concentrated, just as in the private sector. That no longer works.

It's a cliché, but a time of crisis is a time of opportunity. Newfoundland is changing. I've seen government agencies, federal, provincial and municipal, sit down at the same table and talk about issues. They all deal with the same stuff day in, day out, yet they have never met each other before. Now they're being forced to because of fiscal restraint and the crisis we're in. We're seeing municipalities that are neighbours and previously fought over who was going to have the fire truck that year sharing in regional resource use and infrastructure development. We're seeing community development groups partnering and pooling resources in ways they haven't done before. So we can save a lot of money and enhance effectiveness at the same time. The key again, and I harp on this, is to be strategic about it. You don't cut with an axe. You have to do it strategically and in consultation with the people who know what makes sense at the local level and at the regional level.

The ERC, for example, looks at global opportunities and relates them to some of the resources within the province. We've looked at things like small-scale manufacturing. I mentioned the example in Buchans. There's a company in Bay d'Espoir on the south coast of Newfoundland, traditionally dependent on the fishery, where they are using digitizing equipment for digitizing maps and blueprints for General Motors. There are examples of aquaculture industries opening up. With the decline in the traditional harvesting sector, we need to harvest more of the fish by raising it ourselves. We're doing it with shellfish, we're doing it with steelhead trout. They're even trying to farm cod now. Previously our Department of Fisheries couldn't relate to that stuff. Now there's a whole division geared to that need. In fact, we recently changed the Department of Fisheries to become the Department of Fish, Food and Agriculture to enhance that value-added focus on food production, as opposed to just primary resource production for export. In St. John's there's a network of about 50 high-tech firms that are taking their expertise in marine communications and marine use and applying it to space industries. There are companies doing contracts for NASA right here in St. John's.

I had three young engineering students do my business course three years ago. Out of 16 mechanical engineering students in their class, I think only two of them stayed in Newfoundland. They were the ones who did my course. They didn't stay because they did my course, but because they took a project that they developed as one of their design projects in their final year, a stabilizer for a marine satellite system, and are now developing it for commercialization. They've also developed a product in the health-technology sector. And they're employing their unemployed fellow mechanical engineering graduates. So for those who see opportunities in the fact that employment is restructuring, there's no shortage of opportunities. There are lots of reasons to be optimistic.

I don't think we've ever been developed. In fact, we have been bleeding our best and brightest for years. What I see now is opportunity — if we gear the right structures and the right strategies to harness those people at home. Right across the country employers who have employed Newfoundlanders will tell you that they're as hard working and as innovative as anybody. It's when you reward them for staying at home and staying in unproductive activities that you get a bad reputation. So we just need to harness the kinds of capability that are there.

I think staying in Newfoundland is something that is now economically advantageous because of the advantages of the rural economy; it can absorb the vulnerability of subcontracting in the global economy. What we need to do, though, is move people from the traditional sectors, and the traditional activities in those sectors, into more value-added activities. So instead of producing cod block that we send to Boston, which they turn into fish sticks and sell back to us, we should make the fish sticks.

I wouldn't overplay the stereotype that Newfoundlanders are experts at getting money from the government. You show me a company in Canada that doesn't use tax incentives and subsidies to their best advantage. You'd be a fool not to. What Newfoundlanders are is flexible and innovative. We're survivors. There is a Newfoundland identity and there is a quality of life here that is unequalled anywhere. And if we use these reforms in the social programs constructively, there's no shortage of opportunities.

DEANE CRABBE

New Brunswick: Subsidies

Life is easier for many young people growing up in New Brunswick, especially rural New Brunswick, than it is for those growing up in the streets of Toronto, Montreal and the larger cities. They have a big advantage here. It's sad, but that's the way it is. I feel sorry for children in this day and age, especially in the larger cities, because I grew up on a small farm and I was fortunate to grow up in the time that I did. The farm was really small compared to farms today — we had to milk cows, feed hens, feed pigs, carry wood and carry water, all those things. We grew up to be second-class mechanics. We could fix just about anything: all the farm machinery. You can have all the education there is available to you in the world from the school system, but that kind of education in itself is so valuable. It's made life easy for me.

New Brunswick has about 15 million acres of forestland and we're handy to sea transportation. We're well situated for the northeastern U.S. market and I guess it's quite natural that forestry is a big business in this province. Pulp and paper and the lumber mills are the key industries here.

Over the years there's been lots of government assistance available if you wanted it. I guess we've taken a certain amount of pride in trying to stay away from it. We've seen so many instances where government has taken millions and millions of taxpayers' dollars and the money's completely wasted. The feeling around here is that most people know you can go to ACOA with almost any kind of an idea, whether it makes sense or not, and they seem to be keen to spend taxpayers' money. There's all kinds of proof of it.

For example, about three years ago in Grand Falls, the federal government invested somewhere between $15 million and $20 million dollars in a pressed-wood pallet plant. The plant would produce pressed-wood pallets to be shipped down into the American markets. Anybody knowing anything about the forestland in the U.S. knows that they've got cheaper wood down there near the big markets. So the wood would cost more here. Then the transportation costs put us out of the market completely. But they spent their money and the mill operated about five or six weeks; then it went flat.

In the very same year they spent $35 million to $40 million in Saint John to build pressed-metal pallets. Now, they make all kinds of steel in the U.S. Our steel would have to be imported from Hamilton or somewhere in Ontario, so we'd have the high transportation cost on the raw product. Then we'd have to turn around and ship the pallets down into the U.S. to sell them. It made no sense. The money was wasted and the plant didn't operate a month. There's all kinds of horror stories like this.

In my industry some businesses have been heavily subsidized. Some very little, but a fair bit. With our business I guess we've worked hard and we've run it efficiently. We're still here and we're proud that we've done it. We took a subsidy one time, for a change to our planing mill, but we did it kind of against our will. That was quite a few years ago — I'm guessing 20 years. It kind of went against our grain, so to speak, but then some of our accountants and people like that said, "Well, you're foolish not to take it because if you don't take it, somebody else is going to." It was for $110,000 and we spent $85,000 of it. We had a discussion and said, "That's enough of that, we shouldn't have taken it in the first place." And that was that. So we gave in and we've been sorry for it ever since. We could have survived without it. We look around and see other companies similar to ours getting hundreds of thousands of dollars and a half million dollars and a million dollars. And we're still here. We've done pretty much without it.

I don't like when our competitors take subsidies from government. I don't like it at all because I've seen many cases where government, by coaxing people to take their money to start a new business or expand a business, made it more difficult for other people who were in the same business. It's kind of hard to live with. There are times that it makes you quite provoked. We can't even pay the interest on the debt.

The pulp and paper industry in North America, especially in Canada, has gone through some pretty hard times in the last few years. And part of the reason is because Ottawa gave, I'm not talking about millions, I'm talking about billions of dollars to companies to go into the forests in Alberta and build monstrous pulp mills. So what happened was, it made the rest of the industry sick and some of the mills have had to close. Pulp and paper mills in Quebec and other places closed down. So what did you gain by starting a development in one area that put what had already been developed in another area out of business? There's only so much market out there, and when you flood the market somebody's going to pay the price.

In my time the best government in this province was the Hugh John Flemming government from 1952 to 1960. If he had been premier two more years, New Brunswick would have been free of debt. But along comes a small-town lawyer by the name of Louis Robichaud and he promises people they're going to get everything for nothing. Free hospitalization, free this and free that. And he got elected. So then New Brunswick reversed itself and started to go head over heels in debt. He's premier for eight years. He's defeated by Richard Hatfield, a Conservative, and he's premier for 17 or more years and the debt gets worse and worse and worse. Now we're so head over heels in debt that the present government, under Premier Frank McKenna, has got a hard problem to deal with. That's the legacy of Richard Hatfield and Louis Robichaud — a province loaded down with debt.

We go to the federal level. Canada went through the last world war and for years and years they had a Liberal government under Mackenzie King (and some people argue C. D. Howe) and eventually Louis St. Laurent. But within five years after that war was over, Canada at the federal level was absolutely debt-free. That didn't change much. Lester B. Pearson put the country in debt a fraction. But when that good-for-nothing Pierre Trudeau became prime minister, things just went berserk. The debt just went crazy. And then along came Brian Mulroney, and I voted for him twice, I'm sorry to say, and it didn't get better, it got worse. At the federal level today we're in debt over $500 billion. Look what we could have done with the money that's being paid out each year to service that debt. If we didn't have the debt there, this country would be well off. So our problem is not people. Our problem is government.

But there seems to be, I wouldn't say a large majority of people, but too many people who think it's great to get that government money, as if they deserved it. And I guess you'd have to believe that if it's available for everybody else then why shouldn't you take it as well. If there hadn't been that money available in New Brunswick in the last 20 to 30 years, New Brunswick would be out of debt. And if we didn't have the debt, taxes would be lower. I believe that in most cases industry would be more competitive.

The government has so many employees with a whole lot of education and no practical experience. And they don't make very good judgment calls. There's all kinds of proof of that. Down in Nova Scotia they spent $4 million or $5 million to build a furniture factory and put another profitable furniture-making business out. Now they're both closed. If the government had stayed out of it, the other operation would still be in business.

Back in the days when Pierre Trudeau was prime minister of Canada, they sent government people up and down the sidewalks of fishing villages saying to the fishermen, "We've got all kinds of money. Go ahead, buy a bigger boat. Buy a new boat." And to the fish plants, "Build bigger plants." So what did they do? They wasted the taxpayers' dollars. Now the fish are gone and those people are out of work. So I ask you, did it make any sense? No, it didn't. It was stupid. They're reckless because the bureaucracy in charge is keen to spend the money, for whatever reason. They don't seem to be very embarrassed when things don't work out. It almost seems that they feel compelled to spend the money whether it's spent wisely or not. I'd say it's the taxpayer who takes the risk. It's the taxpayers' dollars. I believe that a private person might think twice about taking the risk if he saw somebody else getting government money and setting up beside him or any place where it might affect the market he had hoped to have.

I think there's a lack of understanding in the bureaucracy. For years they've always had a government paycheque. I doubt if they understand risk. If a private person is going to borrow or take money that he already has to invest in some venture, he's going to pretty well convince himself that it's going to be profitable, whatever the venture is, by doing all the exploratory work. Because after all it's his money. When you're spending somebody else's money, you don't have to have the same concern. But most people who grow up in a community would feel pretty embarrassed to start an operation that falls flat on its face in a short while. In plain English, you'd work your butt off to make it successful and be worth something to the community where it's located and to its employees. There's a source of pride there.

I'm not sure I know why government gives out subsidies. I guess I'm always suspicious as to why politicians do certain things, and I have to believe that in most cases they're trying to secure the next election down the road. I think they're more concerned about winning the next election than they are about the future of the country itself. I'm not suggesting for a minute that all subsidies are wrong. There are some instances where subsidies probably would make sense. But I'm saying that subsidies that made no sense initially are wrong. If it was only for political reasons and it didn't make economic sense, then it shouldn't have happened. If government was responsible for subsidizing an industry that started and was poorly planned and failed, then government should accept the responsibility for that decision. Those things happen privately too, but when you see so many instances of government subsidies, and then the industry falls flat within a year, it's kind of sickening. It's money wasted.

Subsidies always make people less resourceful and more dependent. They always do. I've often used the comparison of the deer in the woods. They do quite well on their own if you leave them alone. Sometimes you move into an area where deer yard every winter in certain areas, and for three or four years in a row you cut down all kinds of trees so they can feed on those tops. If all of a sudden that stops, a lot of those deer will starve to death because they've come to depend on someone else to help feed them. I think it's the same way with help in dollars. If you get in a habit of receiving it, you're dependent on it.

ROBERT NIELSEN

New Brunswick: Subsidies

W e're sitting beside the Saint John River, which is a beautiful river and has been important in New Brunswick history. It received a high compliment from the first important European who explored any part of it when Samuel de Champlain, who sailed up it in the early 1600s, called it "the Rhine of America." It has never equalled the Rhine commercially, but it has had some economic importance from time to time. It was useful for paddle-wheel steamers a century ago, especially between Saint John and Fredericton. It was also used for log and pulp-wood drives, but that's a thing of the past now that all of those products are trucked to mills. The river is now used mainly for power, with a series of dams, and that's important. It hosts quite a bit of recreation too, like pleasure boating, and it's still very pleasant to sit beside today.

The government has influenced life in this area in dubious ways. We're looking at one right now: the boardwalk that was put along the river in Perth-Andover two years ago. This is an example of public spending by the wrong governments. It isn't that it cost too much; $140,000 is not a great deal of money these days. But it was provided, 50 percent by the provincial government and 50 percent by the federal government, through ACOA. The municipality, the village of Perth-Andover, paid nothing. Now, I maintain that if an amenity of this kind, strictly local, is wanted by a significant number of local residents, then the local council should take up the matter. And if it decides that it's a good thing to do, then it ought to be willing to face the local ratepayers who'd pay for it. Instead, it's paid for by taxpayers all over Canada. And I don't know why taxpayers all over Canada should be stuck for a boardwalk in Perth-Andover.

When we came out of World War II, Keynesian economics was in its heyday. All of the top civil servants in Ottawa had read Keynes's *General Theory* and believed in it; they believed in both the virtue and the power of government to do all sorts of good things for the country. We soon had the federal government leading the way on national programs, with the idea of creating national standards, making it possible for the provincial governments in all parts of the country to offer their citizens equal standards of public service.

It's an attractive idea and a lot of Canadians still believe in it. The trouble is that we've lost control of the purse, particularly in the last 25 years. Up until 26 years ago when Pierre Trudeau came in, our public finances were manageable. Now they've gone right out of control because of the looseness in public spending. Why does that happen? It's partly due to the regional nature of the country, one region competing against another to get what it regards as its share of the federal goodies. You'll even find that within fairly small areas. Here, for example, Perth-Andover will be watchful to see whether or not it's getting what it regards as its share, as compared with the French-speaking section a bit north of here, Grand Falls, Saint Leonard and so forth.

It would be difficult to count all of the cases of poor judgment, but I'll give you another example, quite close by. About 30 miles from here, just north of Grand Falls, is a good-quality motel complex called Près du Lac. It had very substantial government money, several hundred thousand dollars, to help build it. Then about 10 years ago it was proposed that a place called Lakeside Lodge be built a little south of Grand Falls, within 15 miles of Près du Lac. And I can tell you, Victoria County is not a great magnet for conventions, conferences or things like that. The total population of the county is only around 18,000 to 20,000. Somebody had the idea that they were going to attract Americans over to this place, Lakeside Lodge, although the lake is more of an overgrown pond than a lake. It's really nothing to talk about.

They built quite a glossy building with an ACOA grant of $381,000, plus $225,000 from the provincial Tourism Department. And maybe the initiators of it had to find $100,000 or $150,000 in bank loans. The place went belly-up after a year and a half. And if it had succeeded, it would have taken business away from another government-assisted place, the Près du Lac. It made no sense to build these two quite similar facilities so close together in an area of small population. It was most unlikely that they would ever attract enough business so that both would be going concerns. So one went belly-up. I think it was sold for a song. When I tried to get the present owner on the phone last Saturday, they said his number had been disconnected.

The financial risk for the entrepreneurs involved was a good deal smaller than the risk assumed by the public, by the taxpayer, through ACOA and the Department of Tourism. It was a very small risk, if it was any risk at all. In fact, it was an odd case because it was taken on by the heirs of a very prominent Liberal family at a time when the Conservatives were in power in New Brunswick and in Ottawa as well. They were taking a ride with public money, or taking a flyer, I should say, on an enterprise, one that must have struck most people around here as very unlikely to succeed.

There's another hotel industry example from Sydney, Nova Scotia, which can be briefly told. This is a really horrible example of utterly foolish government spending. ACOA encouraged all of the existing hotels and motels in Sydney to expand, offering them loans or grants on favourable terms, and invited outside hotel chains to come in there. And some of them did, with the result that in five years, from 1985 to 1990, the number of hotel rooms in Sydney increased from approximately 500 to more than 900. So they just about doubled the capacity. And as a result, they all started going broke because Sydney, let's face it, is not a mecca for conventioneers or pleasure-seekers. It has been mainly a great hole in the ground for public funds; and I mean "in the ground" too, in their coal and steel businesses.

So you had a whole bunch of hotels going bust. For the $30 million that was put in, you got a temporary boom in the Sydney building trades, but the long-term effect was that the hotels and motels were right on their uppers. And that was done in the name of economic development. Keddy's, which had been the strongest chain of hotels and motels in the Atlantic provinces, had a motel there that had been a good profit earner, and it sued. I don't know where it got with the suit, but it was going to sue the government for ruining its business.

My opinion on the effects of such regional grants is not expert, but there is an expert opinion, and I'm going to refer to it right now because it's very recent. The report of a study into ACOA came out on October 1, 1994. Its findings were that Atlantic Canada's economy is stalled, and that government intervention won't be enough to restart it. It said that the region is slowly being drawn into a negative cycle of economic activity. Furthermore, it said that ACOA wasn't creating its expected economic results. This report, which was commissioned by ACOA, called into question the very purpose for which ACOA was created. ACOA reacted defensively and said that it had created a lot of jobs. It has created some jobs, but so far as I've been able to observe, most of them are temporary. A lot of ACOA money went to fly-by-night operators who set up little businesses that were gone within a year and a half, just as soon as the government money ran out. They were just temporary things of no lasting value.

Private enterprise in the Atlantic region has certainly gotten used to leaning on government and getting money. And I doubt that even the best-run or most profitable companies are exempt from that statement. For example, McCain, a great success story, has made use of government money in training grants, which were used to profit the company. Harrison McCain himself, the chairman of the board, has defended the government assistance on the grounds that if they didn't get it, they might have to move out of New Brunswick because Florenceville is not the closest place to McCain's biggest markets, which of course are the large cities. I would hesitate to call that a threat, but there certainly was an implied warning in what Harrison McCain said, that if they didn't have this government money, it probably wouldn't make sense for them to stay in New Brunswick, or to keep their head office in New Brunswick.

Even these privately held companies, which never have to show their books to anybody, claim that they must have government money because competitors are getting it. Otherwise their competitors are going to have an advantage. This is the justification that they all use. It's the same phenomenon that you see in the competition between regions and between municipalities. There's a big pot of money there, even if a substantial chunk of it is borrowed money now, and we've got to get our share. And getting our share means getting all we can. There aren't any clear principles to tell you how much should go where.

The atmosphere of dependency is especially marked here, and that has been true for a long time. The Atlantic region has been lagging economically for nearly a century, almost since the days of the sailing ships. This report that ACOA commissioned said that government was creating a culture of dependency, or attitudes of dependency. That's been especially true since we got what can only be called a lavish system of unemployment insurance.

I'll give you an example. Shortly after I came here as a retiree I was asked to edit a local history magazine. It was done as a Canada Works project, so I had to hire from among the unemployed. The project called for two typists and two interviewers. So I went to Canada Manpower, which is now Employment and Immigration Canada, and got lists of unemployed typists. Of the first 10 that I contacted, only two showed up to take dictation tests. One typed at 34 words per minute, inaccurately, and the other typed at 23 words per minute, accurately. Not good enough. Three others said that they already had jobs. These people were listed as unemployed but they already had jobs! One said that she had two jobs. In the end the typists I hired were people who came forward, wanted the jobs and proved competent.

The hiring of the interviewers was even more revealing about the alleged sufferings of the unemployed in this high-unemployment area of Canada. Three of the people on Manpower's lists had left the area. Two of them were working in other parts of New Brunswick. Another was working in Nova Scotia. One had gone to California. One was a farm worker without the slightest experience relevant to the job at hand, and amazed at my calling him. Two others were so utterly unfindable that I suspected their nonexistence. The one who was interested in the job said that he couldn't afford to take it because it paid $23 less than his unemployment insurance. And he was the only one of the 10 who asked what the pay was. So my conclusion was that the sufferings from unemployment weren't very severe for this particular group.

A great many people, not only in New Brunswick but also elsewhere, have gotten used to being on a payroll for 10 weeks and then on unemployment insurance for 40 weeks. I'll tell you how ingrained that is, and by saying this I'm letting a cat out of a bag after 10 years.

Being in a woodlot owners' organization, and also as a producer member of the New Brunswick Forest Products Commission, I was sometimes given access to confidential information. What I heard from a high-level source in the Natural Resources Department was this. After their 10 weeks, which is all that was required in a high-unemployment zone, woods workers were asking contractors for their layoff slips, and if they didn't get their layoff slips, they were going to sabotage the contractors' equipment. Case after case. It was a serious enough matter that it had been brought to the attention of the deputy minister of the province by a number of contractors and woods companies. I don't know how widespread the problem was, but it was presented to us confidentially as symptomatic of an attitude, of something widespread enough to be worrisome to the woods companies. It makes me angry. If I were a young person and knew as much about this situation as I do now, I'd be sore as hell. I'd say that those people are robbing my future, all of them, the entrepreneurs, real and phony, the 10-weeks-a-year workers who deliberately go on unemployment insurance.

But I think the main fault with unemployment insurance is that access is so easy and the benefits are so high that it has become a rational choice for a great many people not to work, instead of taking available work. I suspect that at its peak, when the standard benefit was two-thirds of your previous pay, our unemployment insurance program was the most generous in the world. New Zealand had a welfare state that it couldn't afford and had to take drastic measures to curb. But New Zealand didn't have anything like our level of benefits.

If drastic cutbacks happened suddenly, it would probably mean a considerable outflow of people from the Maritimes to more promising economic areas. But if they happened gradually and were accompanied by reasonably good government, it would mean getting used to a somewhat lower standard of living, which doesn't seem to me to be such a horrible prospect.

I go back to the days (and I didn't actually do it myself, but one of my older brothers did) when men were working in the woods all winter long in New Brunswick for $16 a month. Now, $16 would buy more then than it would today, but it wouldn't be more than $200 a month in today's money. They were sleeping on straw and eating beans three times a day. In 50 years that's where we came from and this is what we've come to, from men working from dawn to dusk in the woods, unable to go home to see their families all winter long (maybe they'd get home at Christmas, but that was all) to the situation where their grandchildren of working age get on a payroll for 10 weeks and then run their snowmobiles, or whatever they choose to do, in the wintertime.

I give a bit of a paddling to my fellow seniors in New Brunswick too. About a year ago the health minister said that New Brunswick would no longer have its medicare fully cover the so-called "snowbirds" when they spend the winter months in the south. He said that the N.B. medicare would cover them up to three months, not up to six months as was previously the case.

Well, this raised a great uproar. There were cries and letters in the paper about how arbitrary this was, that it was illegal. One said, "When is this abuse of seniors going to end?" It was as if the health minister were a cruel hawk, about to swoop down and rob the poor snowbirds of their last savings. Most of the snowbirds almost by definition are among the better-off seniors. I wrote a column about this and said, "This country's treating us old people well, better than it can now afford to." I pointed out that over-65s consume 40 percent of the medicare bill, and that there had to be some economizing done, and I said that here are these better-off people saying, "Economize on somebody else," which is the typical reaction when economic changes are proposed. So then I drew their wrath instead of the government. But they kept enough of it on the government that it backed down. The government has put the matter on hold, which is just a way of burying it, so New Brunswick still pays (at the New Brunswick rates, mind you) for six months' medicare coverage in wintertime. To me, if there's stringency in government accounts, if there's a need for saving, that's an obvious place to save. I'd say, "No coverage outside." Let them get their own private health insurance.

The solution to the problem of dependency, if there is one, is to create more self-reliance. Canada has to get out of this situation. I think we're going to be forced to do so, maybe just by gradually going broke.

PAUL BROWN

Nova Scotia: Transfer Payments

During and after the First World War the federal government decided that this part of Canada would be a source of raw materials and an army outpost, if you will, but that the heart of the industry was going to be in the heart of Canada, which was Ontario. That's the Canadian bargain. We get the money — they get the jobs. The jobs are in Ontario and the money to spend goes to Atlantic Canada and the West. It's kind of a Faustian bargain from our point of view because the trouble is, that's not the way to build communities. That's the way you build dependency and habits, and I think that that has to be broken.

As far as I'm concerned, transfer payments are pay bargains, pure and simple. They work like this: the central part of Canada funnels money to the outlying parts of Canada as payment for having the centre of economic activity in central Canada. Some transfer payments don't allow areas like Nova Scotia to offer a level of services that are of an acceptable Canadian standard without imposing an unacceptably high level of taxation.

Transfer payments have a number of features. There are equalization transfers, federal transfers and personal transfers, like unemployment insurance and family allowance. Then there are economic development transfers, as in spending by the Atlantic Canada Opportunities Agency. It's a mix and you have to separate out which elements of the mix you're going to talk about.

I think ACOA has done some good things, but it's hard to decide whether the overall impact is good or bad. ACOA is often viewed outside the region, particularly from the wealthier parts of Canada, as being an example of the generosity of Canada to the underprivileged parts of Canada in an attempt to spur development. And I'm sure that government feels very good about that. But the reality is the kind of development they want to spur is not development that will compete with anything in particular that's being done there. So it seems to me we're to grow, but we're to grow in a very specific kind of way.

ACOA has produced some jobs but it's always worked under the constraint that it could bring aid to the Maritimes, short of jobs that might go to Ontario or to central Canada. To the extent that it helps us achieve such things as participating in the global information economy, then I'm all for ACOA. But I don't think ACOA speaks to the fundamental changes that have to be made. And that is a change in confidence.

The biggest change with ACOA in recent years has been that the agency has become less involved in making major handouts and much more involved in trying to develop a sense of entrepreneurship on the part of Atlantic Canadian business. If this helps to recover a sense of entrepreneurship, it could have a role. But I don't see it as a role of funnelling all kinds of money. That's not the answer as I see it. The difficulty is in trying to determine how successful it's been.

The most recent development efforts in Atlantic Canada since the 1960s have had one kind of objective, and that is to increase income and employment opportunities. Well, what exactly does that mean? It only makes sense to me if you put some figures where the phrases are. How much income? How many jobs are you suggesting you're going to create? What kind of measures are you going to use to determine whether you've been successful at increasing entrepreneurship? We haven't had those measures, so we've had great difficulty in assessing the impact of the organization and, for that reason, in defending what it's been doing.

If you listened to the Economic Council of Canada, free trade had the potential to produce 484 jobs in Nova Scotia. That was the anticipated benefit. I think it's much more profound than that. Free trade has undercut, perhaps shattered would be a better word, the foundation for the Canadian bargain that saw jobs concentrated in Ontario and money distributed to Atlantic Canada.

What is supposed to be an east-west Canadian sense of nationhood is now going to be north-south. So free trade has changed the ball game, which I think is good for the long term. Our resource-based industries will profit from free trade. But it's going to cause some short-term pain, for sure. I hate to beat on the federal government, but nevertheless, free trade makes it much more difficult for the federal government to use policy and monetary fiscal tools to sustain a bargain that has resulted in having money but no development in our communities. The playing field is now going to be levelled and I think that our inherent entrepreneurship and drive and persistence are going to make us winners in the new economy that's developing, provided we take the right steps to make it happen.

I've looked at literature which suggests that part of the reason the Atlantic provinces are in the state they're in — trapped in a kind of a dependency syndrome, downcast and not very hopeful about the future — is that there is some part of our political culture which leads them to be that way. It suggests that the political culture of other parts of Canada is more dynamic, critical and aggressive. But I've done research that shows that the political culture of Nova Scotia is identical with Sweden's, yet no one would suggest that Sweden is downcast, lacking in confidence or underdeveloped. It suggests to me that we have the basis in political values here which could see us become one of the leading social democracies in the world.

It certainly can be true that a resource-based economy can reach a point where the resource has too many people for what's available. We've certainly got that in the Atlantic Canadian fishery now. Obviously that resource over my lifetime is not going to support the number of people that it once did. That's an economic reality and when it happens you have to adjust.

This happens all over the world. Take Sweden, for example. The Swedish government looks at an industry and it decides that if it doesn't have economic potential for future labour management, they'll undertake the adjustment policy necessary to get people retrained for the opportunities. They don't necessarily have to go away, they can move to another region of Sweden, but they don't have to go to the United States. No. The key point is that the Swedes have a much more realistic view of these things. They don't anticipate that they'll be doing the same thing all their lives, the same thing their fathers and grandfathers did. In terms of opportunity they're looking ahead, not back.

Halifax is a world-class port which has not resulted in a world-class level of economic development. One common explanation is that we're on the periphery of the North American economy and as such we're just a conduit through which things flow. Most ports in other areas of the world produce a lot of economic development around the port itself, but we've never achieved that. I think it's in part because decisions have been that economic development will occur elsewhere and that we'll be a funnel for the flow of resources and products being produced elsewhere, going back and forth. There's always been a difficulty in economic development here because we are on the margins of the continental economy. We've been looked upon as a centre for a supplier of resources that are processed elsewhere.

Nova Scotia has huge supplies of gypsum and it's regularly mined here, but it is sent to the mideastern United States to be processed into wallboard, which is then sold back to us. We're told that the economics of shipping the gypsum and wallboard make it such that the manufacturing has to be elsewhere. We get the low end of the economic activity, which is exploiting and harvesting the resource, and somebody else gets the high end, which is turning those resources into products, which are then sold back to us. One of the tremendous advantages of an information society and economy is that this won't happen anymore. The value of the product lies in the mind of the person. Therefore, if Nova Scotians are generating the information, then the returns will accrue to them and not to somebody else.

I think a better dollars-and-cents example, in terms of the States, would be in the area of pulp and paper. Nova Scotia sells a lot of lumber to European/American markets, where it is manufactured into furniture and sold back to us for 10 times the price. That's the trap you get into if you're going to be a supplier of resources, a hewer of wood and drawer of water — that's the syndrome you get into. And I think it's one that we've been caught up in.

We're on the winds of yet another economic change. For example, it's well known that in Atlantic Canada our economy is 70 percent a service-based economy. I think the winds of change have now decreed that the economy is going to be global and it's going to be service-oriented. It's going to be a computer-based, information-based economy. I believe that if Nova Scotians once set sail and piloted their ships all around the world and had a thriving economy, we can set our sails again to capture the winds of the electronic revolution that's going on now. It's the communications revolution and we can find prosperity again. I have no doubt in the world about that.

But politicians can play on people's fears here in Nova Scotia. They say and do things that get them elected. In Nova Scotia, because in the last 100 years or so we've been resource-based, there is a kind of mystique about resources, so all politicians argue that resource development must be the foundation for Nova Scotia's economic development. They all say this: "We're going to move ahead on the basis of fisheries, forestry, agriculture and the like." But the reality is that the vast majority of our economy is not resource-based, so politicians who are unable to cut the Gordian knot, as it were, who still try to see us as the kind of resource-based society we once were, are not helping the public to make the transition to the information society that we are becoming.

I think there are two things that are happening. If you look at the forestry, the fisheries and some of the mineral sector, you'll find we send huge amounts of resources to the United States. We've also sent people there in the past. So I think our links to the United States, particularly the eastern United States, are very strong.

On the other hand we have an industry that is not a resource industry, the geomatics industry, which is cutting edge in terms of the information economy. Geomatics is an industry centered on the computer-based manipulation of geographic information. It is land-based, marine-based information which brings to bear computer technologies and some fundamental characteristics of our land and resources. It was initiated in Atlantic Canada. It actually started with a federal program, I have to admit, called the Atlantic Canada Surveys and Mapping Program. On that basis we created an agency called the Land Resource Information Service, an Atlantic Canadian agency. Over the years, in its own right and by stimulating private industry, that produced what is now a very aggressive and cutting-edge industry in the Atlantic provinces.

We have a nucleus of firms; actually it's not a nucleus anymore, there are about 70 of them. And if you look at the front-runners amongst these firms, they're exporting all over the globe — Latin America, the Far East — so we're not restricted to north-south ties at all. Globalization means that the world is your marketplace, and if you have the guts to go after it, you can thrive in that marketplace. And I think we do.

I think there are a variety of factors to account for why we're not as confident as we might be in Nova Scotia. One is that we have gone through a long period in which there's been a fundamental discontinuity between our aspirations and our achievements. And beyond that I think what stirs within the hearts of most Nova Scotians is a sense that we really weren't meant to be underdeveloped, we were meant for something better than what we've got. It gets particularly frustrating because you see a lot of Nova Scotians leaving and going elsewhere. I saw that in my own family coming from Cumberland County. That hurts Nova Scotians and it's been true for us since the 1880s. People have gone down the road, as they say.

The first thing I would say to young Nova Scotians to try to keep them here is not to believe what everybody says about you. We're told, and the media emphasizes it, that this is a disadvantaged part of Canada, that it doesn't have many prospects and can only survive through generosity and handouts from the wealthier parts of the country. I think that's a crock. There's nothing at all standing between Nova Scotia and development. All we have to do is rediscover the tradition of entrepreneurship that we once had, that made us famous around the world. "Rediscover your past. It's a very noble past. It's a past of people who did things, who strove and achieved and you could be part of that." That's what I would say.

I think our sense of entrepreneurship is still here, but I think it just got buried a bit for various reasons. The economy changed. People had to adapt, but we in Nova Scotia didn't adapt quickly enough to economic change, particularly the change from being a resource-based economy to a manufacturing-based economy. We didn't achieve that. I think part of the reason was that a greater power than us determined what kind of a role we would play in Canada.

To the hypothetical fisherman, recently laid off and lacking the educational tools for the new economy, I would say that leaving the province isn't the answer. I think the answer is to build opportunities for you in the province. I don't accept, and never have accepted and never will accept, that the answer to the problem of development in this part of Canada is for people to leave. For me it's absolutely a non-starter.

Yet we've heard throughout our history that this is the solution. The Gordon Commission, led by Walter Gordon, who became finance minister in the Pearson government, wrote a report on the economic prospects of Canada in 1958. He said things were quite bad in Atlantic Canada and would be less bad if people who couldn't find opportunity here simply left and went to Ontario. That's suggesting that this part of Canada is not fit for human habitation and I reject that categorically. If the hypothetical fisherman needs assistance, if I were in government I would say, "You've got to be somewhat flexible, but if you're flexible enough to be willing to leave the province, you should be flexible enough to move to another part of the province. I'll give you the money to get educated." I think government has a major role in ensuring that we have the human resource base that we need to thrive in the economy that's now emerging. And I wouldn't think twice about putting that money into people and education.

But people might not be as willing to take that sort of personal responsibility as they're going to have to be. That's probably one of the greatest barriers we have to overcome. People tend to be perhaps too comfortable in the way of life that has been. People don't see clearly enough that major changes, which hold great promise for them, are afoot. But they may have to change in order to seize them. I don't think people are as yet as willing to change and rise to the challenge as they could be because I don't think the challenge has been put to them in a way that lets them see an opportunity.

Nova Scotians are a hardy lot and can absolutely survive on their own. And not just survive: I think we have the capacity to build a society that will be the envy of the world. Perhaps I'm overly dramatic but I really believe that we have a combination of a wonderful natural endowment, in terms of our resources, and a growing information economy. I mean, look around Nova Scotia. Every aspect of the province, every portion of the province is wonderful. The information economy will allow communities to thrive in Nova Scotia whereas now they can't.

People respond to hope. If they have a sense of hope in the future and an expectation that things can be better, then they're prepared to take some of the short-term pain that it takes to get there. That's why we became a society in the first place. People came to Nova Scotia from Ireland and Scotland. They settled here and they faced years of deprivation. It was really difficult work to make a place for themselves but they did it because they had the expectation of a future. If we have an expectation of a future here, then we'll be prepared to take the pain of being weaned off federal grants and handouts. I wouldn't want all transfers to end tomorrow, but I don't anticipate that they'll be around forever. I'm assuming they'll be gone before I live a normal life span.

To tell you the truth, I'm much more inclined to see us doing things on our own, rather than having the federal government play a role in regional development. The federal government has never proven to be a great generator of jobs, except perhaps in Ottawa. I would rather see us do it on our own. Nova Scotia's place in Canada is contributing to the federal government to help other parts of the country, not taking handouts. Let's call that an aspiration, if you will.

Murray Coolican

Nova Scotia: A Changing Economy

There's a perception in the rest of the country that there are no jobs in the Maritimes or Atlantic Canada, that it's a totally depressed region. That nothing is happening, that the entire fishery is closed down, that you shouldn't be eating fish because it's possibly the last one that you're going to get. But there still is a good fishery. It's not necessarily in groundfish, but it's in lobster and scallops and that sort of thing. Our lobster prices are pretty good and the lobster fishery is strong. There are jobs here. There is a vibrant economy. So there's a real misperception about what's happening here, that everything is backwards.

Well, that's not the case, and it hasn't been the case probably ever in the Maritimes. There is an economy here that is working, that is active. One of the things that is happening is that people are recognizing the downsides of dependency and the need to create a stronger economy. I also think that modern technology will make it easier for companies to develop in areas like the Maritimes because people will be looking for a better quality of life, a nicer place to live than large cities, and technology will make it possible for them to work in a region like this without suffering the difficulties of getting products to market because a lot of them will be information-based products. There are a lot of interesting small businesses starting here, based on the initiative of people and on people taking advantage of new technology.

The fishery has too often been used as a tool for social programming, not economic development. In the last 10 to 15 years of the fishery, with the exception of the last, say, three or four years, there was an increase of 10,000 people in the fishery in Atlantic Canada. What allowed that to happen was unemployment insurance, where subsidies allowed people to build small fish plants and to buy bigger boats that could catch more fish. So you had this huge increase of people in the fishery, but not because there was enough fish out there or because it was an efficient business. It was simply because of government subsidies and policies.

It's kind of strange that on the one hand you had federal fisheries ministers trying to reduce the number of small fish that were being caught, and at the same time you had whatever the subsidy department was at the time providing subsidies to small fish plant owners to buy new equipment that would allow them to process smaller and smaller fish. It didn't make any sense.

They did that because, from a social policy and social engineering point of view, the subsidy departments wanted to create jobs. They wanted to create more employment, so they gave these subsidies to fish plant workers to enable them to buy the machines that would allow them to process the small fish that were now being caught. In other cases the government had this notion that fishermen should not have to take all their fish to fish plants owned by the large fish companies, that they should be taking their fish to fish plants that they themselves owned. So you had a program in which the federal government was encouraging fishermen to build their own fish plants. But the government was still subsidizing some of the large fish companies to build fish plants. The increased number of fish plants meant that, first of all, fewer and fewer people could make a good living in the fishery. It also meant that there was too much pressure on the fish stocks, which resulted in a collapse in the fish stocks as well as a collapse on the business side of the fishery.

You had a modern plant in Lockport, Nova Scotia, that was built, I believe, in the late 1970s. The reason it had to close down was because it couldn't get fish from the inshore fishermen anymore because they were taking fish to their own fish plants that had been built with subsidies from the same government that had subsidized Lockport! So that what you wound up with was an overcapacity of fish plants, which created too much demand on the fishery. And eventually the system collapsed and a lot of those fish plants are now closed. Without those subsidies perhaps we would still have a viable fishery here. Again I've used the phrase "the collapse of the fishery," yet there's still a good scallop fishery in Nova Scotia. There is still a good lobster fishery. The collapse is happening in the groundfish fishery.

I think certainly what the government has done through a combination of unemployment insurance and the fishery is create a dependence on something that is not economic. It has encouraged those people who only fish seasonally at certain times of the year to get into the fishery. That creates new jobs but they're only 10-week jobs, so then they can get on unemployment insurance. You have an increased dependence now, so when the government has to cut back and looks to unemployment insurance to cut back, it could have a really negative impact. It means that part of the fishery is not an economic business.

I think false security has been created by unemployment insurance. We've built an economic system in parts of our economy around unemployment insurance. Families, to get annual earnings to allow them to live for a year, will trade UI stamps among themselves. A wife who perhaps gets 25 weeks of work in a fish plant may share her UI stamps with her husband, who may not have work, so that he gets 10 weeks. She may give the extra five to somebody else in the family so that they can get their 10 weeks and then go on unemployment insurance for the rest of the year. They then feel they have an annual salary or an annual income when in effect they don't. What it's based on is 42 weeks a year of unemployment insurance payments. It's more or less widespread, but I think it depends on the fishery in the region, how good it is and how long the season is.

I was involved in the fishery myself and there are lots of stories around of people who do that. There are stories of fish plant owners who will work with their employees to try and make sure that they get enough stamps or can distribute their stamps. It's not only in the fishery where that kind of thing happens, where people are trading around the edges of unemployment insurance. I've known people in business who as employers were asked to say, when an employee left, that they were laid off rather than that they chose to leave the job so that they could go on unemployment insurance.

If you take the subsidies away, it will take millions and millions of dollars out of the economy here and it will be a wrenching experience. It could lead to the collapse of a lot of businesses. So how government responds to that is going to be important because in overcoming one problem you don't want to create another. But in the long run I think it would be better. It would be forcing people to look for other things to do.

When I talked to a fisherman once, an older fellow, about where he got his income, only a certain portion of it came from the fishery purse. He had the skill to build his own boat, so in a sense he was a boat builder as well as a fisherman. He gathered his own fuel, which meant he was in the fuel-supply business, in a sense. He hunted for some of his food. Before the animal rights activists got to it, he was involved in sealing. That also formed a part of his income.

What he sees now is people who were taken out of the fishery and sent to school with the promise of new jobs. But there were no new jobs, so they went back to the fishery, but they didn't learn at school how to do all the other things to make an annual income that you could get by on. They didn't know how to build boats. They didn't know how to gather their fuel. They weren't hunters. We put those people into schools, taking them away from their parents, where they could learn subsistence skills, and prepared them for jobs that don't exist.

Government needs to help the out-of-work fisherman to become more independent rather than dependent, and it may not be a single job that they go to. It may be a number of jobs, a number of activities that they can undertake to supplement their income. But if you continue to provide unemployment insurance, you're never going to get away with that. It's not going to be easy to retrain people, and you can't just cut people off and expect them all of a sudden, after years of depending on something like unemployment insurance, to be able to swim. They will need some assistance. But if we don't start moving away from it, as difficult as it is going to be, we'll just continue in this dependency. There is a program that was begun in southwestern Nova Scotia: the Calmeadow Foundation, along with the banks, assisted small entrepreneurs with capital to get them going. We're not talking millions of dollars; we're talking about $1,000 here, $2,000 there, to assist with capital to allow people to start small businesses.

In terms of ACOA and the like, I think it depends how regional development programs are structured. They do take more money out of the taxpayer and often they're not successful in creating employment. Perhaps more of that money should be put into teaching entrepreneurial skills and training people to take advantage of the opportunities that are here or are going to be here in the next 10 or 15 years, rather than creating artificial situations that encourage a company to locate here just as long as the artificial subsidy remains.

There are a lot of things happening in this region in terms of economic development and activity that bear no relation at all to government subsidies, that bear no relation at all to government economic development strategies. It's just people taking initiative and going out and doing things with what's around them. There was a story on the radio this morning about a guy who had been laid off who has now developed a pet cemetery. He's now earning a living for himself, getting away from his dependence on unemployment insurance.

You could say that UI has created something of an underground economy, but it's not just fraudulent activity. There are some people in the fishery who earn a very good living, you know, $100,000, $150,000 a year. At the end of the season they go on unemployment. And they do it quite legally. It's within the system. I know people who work in Halifax who have a contract for a certain period of the year, then go on unemployment for the rest of the year, and the contract is renewed the next year. That's just working with the system in the same way that a businessman or another Canadian would. They do whatever they can with the tax system to decrease the amount they have to pay in taxes. It's not illegal, what they're doing; they're just using the system that exists to their full advantage.

There are a lot of Canadians who are involved in dependence on government incomes and we can't afford that anymore, so we all have a responsibility to try and get people in Canada, not just in the Atlantic provinces, away from this dependency. But I think people have to avoid the easy answer, either as a Maritimer or somebody living in another part of the country, that Ottawa or somebody else has a major role to play in getting us off dependence on them. It's in a sense a new kind of dependence, which says we can't get off this unless we have help from Ottawa to get us off it.

One of the problems for Atlantic Canada is that as a result of the extent of our dependency and the amount of money that flows to Atlantic Canada from the government, people in other parts of the country are going to lose patience. They have a perception that nothing happens here except for the money that flows from Ottawa. They're going to say, "Hey, why do we keep sending all this money to Atlantic Canada and there's nothing happening down there?" We're going to be cut off at some point.

But Western Canadians can't say Atlantic Canada is the only region that has received heavy transfer payments because it's not just in Atlantic Canada. Take a look at the railroads. Most of their activity in terms of freight and passengers is in central Canada and Western Canada. The railroad unions have contracts that if someone is laid off, they get paid for the rest of their working life, and when they reach retirement age they get their full pension. Who else in Canada has that? Certainly not people working in the fishery. Is that fair?

There are some subsidies to Eastern Canada that actually benefit central Canada more than they benefit Atlantic Canada, like the subsidies to Hibernia in Newfoundland. Most of the equipment that is being purchased to put together the Hibernia oil development is being manufactured, not in Atlantic Canada or Newfoundland, but in Ontario and Quebec and other parts of the world. So if you were to look at the economic spinoff benefits from that subsidy, you'd find a lot of it goes back to jobs in Ontario and Quebec and a certain number in Western Canada, particularly in Alberta.

Maritimers have got to learn, like the rest of the world, that we're in a changing world; we're in a changing environment. It means learning. It means going back to some of the independent and outward-looking ideas that Maritimers had in their history. Before Confederation this was a very strong trading region that looked out to the world to make its living. There were a lot of entrepreneurs, a lot of people who worked hard. I think we have to rekindle some of that spirit. Obviously not with trading in schooners with sails, but perhaps by becoming adept at trading in the new technology era, where you'll be able to access people through computer networks just as easily from Yarmouth as from Tokyo.

RON WHYNACHT

Nova Scotia: Modernizing the Fishing Industry

National Sea Products is one of Canada's oldest fishing companies, founded in 1898, and was quite large until a few years ago. In 1987 we processed about 300 million pounds of fish, and this year, 1994, we'll probably land 24 million pounds.

In the mid-1980s the industry was still growing. Ships and plants were being built. We were very much in an expansionary mode at that time, but the collapse of the fishery in the late 1980s caused the whole industry to rethink itself, and our company was no different than others. We went from somewhere in the vicinity of 7,500 employees down to about 1,200. So if success is generated by the pounds of fish that you land, we haven't been successful lately. We went through a shakeup in the last couple of years as a result of the downturn in the northern cod fishery. It forced us to sell off many of our businesses.

It's not clear what was the single biggest cause of the downturn in the cod fisheries, or where the codfish went, whether it was entirely caught, or it moved, or it failed to reproduce as it normally would because of the environment. The most popular theory is a combination of several factors, including overharvesting, the environment and the predator-prey relationship. The combination of all those things, including overfishing by foreign nations, has been a formula for disaster. If a mistake was made, it was that the industry lacked a lot of research and scientific advice in terms of what was going on in the fishery. This thing sneaked up on people. There are fishermen and other people in the industry who would tell you that they saw this coming, but while they were saying that, the government, the scientific community, companies and people at large were continuing to forge ahead.

Fishermen and fishing companies basically rely, and certainly we did, on the Department of Fisheries and Oceans, and it's a different department today than it was 10 years ago, but I don't think they were thinking about short-term profit so much as just trying to manage the fishery. It's a very complicated fishery, and I suspect in my heart that the people who were responsible in those days were doing what they thought was the right job, and that the fishing companies were following the plans, quotas and regulations that were set out.

One of the major problems that occurred as a result of this downturn was that people started losing their jobs. Fishermen had no fish to catch, and their boats stayed in port. Then it started to spread to the processing plants. There wasn't enough fish to process, so the plants started closing. A lot of social and community problems started to develop. How were these people going to live? Where were they going to go? Many people in the fishery were not trained and did not have the skills to do jobs other than fishing and processing fish. In many of the rural communities the hardship was unbelievable. In some of the bigger communities, like the one here in Lunenburg where we'd already started to diversify quite a few years ago, there was work available.

Before that point a lot of people just weren't giving it much thought. The fisheries seemed good and people hung on to the traditional side of the fishery, probably for too long. It's not easy today. Capital is short. People don't want to invest in the seafood business, or haven't wanted to do so up to this point because we've still been in a downturn. We were always thinking every year that this was the bottom, and then we'd find out the next year that there was even more bad news. People have been looking at underutilized species and at new kinds of fisheries. They've been looking at ways to get around this crisis, but it hasn't resulted in a lot of success so far.

We were very close to being in serious trouble. The company had debts in excess of $100 million. And these were all debt-financed; very little was equity-financed. This came from our expansion through the 1980s, when the fishery was quite healthy. We had to financially restructure our business. We had to sell off many of our foreign operations, including a very big food service business in the United States. Our company wrote off $50 million of assets last year; that came right out of shareholders' equity. So it was tough sledding. It still is tough sledding. It's a very tough business.

What we did differently here in Lunenburg to survive the downturn was refocus our business primarily on our Canadian customers. The emphasis there was to be the best in our class in terms of customer satisfaction. We weren't able to satisfy all of the customers in all of the markets, so we refocused our business very narrowly during that period. We also scoured the world to find fish, to find raw material that we could bring into this plant to keep it going. Having invested in the international marketplace, we had good contacts in terms of where we could go to get fish. That really helped us turn the corner. I think that other companies could learn a lot from what we've done in terms of sourcing, externally trying new things and value-adding. But all of these things do take investment, and in an industry that's broke it's hard to raise that kind of capital. We've been fortunate in our company to have loyal, primarily Atlantic Canadian investors who've stuck with us. That's part of the reason we've been able to survive the downturn.

The town of Lunenburg has only 3,000 people. But a very small percentage of our workers actually live in the town of Lunenburg; most of them are from the outlying areas. We're in a medium-sized populated area in this part of Nova Scotia and people seem particularly willing to travel upwards of 75 or 80 miles to come to work here every day. In some of the other rural communities the population is so spread out that it's difficult, the commute would just be too long. However, I think that the long-term work opportunities for people in those rural communities aren't out there. They're going to realize that they have to give up that way of life, as tragic as it may seem. And as hard as it may be, commuting is one way around that. They'll come to realize that people have to gravitate to those centres where there is work, where there do appear to be job opportunities. And there has been some reluctance in Atlantic Canada to do so.

Nevertheless, there is work. Next week in this plant, which employs about 850 people, we're actually going to be hiring back some more, about 20 people. Now, they won't be permanent jobs, but there will probably be work here until early in the new year. Most of our laid-off people in this particular area have been called back and many of the people commute to get that work.

The town of Lunenburg is quite fortunate. We like to consider ourselves the fishing capital of Canada. The Canadian scallop fleet is headquartered here; National Sea Products is still one of Canada's largest and most diversified fish processing operations. When we did lay people off here in Lunenburg, and at one point we laid off about 350 people in total, there was a lot of shock in the community. With National Sea in Lunenburg people always felt, "At least they're still going," but when they heard that we were laying people off and were in trouble, people felt that this was really the end. Morale was bad, but again not as bad, I think, as at some of our other fish plants in rural communities, in Newfoundland and Cape Breton, where they really didn't have many other options.

We keep hearing the question over and over again, "Are there too many fishermen for too few fish?" And the answer is definitely yes. That's why the Government of Canada is working so aggressively through the Human Resources Department and the fisheries to get some of the older people, particularly, out of the industry, and also to retrain some of the younger people.

In areas where the downturn hit the hardest, people in Atlantic Canada have to change their way of thinking. That's tragic in most cases because it tears at the roots of the people, their culture and the way they were brought up. It's not just transferring to a different industry. It's really a whole different way of life. It's going to be very, very difficult, as we found out, to retrain people and to get them to move.

But I think that when all is said and done that's the only answer. A few communities will diversify. Some form of new fishery will come in. People will bide their time until the fishery returns, but they will have to move to where the work is. Transfer payments from Ottawa do help the fishermen and plant workers in these communities, but we have to be careful not to set up a false sense of security. A lot of people in the rest of Canada sense that. It is a difficult issue, and there aren't a lot of options for these people. Financial support from the federal government will be important in the short term, but it's not something that we can afford to do long term. The Canadian taxpayer can't afford to continue to support these communities for the long haul. It's a humanistic issue. People are genuinely feeling bad for people in Atlantic Canada, particularly those of us who are still working here, for those brothers and sisters who aren't working. It is a very humanistic, gut-wrenching issue. We're all striving to find a solution that works.

We don't know when the fish are going to come back. I'd like to think that they will come back, but we don't know if that will take five years or 10 years, and that's a long time. What we need are some assurances that we're going to have fish, raw material to continue to operate here. And what concerns us is that fish will be moved around to other parts of Atlantic Canada to help out other communities, and then we'll have another economic disaster.

Over the last 10 years a significant amount of the fish that was harvested by some of the offshore companies has been transferred inshore, and that's something that we continue to see, into these smaller communities. But that puts some of the major, vertically integrated companies at a degree of risk. It has affected our company. We've had to shut down a lot of our other fish processing plants in smaller communities. We'd concentrate our fish into one plant to make it viable; otherwise we'd have two or three plants closing their doors. So we've had to retrench around our strongest, best and most diversified plants.

I think that the government has a responsibility to keep the healthy businesses healthy. Otherwise the whole East Coast Atlantic fishery is in jeopardy.

JOHN ELDON GREEN

Prince Edward Island: Education and Jobs

Government should be involved in the business of creating government jobs. They do a very good job of that. I have a little difficulty with the idea that government can create the kind of jobs that they now talk about. I've been watching that for 25 years, since the days when the Department of Manpower was created, when it was the federal government's initiative to generate jobs for the economy. I wasn't privy to what was going on across the country but I presume it was very much the same as what happened here. The new department hired new university graduates. I saw young people being hired straight out of university whose mandate was to create jobs. And I wondered how that was going to work. Twenty-five years later I'm still wondering how that works.

The island's best and brightest are courted by the central Canadian accounting firms. They'll come down here in the spring and they'll interview the graduating students from the business administration program and they'll pick off the best and off they go. But we're not losing new entrepreneurs in that fashion because the new entrepreneurs really aren't graduating from university. Very few people who go through that program will start new businesses.

The whole school system is geared to get people to university. They say education is the key to the economy but when I look around to see who's generating jobs, it's people who haven't got university degrees. But you get people who have their bachelor's in business administration and who are not getting work. They go and get their MBAs and then they come out of university with a major debt load and they go work for other people. They wind up working for people who had the good sense to leave school early and to start a business. In fact, the biggest entrepreneurs here are people who left school early. But government continues to emphasize degrees. If you haven't got a degree, you don't get in the line-up.

So you have government emphasizing that we need economists because they're the ones who can tell us about the economy and they're the ones who can help us generate jobs. That's not what economists do. They measure jobs that other people create. But there is no evidence that people with degrees are very good at generating new jobs. They only get to the front of the line to get the jobs that are created. Jobs are created by the risk takers, by the entrepreneurs, the gamblers. People who can afford to take a loss, who have the time. They're young and they take the time. My daughter's fiancé left school. I don't think he finished high school. He got himself a backhoe and started digging trenches.

This is how it happens. You get a backhoe, then you get another backhoe, and then you get a truck to go with the backhoe, and then you start getting small contracts. Then you start getting big contracts and you're building houses, and then you're hiring engineers and architects to work for you.

You do an analysis of the members of Cabinets across the country and find how many of them are major employers. There are a lot of professional people. You've got a lot of teachers. You've got people like me. I don't generate work. I hire three or four people a year, maybe five or six, depending on how many contracts I get. I'm not an entrepreneur. I'm a professional man offering a service to the community. I'm not bringing in whole lot of new money to the island. So I just don't see how that can happen.

I have a story for you. I was at a conference with the premier. It was the premiers' conference when the premiers all agreed that government should now be creating jobs; that would be the new initiative right across the country. So they dispatched a group to prepare the press statement that this was the new thrust of governments right across the country. At the break I turned to our premier and I said, "I have a little bit of a problem with that, Premier. When you go back to the island now, your news statement is that you're going to generate jobs and then you're going to turn around and say, 'We've got to do this.' But who is going to do it? You turn to people like me and you say, 'No, we'd like you to start creating jobs.' I have to tell you that if I was any good at creating jobs, I wouldn't be working for you, I'd be out there making money creating jobs because that's how you make money."

I told him about the kind of jobs I could create, which weren't the kind of jobs he was interested in. I wanted probation workers and homemakers and things like that. He said there were other people in government who had different gifts, the people in the economic development sector, and he presumed that they would be able to do this. I said, "OK, Premier, that begs the question: if they are good at creating jobs, then why are they working for you? Why aren't they out there creating jobs? So I have to say they're not very smart because they could be making money and here they are working for you." So the premier turned and walked away from me and that was the end of that conversation.

I turned to a minister from another province and I said, "I want to put the same question to you that I just put to the premier. Do you have people working in your government who are good at creating jobs? If that's the case, I have to say they're kind of boobs. Why aren't they creating jobs and making money?" And there was no answer. He said, "Well, you know, that's how it works." And I know that's how it works. This commitment had no substance because there wasn't the capability of doing it. So that's a long answer. Twenty years later I still haven't seen that ministers or deputies or government officials are very good at creating jobs.

If you've driven through the island, you don't get the impression of a have-not province. It's a have-not government rather than a have-not province. The business community here on the island consists of small businesses. There are no major initiatives. We have Cavendish Farms and McCain doing potato processing. We have a few major operators but we're all busy trying to get another contract, trying to meet our cash flow needs to get through the day. We don't have spare people who can do this heavy kind of thinking for us. I presume it's the same in the other Atlantic provinces: the small businesses have difficulty in visionary, forward thinking. But when you see opportunities there, we have to move on them.

During the province's big comprehensive development plan back in 1969, it was necessary to make some changes to the structure of the island economy. We had a lot of farms that weren't going to survive with 100 acres, 120 acres, with 40, 50 acres of potato production. We had too many fishermen. We had too many wharves. We had too many people taking small bites. So the development plan restructured some of the components of the economy, and government was very good at that. They had the information and they could put in incentives to make that happen.

Let me describe the phenomenon of "Other People's Money" and what it means to the island. Let's start with equalization. With the development plan there was a lot of money in incentives for businesses to get established. We started the development plan with incentives to encourage people to start new businesses because, as we consolidated the farms and consolidated the fisheries, there were a lot of people that couldn't find work. And as the farmers were getting more and more mechanized, there had to be some way of getting new types of businesses to start up.

So the incentives to do market studies and feasibility studies were there. Fifty percent of the money was there for start-up incentives. There were some loans, some grants, and as time went on it would have been very foolish to not take advantage of that money. I haven't had a whole lot of experience in dealing with banks, but the extent to which the government is going to guarantee the loan would decide whether or not the banks would invest. High-risk investments were left to government. The banks were not risking any more. And when the banks stop risking it's really hard to expect an individual entrepreneur to risk.

It got to be that the business initiatives were highly dependent on the extent to which government money was available. So we finished the development plan in 1984. The different governments in place would come up with a new approach for the next series of five-year agreements. We're into another series that's now coming to an end with ACOA. There have been some changes. We had DREE, which became DRIE, which became ACOA, and now we're in little bit of nervousness whether or not we will have another agreement with more incentives. So we've had 25 years now of becoming addicted to grants, and "addicted" is the closest way to describe it. It was pretty hard to do anything without getting a grant. You hear people in business who are opposed to the whole concept that governments should do this, but they say, "I'd be foolish not to do it because the other guy, the competition, has an advantage." After 25 years it's very difficult all of a sudden to say we're not going to do that anymore. Where do you go with it? Particularly with the banks being as cautious as they are, never having to get into these risk areas.

I have to tell you I don't understand the debt. I'm the last person in the world to give you a sensible answer on that. The young people on the island, they're not conscious of the debt. It's a political problem. If you're in politics and you want to do new things and the money's all eaten up by maintaining current services, then you've got to find room to do new things. You have to start putting the squeeze on. The debt is a fairly convenient argument because really the big problem is, what do you do? You don't get elected to baby-sit government. You get elected to do important new things and then you get in there and find the money's all gone. I have to tell you there's a touch of cynicism in me.

When it looked like the fixed link (Confederation Bridge) was about to be built, I had a contract with Public Works, so I attended the hearings and realized that this bridge is going to be built. It's going to take some time but they're going to build a bridge. There's no reason not to build a bridge. So I started nagging people that we should start preparing for business opportunities coming out of the fixed link. I was embarrassing myself because I'm going around creating this urgency. So the local business community met with the premier and he gave them his assurances that the bridge wasn't that imminent and that they would be looked after. So he appointed several civil servants to look into business opportunities coming out of the link.

I was looking for a contract but it was really that I wanted to see the opportunity realized. Trying to impress upon the business community that when they get a contract to build a bridge they'll need bridge builders, not economic development people. They're going to give jobs to whoever shows up with the capability of giving jobs. So they have a commitment to provide so many jobs in the region but they can say, "Look, sorry guys, you don't have anyone qualified."

I was trying to get the province and the business community to prepare for this sort of thing and it didn't happen because the premier said, "We're looking after this." I used to say, "Who's Joe Ghiz?" And people would say, "Joe's the premier," but I said, "OK, but who is Joe Ghiz? Tell me how he's going to do this." Well, now when I say, "Who's Joe Ghiz?" they understand what I mean because he's not here anymore. So we didn't do a whole lot to prepare ourselves for the bridge.

I mean, this thing is costing around $800 million to build. There's a lot of money bleeding out of that, so you have to be ready to meet the demands of the builder if you want it to work. It'll be opening next month and we're going to have a flood of new tourists coming here because of the bridge. Now the projections are conservative about the additional visitors each year. It's about 125,000 more. And that's conservative. We need to start preparing for all these visitors because this summer we had people sleeping in their cars. They couldn't find a place to stay on the island. There are people who went back to the mainland because they couldn't get accommodations. But with the bridge they can back out an awful lot faster. They come over, see the island and get back to the mainland. So we have to start preparing the tourism industry for the bridge. I don't see that happening.

I think the problem is that the business community has gotten so used to the assurance of government saying they're on top of things, that they're going to look after it, that they're doing the planning that's necessary. They wait for those people to begin the planning because they have the money. They have the ACOA, the co-operation agreement money to initiate projects. I think this is the danger of "Other People's Money" that we're not preparing ourselves for.

There's a fortune in the economic future of P.E.I. but we've got to be smarter about understanding the world market. I heard a man being interviewed this morning on CBC who spoke of people who travel outside the sector and come back with new ideas. But we don't have to travel outside the island, outside the Maritimes, to get new ideas. For example, we're still processing lobsters the way we did 30 years ago, by hand. We're discarding waste that we could make use of through technology. We can use all of the fish except the part that we fillet. We don't use all of the other parts. We need to upgrade what we do well, our food sector. Beyond that we can find ways of bringing people that can teach us how to make the new technology work for us.

I have to say that the business community here isn't really with it, certainly in that area.

I read these magazines and they tell me, and I believe it's true, that the future is going to be based on computer technology. Your understanding of computer systems, communications and computer technology is the key to the future. We have school systems without computers. The kids are not being taught this important tool and the various ways of using it. I'm not even sure how well it's being done at university. I can't speak to that.

We're generating now a new elite in the school system — those who have computers at home and those who don't have computers at home. The other day I was talking to a very prominent politician and I raised the question of fax communication with the MLAs. I was told that the MLAs don't have fax equipment at home. I thought, that's interesting, that's as important as the telephone now. Then I asked about e-mail and he told me he doubted that the MLAs had computers at home.

I suspect the same would be true of politicians in other areas as well because they are not in business. They're professional people; they have this equipment at their office. So we have people deciding public policy for the new economy who don't themselves understand computer technology. I find that a little strange, if you're making decisions on educational policy, for example, yet you don't understand the importance of the technical people. It's their mindset, not understanding the importance of computers or why you should bother learning about it. If the mindset's not there and you say, "That's a threatening instrument over there in the corner," then you don't get into it. You start thinking in terms of growing more potatoes and doing the things we've always done while we're talking about the new economy. We're very proud of what's happened in Summerside at the defunct Armed Forces base. We're very proud of the new aerospace sector but we're not learning from it. It's kind of rough to accept that we haven't the least clue as to what all that means. It's a very sad thing.

This is an interesting place. I'm very proud of this place. My people have been here for a couple of hundred years. My roots are fairly deep. We often hear about P.E.I. being compared to a small Ontario town. Why should P.E.I. be a province if it's only got the population of a small Ontario town? Well, it's a small Ontario town with international trade in potatoes, international trade in the fishery and international tourism.

We quadruple our population in the summertime because people come here to enjoy the place. It's a small Ontario town with 45 high schools and elementary schools all over the place. There are 90 municipalities. We do a major job of pulling this together and we do a lot of wonderful things. But we can't continue to compete in the world economy based on French fries.

In my family we have seven children; the youngest and the oldest are on the island. Of the others, three are in Toronto, one in Calgary and one in Singapore. The one in Singapore came with her husband hoping to work here. She was lonesome being that far away. She's an excellent teacher, she teaches English as a second language. She spent five months trying to get interviews across the country. She couldn't get a job, let alone an interview. Her husband came here looking all over the place. He's very bright and personable and very talented. He said to her, "Moira, there is 13 percent unemployment in Canada, 18 percent unemployment in P.E.I. and three percent unemployment in Singapore." There's no argument. So they went back to Singapore. Within three weeks she had five job offers. So that's what happens. My wife would like to have them close to us. I'd like to have them where they're doing well. There are 11 in my own family and three of us on the island and eight across the country. And that's the way it is for Islanders, although we're not having those seven- and 11-children families anymore.

Retraining seasonal workers is a trick. It's like education is a trick. I have an op-ed piece coming out in *The Guardian* shortly, observing that when I was a kid I was the smartest kid in our village. Hands down, the smartest kid in the village. I finished Grade 8 when I was 11 years old, no trouble. I zipped through school and I was ahead of people who were four or five years older than I was. It took me years to realize that I was only smarter at what I was smart at. All of the kids who dropped out of school were smarter and knew they were smarter than I was. They could take cars apart and put them back together again. I didn't know a wrench from a screwdriver. They could do the same things with bicycles. I never learned that. If it wasn't in a book, I didn't know it.

The school system is geared toward people like me. Not only is it geared toward people like me, it's geared toward people who aren't like me who consider themselves a failure. So you go out having failed to achieve what people like me do, and I'm good around books. You can't change that because the teachers are taught in an academic environment to emphasize academics.

The fellow who looks after my horse is a Grade 10 dropout. He's not highly regarded for his academic skills but he knows the 12 horses he looks after. He knows everything about those 12 horses. He knows more than the vets do about those horses. He knows more than I do. He's more intelligent in his business than I am in mine, but the world and the teaching system hasn't recognized that. I'm afraid the idea of retraining is going to do more of the same thing. That's a difficulty. They also come out of an academic environment. They understand training in academics. Now they're saying, "OK, everybody's got to understand computers," so they teach them how to work with computers. Well, that's not going to get you a job.

I get very annoyed over this attitude toward people on unemployment and the people on welfare. I know these people. I know their faces. I live among those people. They don't have to be teased to go back to work. They don't have to be bribed to go back to work. And this is a misunderstanding of people in government. Ordinarily you don't have to bribe people to work.

Last night I met my nephew at a hockey game. He has a fairly substantial potato producing operation, and I asked him if he has trouble getting people to work. He said, "No, I never have trouble." "What about cropping and harvesting?" I said. "No, no problem," he said. I said, "They tell me that you can't get people to work for you anymore, so how come you can get people to work for you?" He said, "Simple, treat them half decent and pay them half decent." And with my experience, I could have answered the question for him because I know that.

We have people who are willing to work because it's more interesting than being home all the time. Are we going to say people have to get retrained? Are we going to retrain people and say they can get unemployment and tell them to go and get work? These people can't generate work. If I can't generate work, and I'm a smart man, how can people on welfare go generate jobs for themselves? A lot of the guys on unemployment insurance are the ones I told you about, whose skills were not reinforced at school 'cause they were busy reinforcing mine. What a smart fellow I was! So you have all the people who are technically oriented or trades oriented who might have made something of themselves in a different environment and they're not doing that. This is why, if we're going to do retraining, we better think hard about the trainers because the trainers will keep on doing what they've always done, as the teachers have always done.

Critics are constantly commenting on the people who don't want to work for a living, who want to lay back and draw unemployment. There are people I know that are drawing unemployment who are personal friends of mine who would rather do anything but draw unemployment. It's just the lack of opportunity. I do workshops on retirement and I warn people about hobbies, about leisure activities. Leisure is valuable as a counterpoint to work. If you're not working, leisure becomes work. So you need the work to make your off-time enjoyable. If all you do is go to hockey games, hockey games get boring. People on welfare, people on employment insurance understand that. Retired people understand that. Life gets boring. There's no problem, but the editorialists and the critics assume the worst without knowing these people.

You cannot change their minds, no matter how much you tell them. For example, when I was a deputy about 85 percent of the people on welfare were women and children. The 15 percent of males were mostly physically or mentally disabled. And yet the criticism is everywhere because every now and then an apparently employable male with a personality disorder, whom nobody liked and no one would hire, would show up on welfare, but they thought he shouldn't be on welfare. We have no exile. We have no place to put them. And so the critics simply don't know the programs. They don't know the people. They don't know what they're talking about. I worked in the field. I know these people.

I have a couplet that I've used many times:

The man convinced against his will,
Is of the same opinion still.

I had a rule with the critics. "If they knew what I knew, they'd do what I do." So I ignored the critics. The only exception was that if I could find one trying to make me look good, I'd pay attention, but I didn't come across a lot of them.

It's an Ottawa phenomenon and a media phenomenon too. It's one way of getting attention. They're going to do something about the minimum wage. We really should turn back the minimum wage, they say.

We'll go on to build an economy on jobs that are worth $5 an hour. We have fairly prominent people that still talk about the curse of the minimum wage. My nephew is paying well above the minimum wage. He's not a rich man, but he's living with his neighbours in peace and he feels good about it. The critics who are talking about the minimum wage should be ashamed of themselves. Who would live on $5 an hour? When I hear a critic talking about minimum wage, I write him off.

There are remedies for seasonal workers who are getting benefits when they could be doing something else. That's a bit of a trick. The answer is addressing seasonal labour in a different fashion. We have to say that if we're not going to have seasonal people, then we don't have a fishery at all. And we're not going to have a forest industry at all because that's seasonal by nature, and we're not going to have a tourism industry at all because that's seasonal too. We're going to create a great economy out of this?

HARRY O'CONNELL

Prince Edward Island: Self-Reliance

Angus MacLean was elected in 1979 on a mandate of community revitalization. We had been 10 years into a comprehensive development plan at the time. His government got elected during the 1979 election on the basis of the need to decentralize some of the development possibilities into the local rural communities of P.E.I., and that theme of community revitalization was a key theme in his campaign. He started a new department of government called the Department of Community Affairs. He asked me to join the government as deputy minister of that department, with a view toward starting a strategy in that regard.

That kind of a strategy requires a long-term process to make sure it takes hold. To revitalize any business it takes three to five years to get it off the ground. There were some successes in developing some businesses in small areas, but that kind of process takes such a long period of time and it needs a lot of support from people. Some of the businesses that were contemplated would have required a long-term effort as a key part of the process. So a lot of elements had to go together and it would have required a long period of time, and we just didn't have that.

My belief is that during the late 1960s, and all through the 1970s and 1980s, government grew too big. In fact, there was a belief at that time that government's role could be designed to stabilize and develop the economy. The comprehensive development plan for Prince Edward Island was a key element in that belief. As a result we became bigger as a government. We needed more taxes to run it and the people became more dependent as that process went on. We now have much more government than we need, we have many more dependants than we need. We have much more taxation than the economy can stand to develop itself on its own.

One of the goals of the development plan was to make boost in the economy such that people would earn more income, rather than depend on government for transfers. I recall in 1969 when the development plan was signed, P.E.I.'s total transfers to individuals were in the 69 percent range. The idea was that we would move up the earned income of individuals rather than the transfer income of individuals, which would move downward from that 69 percent to 60, maybe even 55. As it turns out, the net result today is that we are very close to 80 percent government domination in the economy.

Once you start the process of dependency, once you have a belief that a government can stabilize the economy and provide the necessary benefits and transfer to individuals the necessary standard of living, then you grow the government sectors so as to accommodate it. Such payments as medicare, UI and other various payments blossomed through that period in order to equalize the standard of living, to the point where the medicine, while good at the time, has now had major side effects, such as too much taxation, too much government and too much dependence. Once you transfer to individuals, that dependency grows and the individual has less need to be self-sufficient, self-reliant or entrepreneurial in nature.

There are so many areas that government now possesses that there are great opportunities within the government to privatize many of the services they have. Even health services and social services could be privatized and the individuals that are currently employed would make excellent proprietors of those businesses. There is a great possibility to reduce the role of government by privatizing many of the functions that are already in government that are adaptable to the private sector, using the employees that are already there to run it.

I don't think the government is inhibiting the growth of the technological sector right now because it's so very new that they haven't really got into it. Government employees have a lot of computers, and within the government employee ranks there are probably great pockets of innovation. These people probably would go into business and do very well at it because they have the time to develop some of the innovative ideas. But by and large innovation is best created by somebody who has a need to make a business go, to make a business out of the product that he's thinking of and to make himself self-reliant as a result of the product know-how that he has. It is not usual that one looks within the bowels of government for that innovation. It's usual that you look at individuals who graduate from colleges and high schools and university who are now on the search for, "What am I going to do with my life? How can I build a business around what I want to do?"

We're already well into a new major sector called the technological communication area. That's going to go on for some time. It's an area that makes up maybe five percent of the economy today. It will probably grow to 30 or 40 percent of the economy over the next 10 to 20 years. The government is largely not involved in that sector at this time. And that is right and just. It should not be involved in that sector. It should not attempt to regulate it. It should not attempt to urge people to go into that business. In fact, the very nature of technological development is that an individual conceives of a software program that he wants to create on his own and sell to the world. So let's not interfere with that. Let's let that happen. Let individuals develop their own expertise, their own entrepreneurial skills, and they will develop that small business necessary to dominate that sector.

If Canada can develop major products for the world in that sector in the next 10 to 20 years, then we will grow our economy —if government is not so much involved in the new economy, not even in the regulation of that new economy. I would suspect that we ought not to have much regulation in that new economy. Then that area will expand, the private sector will expand to be 30 or 40 percent of the total economy, and we will grow out of this problem.

I'll give you an example of how regulation can burden business and job growth in Canada. We have a little business in Charlottetown here of 15 individuals. I would safely say that two to three people of the firm work full time with the various paperwork and requirements of government. The GST, the taxation collection, the tracking of things for income tax and tax purposes: all of those activities would take a good portion of our employees. That's a major overhead that we have to have on staff in order to accommodate government requirements.

We can learn from the last 25 years that government cannot create jobs. The creation of jobs is not the role of government. Nor can government provide the individual extension services to assist an individual to go into business. That is something that you as an individual gather as you go through your life. It's something that comes from your own genes and not something that someone forces you to do. As a result, government's role is perhaps more in providing the context to allow you to go into business. It's not to ask you or to develop you to get into the business, but it's to provide the context: a low-interest-rate economy, good services, good freight, good highways, good transportation and communication. That's the role of government. It's not in the development process of providing individual entrepreneurship.

One of the things I've noticed over a period of time, in the last 20 years, is that government assistance programs in the area of development or to private business have always been in capital assistance to build a new plant, usually in processing and manufacturing. We have a large number of plants established in Atlantic Canada, for example, because there were 50¢ dollars or 75¢ dollars available that would build a plant. But in actual fact the problem that affects business, the difficulty for any business, is, what is your unit cost to produce a ski, to produce a pound of fish? How much does it cost to produce one of anything in a fish plant or in a ski plant or a manufacturing plant?

It is the overhead costs that are the dominant aspects of that cost. For example, labour is about 50 percent of the unit cost of producing a pound of fish, or a ski, or a medical device. Labour is a major cost. Interest rates are another major cost. Thus the banking service and electricity, power rates, these overhead operating costs are the dominant things that tell you whether you will succeed or fail with your product. It's not so much the capital; the capital is only a small part of your unit cost. So if governments had a role at all in the future, it would be to provide a context for you to keep your operating costs down, i.e., a low tax rate. The tax rate is one of the dominant things that are part of your overhead. A low interest rate is another key lever in making sure your unit costs are kept low so that you can compete with others in the world.

There are a number of examples where capital buildings have been built and currently stand empty, and many of those projects have been written about over time. Suffice it to say that, perhaps as a result of investing in capital outlays as opposed to operating outlays, many buildings now stand in Atlantic Canada that could house operations that would start up with decent overheads. While capital is good up front, the key thing to keep your eye on is the unit cost over a period of time.

There are a number of government-funded buildings sitting vacant here in P.E.I. Because they're vacant, they are very easy to come by now and the rent is very low even if you don't purchase them, although some can even be purchased for as low as a dollar. But even if you don't purchase them and you're just renting them, you're basically renting them for the lights and the operating cost associated with that building. So there's a great opportunity for island entrepreneurs to begin their operations in those cheap buildings with a view toward keeping their operating costs down. There are many small businesses that I'm aware of that have divided the larger building into several spots and are operating seven small unit businesses out of that building. The other interesting thing is that these seven new businesses that are formed in that old building tend to be more based on indigenous resources, such as agriculture and fisheries, as opposed to some product that is new to our province.

Within the current public debt that we have are the write-offs on many of those businesses over a period of time. So there is the debt resulting from the closure of the businesses, but also the people have been laid off and that causes the government to raise its transfers to individuals. So it has a double-whammy effect that adds up in the total debt.

If government stays largely out of the regulation area, then there is a great opportunity for individuals to succeed in small business. As that happens government ought to peel back its services so that it gets back to its basics, which is providing service to its citizens as opposed to the developmental role. If it does that, it will automatically reduce its need for drawing off the resources that people have — taxation. It will leave more money in people's hands, more disposable income to spend, and thus create more business activity. The other major side effect is that it will leave the people less dependent on the state for their sustenance.

They will be able to develop their own entrepreneurial skills out of necessity because they will have fewer transfers. They will be looking for more earned income than transferred income.

However, if federal transfers to P.E.I. were cut too quickly it would be a catastrophe. We have to take the time. This did not happen overnight. This happened over a long period of time. As a result we're going to have to gradually, by increments of one and two and three percent per year, get back to the earned income rising. It's not unlike Quebec, which was very dependent back in the 1970s and which made a conscious decision to invest in their own people so as to be less dependent on transfers.

A similar thing can happen in Atlantic Canada if we use our resources. On Prince Edward Island, for example, we have a one-million-acre farm. The richest soil east of Niagara Falls, number-one, Canada-class soil. If I was given that as a farm today, surely I could make a living out of it. Surely I could hire people that would also make a living out of it. There's no reason why a province with an acreage that we have should be dependent on anybody. We should be able to produce enough in the long run so that we would pay our own way. And we have the ability to do that, but we're going to need a lot of time to take us away from the dependency we have and gradually get us into a self-reliance role.

It's very important for us to go easy with how we wean ourselves off. We'll have to do it over a period of time, but only with a concrete strategy as to how to get there. I believe that down deep in the ethos of any Islander is, "I'd love to be able to do it on my own. I'd love to be able to make my own way rather than depend on unemployment insurance or any other transfers that we have." Most people would love to work year round. Most people would love to work for a decent wage, in a decent job of their own. The potential is very great for that to happen, not led by government, but by the people themselves and their organizations, and supported by and provided with a proper context by government.

Let the information highway develop so that it becomes a form of self-regulation. As a result, 95 to 97 percent of all citizens will regulate themselves. It's the two or three or four or five percent of the citizens who will try to get around regulation. In the days before government had a lot of regulations, people in the community regulated those two or three or four percent. We should perhaps get back to that. There are a lot of individuals in the 95 percent or the 97 percent who will regulate the two or three percent. Let it happen. Don't regulate 100 percent for the sake of the two percent. It costs you too much. I believe that there is a good deal of regulation that we do not need to have because people will normally regulate the community themselves.

We used to have a dance floor here, and as on any dance floor, from time to time there would be a scuffle or a fight. Currently we have great legions of security services who rush in and break up the fight and a lot of people then get involved in the melee, and it costs great money to keep that kind of a level of security. Back then the people at the dance themselves took care of the situation. They would let the encounter develop to its logical conclusion and then take care of it. Once it was out of people's systems then it never happened again. If you stop things too early, then the next night and the following night you will have a rematch.

MICHAEL MACDONALD

Nova Scotia: Intervention Disasters

My father worked in the mines and so did most of my relatives. The whole culture there was to really work hard at school and make sure your kids did well so they would leave. My generation grew up to out-migrate. I went to high school in the early 1960s and ended up at the age of 16 going to the University of Toronto because I got a scholarship. When I look back at Cape Breton and all of the Maritimes, I see a part of Canada that invested its own young people in Canada as its contribution.

If you go back to the 1960s when the coal mines closed, the federal government intervened to set up the Cape Breton Development Corporation, which was designed by a group of Cambridge technocrats in Ottawa who moved in to set up some interesting projects. So you have, for example, a minister who's a very charismatic minister, fighting to have things like heavy-water plants and pulp mills and to set up things like Scotland because we have sheep farms. And if you have sheep farms, "Let's have a woolen mill, let's make sweaters. Let's have a trout farm. Let's use the Bras d'Or Lakes as a trout farm." When you look at that today, there's nothing there. Several billions of dollars and several lives, and a generation later the whole intervention by the government has been a disaster. You can say, "Well, the people are still living there," but the fact of the matter is that economically they're still trying to recover. You see the same thing in the closure of the Sydney Steel Corporation, where the government intervenes again under political pressure, and instead of letting the plant close and the economy diversify, it still goes on.

Up until recently Cape Breton has had a very poor level of entrepreneurship. What's interesting in the last 10 years is the number of small businesses being started and the development of the University College of Cape Breton. You have more women starting businesses, and you have entrepreneurship on the rise. From that point of view I'd say the prognosis for Cape Breton is looking good, but I don't want to give you the impression that it's great.

What really concerns me is the pain that my people are going to go through in the next decade. They have become dependent on a system that they did not design. I suppose that's the essence of my problem with how Canada has been structured. It's the bureaucracy in Ottawa. Politicians come and go but the bureaucracy is still there. It will design short-term reactive systems to solve certain political problems and these will go on and on and on.

If you have unemployment insurance where people need 10 weeks to draw 40 weeks of unemployment, the economy will build itself around the system. For example, in Cape Breton you have great difficulties extending the tourism season into September, October and November. But the three months of autumn are three of the finest months in Nova Scotia. We have a lousy spring but a beautiful autumn. But you have motel owners having difficulty getting people to work there because they've got their stamps. The economy follows the line of least resistance and builds around structures. I don't find unemployment insurance to be a moral problem. I know a lot of bureaucrats do but if Maritimers or Albertans or people in Northern Ontario have been able to use the system for their own advantage, that's very entrepreneurial. That's good. They didn't design the system but they knew how to use the system. I'm very optimistic about that.

And let's not have a morally superior point of view. If you and I had been politicians in the 1960s, we would have designed the system in the same way. I mean, there is a basic concern for people. How are people going to earn a living in those other 40 weeks if there's so little to do? Instead of taking a really gutsy solution, let's say, like an annual wage or even a guaranteed income, they designed a system that works in the short term. It's the impacts on the system that are terrible, the structures of the economy, the nature of work, the lack of entrepreneurship and just gross dependency. In the long term, if you live every two weeks by a cheque with a red maple leaf on it that comes from Ottawa, that doesn't seem to me to be very good. In the short term it's OK.

The Atlantic Canada Opportunities Agency is one in a long line of regional or economic development strategies by Ottawa. We've had DREE and DRIE and for the most part they've all been defined by ultimate failure. Along the way they did some good things, especially infrastructure development. ACOA started out differently because for the first time since Confederation a deputy minister was appointed outside Ottawa. The president of ACOA and the agency was given a billion-dollar budget to spend outside Ottawa, mainly under the control of Atlantic Canadians. It was focused not on pulp mills and big projects, but on entrepreneurial renewal and small business development. So it had a cultural point of view.

Back in the mid-1980s that was leading-edge thinking. In its design ACOA was excellent, and it was diversified in the different provinces and there were a lot of good things done. However, almost a day after it was invented the Treasury Board officials in the Department of Finance in Ottawa started to go after it. There was an immediate attempt by the central bureaucracy to get control over that budget and agency. So the agency, being constantly accountable to Ottawa, ends up being audited all the time. Your projects are constantly being watched. You're monitored, your budget's cut back and you can't make your commitments. Here was an independent ministry outside Ottawa for the first time. If it had been wildly successful, I think the whole system would have been in trouble.

ACOA had some spectacular failures, and the press of course is more interested in failures in which governments are involved than, say, spectacular failures in which banks are involved. These spectacular failures were the result of all the reasons why businesses fail everywhere. There was political involvement in some, but in the early years of ACOA there was less political involvement than the press has led us to believe.

What was interesting about ACOA, however, is what it did in areas which were not of interest to the media. For example, it invested almost $80 million in universities in terms of research. It set up food technology centres, in P.E.I. on the potato industry and on the fishery at Moncton, and it set up a fisheries and marine institute in Newfoundland. What is most significant about ACOA is that it focused on entrepreneurship and promoted women in business. There was a change in the direction of the business schools, which focused on accounting. An entrepreneurial development curriculum was introduced in the schools. That's new. That's progress.

There's a growing spirit of entrepreneurship in Atlantic Canada, especially in Nova Scotia. The rates of small business start-ups tell you that, and the participation of women and minorities in business. Those are the indices that you use to measure entrepreneurial health in a culture. I was speaking at Dalhousie recently to some students and I told them, rather sadly, that there are very few jobs out there but there's lots of work. So you'll find a lot of people today have sole proprietorships, small businesses, and they're grouping together in co-ops. This is the result of Nova Scotians and Atlantic Canadians finally realizing that the government is not going to save them. The government really has become impotent.

Regional development and federal economic development are really one of the big insights into how Canada works. My experience is that the federal bureaucracy is not interested in economic development. It's interested in economic dependency. If you rely on somebody else for their ideas and direction and dollars and continued support, you pay a phenomenal personal, cultural and moral price. If you're dependent, basically you have no future and you certainly don't have any sense of destiny.

I think it all goes back to the 19th-century tradition of tough, resilient Maritimers. We're the people of the sea. You can't be a pussycat and live here and do well. You've got to be really tough. And the new generation of Maritimers is beginning to see that they're going to have to get out there and scratch and fight for themselves. What's really interesting with this new generation is that they're not as disposed to out-migrate as my generation was. They're fighting to stay here, to find jobs here and create new work. They're trying to make a dollar here, have babies here, and that's very, very important. They're having trouble getting jobs, but there's trouble getting jobs in Toronto and Vancouver too. They leave if they have to leave. Many of them are going to other parts of Canada but they're buying land here, so their whole life horizon has the Maritimes or Nova Scotia built into a place in their lives. That's very exciting and optimistic. I'm optimistic because there's no alternative. The thing that scares me most, terrifies me, is youth unemployment. I don't think I have a solution for that but I'd rather talk about solving youth unemployment than attacking unemployment. The question of youth unemployment is very complex — we'd need a couple of days. The point is that a lot of the old jobs have disappeared, and a whole generation of Canadians have been trained, or not trained, for an economy that is dead.

When Paul Martin was down here before he gave his first budget, he got one message here in Halifax and that was, "Get out of our way. You're in a province which has a million people. We have municipal governments and mayors. We have a premier and a Cabinet. We have a legislature over there full of almost 50 people. We have a federal government. We have a federal bureaucracy. Basically we're governed to death. We're regulated to death, whether it's the environment or the fire marshal or the taxman or the GST person. Try starting a business in Canada, you'll see what it's like — it's pretty tough."

In terms of responsibility we are responsible for ourselves. We shouldn't blame Ottawa. We did it. We wanted it. We collaborated in the weakening of our country. We're collaborators. We're all to blame because we're all collaborators in this dependency syndrome we have created in Canada. We didn't design it but we didn't say no.

The decline of the Atlantic fishery is a national crisis that all Canadians should understand. It's probably one of the worst tragedies in the history of our country. It's very fashionable to blame somebody but there's a whole myriad of reasons, one of which is overfishing. One of the issues we have to face is that for over 20 years the government used the fishery in terms of implementing a social policy. It encouraged the development of fish processing facilities and small fisheries all along the coastlines of these communities. Had these industries been the result of market development, they would have survived. But as soon as the resources shrank, the communities collapsed.

The really diabolical effect of unemployment insurance (and by the way, unemployment insurance works because people spend the money and it goes into the community) was that in a typical fishing community people have been seasonal workers for perhaps 300 to 400 years. Their whole culture, their whole daily way of life is built on this. So you would have fishermen who would work the fishery, they would return home and spend the other months logging or farming or repairing houses or repairing their boats or making their nets and just recovering. With unemployment insurance, of course, they work their 12 or 14 weeks and then it's over. So a coherent annual cycle of culture and economy and life collapsed. And that is a terrible thing.

The disappearance or revamping of the unemployment insurance program will be a heart-wrenching experience and cause profound pain and nobody should feel smug about that. However, the good side of that is that people will begin to distrust government and rediscover those virtues of self-reliance again. They'll realize the price of dependency. They'll realize that in order to survive and live in the communities they love, they're going to have to discover work and a way of making a living. And I'm confident that, especially with this new generation of Nova Scotians, they have the wherewithal to do that. Remember, the whole cycle of economic dependency in Canada, these programs which are supposedly so much a part of our national heritage, are only about 30 years old. Newfoundland, for example, came reluctantly into Confederation. Joey Smallwood promised Newfoundlanders the baby bonus and several cheques from Ottawa. It was only after that event that Smallwood got the federal government to put the fishery in the unemployment insurance cycle. And that was the beginning of the end.

If you look at Canada at face value, you'll say, "Oh, look at all the federal initiatives to support economic development." But if you look at the history of all these agencies and initiatives and federal programs, it's not cynical to conclude that the Government of Canada is not in the economic development business, it's in the dependency business. Economic development means independence. It means power to the regions. And that hasn't happened in Canada. Dependency is a terrible thing because it obliterates culture. It obliterates independence and has a profound effect on spiritual values, which you sometimes don't measure. You say these people have become lazy; they're not lazy, they've become dispirited. There's a dead end there. There's no payback. People do things if there's a payback.

With the new generations of Nova Scotians I find a resilience, a new cynicism about government, a kind of self-reliance, an understanding of the precious life we have here, the quality of life, the fragility of our environment. People realize they're on their own and nobody's going to save them. Nobody's going to be there to protect them if they're stupid and lazy and lack initiative.

There are three levers for growing an economy. One is education and training. We've got lots of universities and a tradition of education here that is very solid, very traditional and very old. We have more people coming to Nova Scotia to be educated than Nova Scotians. The second lever is immigration. We have been betrayed on that program because Canada has sat back for 50 years and allowed most of the immigrants in this country to flow into two or three cities. We need immigration. We have to use it as an economic development strategy. The economy of British Columbia is growing because of immigrants, the economy of Toronto is reviving because of immigrants. Yes, there are problems with some immigrant communities, but we can't let a minor racist slant detract from the fact that immigration is the lifeblood of our country and has been since 1603.

The third lever is investment and I think you have to look at the issue of trade. One of the issues that Canadians have not yet learned to talk positively about is free trade. The elites in our country objected to free trade because they thought we were going to lose our culture. Well, welcome to the heartland of English Canada. We haven't lost our culture and we will never lose our culture. As a matter of fact we have more in common with the people five hours south of us on the Atlantic Coast of New England because basically Nova Scotia is the 14th colony. But we happen to be part of Canada. We have to begin to look at the free trade agreement positively as an economic business opportunity. I was in government when we were negotiating the free trade agreement and I had severe reservations about it. But I bought in for this simple fact. In my region of Canada we have two million people. With this agreement, overnight we had a market of 50 million of the richest consumers in the world. For the first time since Confederation we have equal access to New England.

We've been brainwashed for so many years about the Pacific Rim. I don't live there and I probably never will. Part of my country is there but I live on the Atlantic Rim. And just because the Pacific Rim is growing doesn't mean the Atlantic Rim is dying. If we can't build industries and markets, we deserve to be poor. That's why the entrepreneurial spirit of the new generation, their resilience, their cynicism about government, their disbelief in dependency, is a cause for hope here.

To a member of the Toronto elite, especially the literary and artistic elite, free trade is bad because they think they're losing their culture. But that isn't so. Basically Margaret Atwood is losing control of my culture. If I chose to go to Boston or to look at PBS or get my news from CNN, I am free to do that. I just happen to like the CBC.

I hate the word "have-not." Have not what? Do you have this in Toronto? Do you have this in Moose Jaw? Have not what? Have not what you've got? It infuriates me and it insults me. Have not what you've got, I mean, that's a part of the Canadian polarities. We've put the French against the English, the immigrant against the citizen and the poorer regions against the richer provinces. But the rich need the poor. That's how the Canadian system works. And Canada's system of transfers has been very good in our nation. I don't think we should let basic things like health-care facilities and support for education disintegrate. These are what keep us together. However, the government has got to get out of almost everything else. Canada was a federation of independent states, colonies for the most part, and basically the federal government had a very minimal role. Over the years departments in government have grown and grown. We have more bureaucrats in the Department of Fisheries and Oceans than we do fishermen. We have more bureaucrats in the Department of Agriculture than we have farmers. We have government involved in support for business. Get out of there. Get away, get out, get off our backs!

The fact of the matter is, we have to live with the consequences now and get out from under this. Transfers have done a lot of good things in Canada. We have spread the wealth around, you know, we have good post-secondary education, we have good hospitals. But we don't have good roads. We don't have a national highway system, for example, which is kind of crazy, isn't it?

I can't describe what the pain is like to leave a Maritime community to find work elsewhere because I didn't do that. I stayed in Nova Scotia. All I know is when I look at the literature of Atlantic Canada it's often about the nightmare of migration. If you look at the paintings of Alex Colville and Christopher Pratt or Mary Pratt, they're all looking out through windows. It's "Goin' Down the Road." The dislocation of people from the sea is terribly painful but out of it has come great literature and poetry, and the new generation of young people are not going away forever. They're going away to earn a couple of bucks to come back.

When I was a kid my grandfather used to say to me, "The railway doesn't run from Vancouver to Halifax, it runs from Halifax to Toronto and Vancouver to Toronto." That's how Canada works. I'm very optimistic about Canada but the system of the centre sucking both ends dry is dead!

ARNIE PATTERSON

Cape Breton, Nova Scotia: SYSCO and More

People worry about Atlantic Canada but we've survived for 300 years. It's an old economy, you know. We've been here a long time and our greatest source of wealth of course has always been the ocean. You can't move it to Toronto. It's too big.

I suppose there have been 50 commissions and expert groups for the last 100 years studying the Atlantic economy. There have been all sorts of programs, the Atlantic Development Board, ACOA, different provincial incentives, all to create new industry. In reading history I think we're never going to have a dramatic booming growth. We will grow with Canada, which we've done, but I don't see any major new industries of consequence coming. I do see, however, new secondary industry coming.

The Dominion Steel and Coal Corporation, DOSCO, was founded in Cape Breton at the beginning of the last century, in 1900, when they built the steel plant at Sydney. It was a merger of the local coal industry and steel. At that time the steel industry made great sense at this location because Sydney was on tide water and the major markets for steel were in Europe. Secondly, there was coking coal in Cape Breton and iron ore in Pictou County and major deposits in nearby Newfoundland. So it was a natural. Most of the money that went into that development in 1900 was British money. In fact, the company was first known as the British Empire Steel and Coal Corporation (BESCO). It struggled along — certain people made money and it did provide a lot of employment. I think that at one time BESCO and later DOSCO had more than 20,000 employees.

The company was relatively prosperous but it always needed government support. The coal industry, particularly after 1950, was on a downward trend and it was only subsidies that kept it buoyant. SYSCO was formed after 1967, when Hawker Siddeley, the company that then owned DOSCO, decided to close the steel plant because they thought it was not viable any longer. They were faced with a massive capital expenditure to improve and modernize the plant and they opted not to do that. They thought the plant was losing money and that they would never get their capital back. So they opted not to do it. Given the fact that there has since been $2 billion or more poured into Sydney Steel without any return, people wouldn't agree with this, but they probably made the right decision. The provincial government stepped in, led by Robert Stanfield, as a social saviour. At that time there were a couple of thousand jobs involved.

At that time, and we're going back to October 1967, the steel plant had been the major muscle in the Cape Breton economy for 67 years. It involved thousands and thousands of people and their dependants and the government thought they could probably run it better. The unions were of course militant and wanting them to take it over. Also, the takeover was a social measure, one that unfortunately didn't work that well. Although the plant has survived for 27 years, I don't think it's ever made a profit since the government took it over. There've been other failures in the Atlantic provinces, but nothing as significant as that.

I'd say the government did not make a worthwhile choice. They could have cut it off years ago. But those decisions are tough to go back over because they're not totally economic decisions; they're political decisions. It was a social welfare decision, which probably was right at the time and right for a long while.

There was a time when there were 5,000 people in the steel plant. It's going to be a tough relocation but people will have to relocate. That has happened in the coal mines and in mining companies in Northern Ontario and northern Quebec for the last 75 years. They are tough decisions but decisions that will probably have to be faced down the road.

The reason why the government allowed SYSCO to continue for so long without a profit was largely a social decision. The fact that industrial Cape Breton was so dependent on steel and coal made it a social decision. But now the taxpayers in Nova Scotia are paying for it and indirectly, to some degree, the taxpayers of Canada are paying for it because of the equalization grants and the other things that allow us to sustain the level of life that we have.

Equalization grants have a rationale in our history going back to the time of Confederation. Certain promises were made then to entice the distant parts such as Nova Scotia to go into Confederation. Freight rate subsidies and other things were part of the promise. Equalization grants, a more modern mechanism, have been important in sustaining us. This is the whole idea of Confederation, that we try to have equality in education and transportation and all these other things. That's what equalization grants are supposed to do. Now it would be tougher without them, but we'd still survive.

The old Atlantic Development Board, which was created by John Diefenbaker in the late 1950s, made sense in that they put money into infrastructure, the roads and transportation systems. That really made it easier to create wealth, rather than direct loans or grants to industry. But giving grants outright to entrepreneurs is wrong because I don't think it's ever worked. I could probably name 100 instances where through various agencies, whether it be ACOA or the provincial loan boards, the government has tried to entice someone from Ontario or Quebec to come here and operate or open a plant. And they've failed.

The direction of regional development in Canada should change. I would rather see the money spent on infrastructure than on individuals in the form of either grants or loans. To me, if the Royal Bank of Canada or the Bank of Nova Scotia won't fund your new business, then there's not much chance that you should be starting a business. If the bank turns you down, there's not much chance of success. It's kind of foolhardy for the governments to jump in and start throwing money hoping that they're going to create jobs.

I'll give you an example of a failed government intervention in free enterprise. Thirty years ago Frank Sobey, the great entrepreneur who founded the supermarket chain, brought in a man who was promoting Clairtone, which made television and radio sets. They put in a very lush modern plant at Stellarton, Nova Scotia, which was Sobey's hometown. It was funded with federal money and I visited the plant 25 years ago and it was almost staggering, it was such a beautiful plant.

But for every reason why you should put it in Stellarton, there were 50 reasons why you should put it in Halifax where there was some market. But there were also 500 reasons why you should put it on the 401 in Toronto where the market really existed for that product. That plant went bankrupt and that debt was never paid. Doubtless the province of Nova Scotia and the taxpayers took the major loss. I think it's something we may have learned by now, that many of government's intrusions into public sector financing for private organizations have failed.

Free trade is still a mystery to all of us. We haven't had enough experience with it anywhere in Canada to make a final judgment. But I don't think free trade is going to have as much effect here in Atlantic Canada as it will elsewhere, other than we may get products a little cheaper. It's far more of a challenge in places where industry exists, such as Ontario and, in part, Quebec. I don't see it as being a major benefit to Atlantic Canada, but it shouldn't hurt us much.

The 100 percent free-enterprising people would say, "Let everyone go on their own." But Canada is a little different than the United States. We talk about a free economy and we talk about free enterprise, but my experience, having lived in different parts of Canada, is that we have had a social economy, not only here in Atlantic Canada but throughout Canada. We have had a very strong social welfare economy.

The Americans would never suggest that we are free-enterprising people in the same sense that they are. If the SYSCO steel plant in Sydney were in Wheeling, West Virginia, it would have been closed 25 years ago because the Americans make those decisions on the basis of a profit-and-loss statement. Our way, and it might be a better way, is more humane. We're a little slower to arrive at those decisions because we deal with them on a political basis and we deal with them on the basis of social welfare. In Wheeling, West Virginia, they closed the steel plant after it had losses for about three years. Ohio was once one of the great steel centres of the United States. Even in Pittsburgh there are vacant spaces where the great steel plants were 40 years ago.

It's tough to say when the government should step in and decide it's time for this or that industry to fail. It's always a political decision. It's never an easy one because the people who make those decisions have to be elected. It's tough for a politician to say, "Let's stop."

Ralph Hindson

Cape Breton, Nova Scotia: SYSCO Subsidies

My first involvement with SYSCO would be probably around 1940 when I was at the Steel Company of Canada. At that time we had close relationships with all the various steel producers in Canada, there were really only four, and I got to know their people and their plants. The war was on so everybody was producing as much as possible. SYSCO was an obsolete old plant then, hardly comparable to Stelco or Algoma or Dofasco.

The people who lived in Sydney had a very emotional involvement with Sydney Steel and perhaps wouldn't know much about the steel industry because they had no other experience but with Sydney Steel. It was the biggest employer in Nova Scotia by far, and very important to their lives because in many cases their fathers had worked there, their families had worked there, and it was a way of life for those people. There was a lot of pride and sometimes their emotional connection to SYSCO took away from rational thinking. The working force at Sydney Steel in those times, and even later, did not travel around as much as the employees, say, at Stelco did. I had seen many steel plants in Canada and the United States, so I had an opportunity to compare the operations with the operations at Stelco, whereas the people at Sydney didn't have that same opportunity, or weren't given that opportunity.

Before 1967, before we knew that the province was taking it over, I instigated a study called the *Sydney Steel-Making Study* in my capacity as general director of the materials branch, which is that part of the government that had responsibility for the steel industry. In that study we involved the Atlantic Development Board, the province of Nova Scotia, the Voluntary Planning Board of Nova Scotia and DOSCO itself, which owned the plant at that time. The president of DOSCO was involved and the deputy minister of finance of Nova Scotia was involved and so on. Anyway, we did a major study, which took two years, determining the problems and the future of Sydney Steel.

The study was published early in October 1967, and it clearly showed that the company had no real future, mainly because of its distance from its markets. It showed the high cost of production, the high cost of producing steel, the high cost of rolling steel. It was a very negative report and it was about the fifth or sixth report of this kind, all the others showing the same thing over the years. Three weeks after the report was put out DOSCO announced that it was closing Sydney Steel. Of course the people in Sydney and the premier of Nova Scotia were pretty shocked and all hell broke loose, as you can imagine.

After what they called Black Friday, when DOSCO announced the closure of Sydney Steel in October 1967, the Government of Nova Scotia considered the possibility of taking it over at least for a short time. The unfortunate part, I suppose, was that Ike Smith was the interim premier of Nova Scotia because at that time Robert Stanfield was on the hustings for the leadership campaign for the Progressive Conservative Party. Smith was faced with the greatest problem one could probably face in Nova Scotia because this was the province's major employer. He had a meeting of his Cabinet along with consultants they had hired, the firm of Arthur G. McKee & Company. This was a group of well-known American consultants on the iron and steel industry, one of the best consultants at that time. Smith had been in touch with the prime minister, Mr. Pearson. As a result Mr. Pearson sent me and one other chap down to attend the meeting as observers, which we did. We attended the meeting with Ike Smith and his Cabinet and listened to the Arthur G. McKee people give the report and that report very clearly outlined the fact that the Government of Nova Scotia should not take it over. It was not a viable operation. I remember their words, that Sydney Steel is not a viable operation now and never will be.

Again the report stressed, among other things, their distance from markets. They were over 1,000 miles from their principal market, compared to the other steel companies, who were only 100 to 200 miles from their principal markets, and you can't win in a situation like that. Anyway, I attempted to say something at the meeting because the man presenting the report knew me and didn't know I was with the government. He thought I was still with the Steel Company of Canada and he addressed some questions to me and I commented, but the premier quickly reminded me that I was there as an observer, which means you don't say anything.

But as I've said, the report very clearly advised the Government of Nova Scotia not to take it over, that the steel plant was not viable now and never would be viable, and they gave all the reasons why this was so. It was a very, very good report. I might add that same company had done a report on Sydney in 1944, 23 years before, in which the same things were said. That report in 1944 was ignored just as their report was in 1967. But it was not ignored by Mr. Pearson because in spite of great pressure by the Government of Nova Scotia and Premier Ike Smith, Pearson said the most that the Canadian government would give would be $2 million. Plus, he would pay for half the costs of another study, if they wanted to do one, plus a few little incidentals. But he set a positive maximum on that, which changed as years went on.

This happens so often, the opinion of experts is often put aside and people believe what they want to believe. As an engineer I find it very surprising when people who know the subject are not listened to. It's like if you had six or seven people in this room. Let's say one was a gynecologist and we're all talking about whether your wife should have a hysterectomy. And you don't listen to the gynecologist but you listen to all these other people who don't know anything about it at all, and you make your decision on what they say. That's what happens. The expert's view is ignored because it isn't pleasant.

It wasn't just my view, of course, but those views had been expressed going back for many years. Unfortunately they were always ignored. They were ignored because you have the church, the unions, the merchants, the steel plant — where most people are employed, directly or indirectly — and it forms a monolithic group who collectively have great force and put pressure on the provincial government and the federal government. They have a fair amount of political clout and politicians have vested interests. In a municipality or in a company, if a subject comes up and if you have a conflict of interest, you step out while it's being decided. That doesn't happen in government. The politicians directly involved get even more involved, which I've often wondered about.

SYSCO was really a plant designed for the 1800s, when the theory was that you'd be close to the raw materials. I'm not suggesting this was right, but the world view in the industry was to build steel-making plants as close to raw materials as possible because in those days you had to use a great deal more iron ore and a great deal more coking coal to produce a ton of steel than you do today. I'm talking about the 1890s. Technology then changed. Now you only need a small portion of the coal and higher-grade ores than you used to use, and there are much higher-grade ores around the world that are much more economical to use than a local ore of very low quality. The ore from Wobana, Newfoundland, was not of a very high quality. So the plant at Sydney was obsolete the day it was built in 1901. There was no real advantage you could identify for a steel producing plant being located in Sydney. Not one.

I'll say this for Mr. Ike Smith, who is now a senator: I think he was very worried. When the act was finally passed he had only been a premier in his own right for a few weeks, but you could see he was very concerned by the things he said. The act, establishing how the Sydney Steel Corporation was being taken over by the Government of Nova Scotia, clearly states that its only purpose and objective was to take over the Sydney Steel Corporation and to assess its future and to put that assessment into action. In other words, Ike Smith's idea was to take it over for a short period. He was greatly worried about what it was going to cost him, even for that short period, and it was obvious, in his mind, that this was not going to take long. The act clearly stated that the government was there to assess the possibilities of Sydney proceeding and to put into effect that assessment. The act clearly says the steps were taken to rationalize that industry.

Why Canadians don't do anything about this, I'm not sure. I've made the suggestion of a class action suit where people could take action against the government for doing some things that they feel are not correct. You could take a class action suit against them for that act because they're not doing what the act says they should be doing.

In 1974 I was asked to go down and meet Premier Regan. We had many conversations and I then went down periodically to give them advice on Sydney Steel. I was going down enough, I guess, that someone in the Quebec government objected to my spending this amount of time with Premier Regan and Sydney Steel. At that time Sidbec in Quebec was having its problems, but I don't know whether that was the motivating reason. I suppose it was the fact that they thought I should be spending more time with Sidbec. The problems of Sidbec were not at all as great as those of Sydney Steel, I might add. They raised objections with my minister and I either had to stop altogether or go down on a permanent basis. So I went down on a permanent basis as principal advisor to the premier on iron and steel policy and related matters. I never quite found out what related matters were, but I didn't change my position on SYSCO at all. The premier was quite open on that.

One of the reasons Sydney Steel got into very serious troubles in 1974–1975 was because shortly after the Government of Nova Scotia took it over, the personnel that were running SYSCO made a big hullabaloo about how successful they were, which in fact was greatly exaggerated, but they persuaded the government to allow them to spend, I've forgotten how much, I think it was in the neighbourhood of $125 million, in modernizing the plant. That was a great mistake because it contributed greatly to the future problems of Sydney, in that they couldn't make enough out of that expenditure to even pay the interest on the money.

To spend that kind of money you must know whether you can get it returned from the sales of the product you're going to produce. Well, obviously in Sydney's case you could not. So that money and the debt hung over Sydney Steel's head and has been a major problem for Nova Scotia ever since.

In 1975 when I went down on a permanent basis, the same problem existed, and Mr. Regan was quite aware that he wasn't going to solve the problem by throwing money at that plant. There was no argument on that. That's when the Cansteel project came into being. It was the plan for a brand-new plant, not far from Sydney Steel. Other partners would join in and operate that plant with coal, particularly with the coal in the area with the deep-sea port, and produce steel for the four partners. In this case we had two Europeans, one American and one Canadian involved. That was the only practical solution that we had for Sydney Steel, and if that had gone ahead, then Sydney Steel would have been shut down.

But you see, the real problem is, if you had built a brand-new steel plant in Sydney, the whole plant brand-new to produce one million tons a year, it still would have failed because it wasn't competitive, because it had to ship 85 to 90 percent of its steel to markets 1,000 miles away and there was no local market to pay for the fixed costs of operating that plant. Any steel company needs a natural home market to cover its fixed costs. In Sydney's case it didn't have that. The consumption of steel in Nova Scotia was only a little over two percent. That is not very much steel. And they mostly consumed products Sydney Steel didn't make. There was no way a brand-new plant would have succeeded. It would have failed.

By the way, Mr. Regan did not throw money at Sydney Steel. He did his best to keep it going but he didn't throw money at it. But as soon as Premier Buchanan, who came from Sydney, worked in Sydney Steel when he was young, and whose family worked in Sydney Steel, came into power in Nova Scotia, they embarked again on another modernization program.

Government should not be involved in part or full ownership of businesses — not at all. That's one thing I'm very clear on. Companies have a right to die too, you know. They do, and I don't think politicians should be allowed to get involved in the giving of grants and large subsidies to companies — for their own sake, not just for the sake of all Canadians. If I were a politician, I would like to be protected against having to do that. They're not the ones that should be making those decisions. But this is the problem. How do you get around that?

If the future had a vote, most of these things wouldn't have been done. When these decisions are made I'm not sure the people who make them are thinking of the future. They're thinking more of themselves and how they feel. They're going to feel good by doing this. But do they spend much time thinking about the impact this is going to have on future generations? I doubt it very much and I think that's too bad. If we could devise some way, some means of bringing the future into the decision-making process, that would be very good.

The Harvard case study method takes an example of something that happened in the world. They dissect it and then they present it to the students and the students get together and provide suggestions as to how they would have handled this thing. The Sydney Steel situation to me probably presents the best opportunity for a major case study the way they do it in Harvard. It's a very familiar way of teaching economics and it's got so much to it that it would be a good example for governments to use.

The main thing is that all governments in Canada should understand, number one, that companies have a right to die. Number two, that by supporting one company that is in difficulty, government is not helping the rest of the industry. We have a recent example of that on the Davie shipyards. In a study done, I think in the *Financial Post*, not too long ago, they showed the Davie shipyard as the least efficient of all the shipyards in Canada. Here is the government wanting to involve them on the bidding for the work to be done on the Hibernia oil rig. The effect of that on the more efficient companies will be to bring them down to the lower one's level. They wanted to bring it down and let it go to the least efficient one, so what's the point in being efficient?

Bringing down the shipbuilding industry to an inefficient level is an example of something that is absolutely endemic in Canadian thinking. It applies to all the examples — all of them. With the shipbuilding industry in Cape Breton we had three companies. We had the Sydney Steel Corporation, we had Devco and we had the heavy-water plant. The heavy-water plant was quite a scandal a few years ago. The Government of Canada threw $100 million in that heavy-water plant and it finally went up. Trudeau said the government has no business in the bedchambers of Canadians. I say the government has no business in the business community either. The government should keep out of subsidy or financial support to industry. I can hardly think of a case where they have thrown money at an industry where it's been helpful.

DOSCO had no choice because if they hadn't shut it down, Hawker Siddeley, who owned DOSCO at the time, would have lost all their operations around the world. It would have gone defunct and they would have been out of business. So if one is faced with bankruptcy, one can do these things even though they're very difficult at the time. But how do you make the government go bankrupt if they make a mistake?

DOSCO owned Wobana in Newfoundland, and they were trying to get rid of it when they closed Sydney Steel. This is also in 1967. They came to Mr. Smallwood and they wanted him to buy it. I was advising

Mr. Smallwood at the time and I said "If you want to take it over, do so, but don't give them anything for it because there's nothing they can do with it. It isn't worth anything. It would cost them more to dismantle it than it would for you taking it over." I sat in an adjoining office from his and he negotiated with them by himself, which is what he always did. Every half an hour he would come into my office and tell me what was going on and ask me how he was doing and then he'd go back. He was a very peripatetic man. He would walk around all over the place.

He finally got it for nothing and then asked me what we could do with it. I said there were only one or two companies in the world that could use that ore and those were people operating a Thomas converter, which we don't operate in North America. He said, "What are the chances?" I said, "Five percent." He said, "That's good enough for me." And the next day we were on a plane going to Germany. To make a long story short, these people did come, they were interested, they signed an agreement to take it over and they were coming to Newfoundland for a major signing ceremony. But they had to back off because de Gaulle, the president of France, interjected. The reason for that was that this company in Germany was using French ores and producing steel in Germany and shipping their steel to France. De Gaulle told them if they took on Wobana iron ore instead of the ores from France, they wouldn't sell another pound of steel in France and they had to bow out. But Joey wisely didn't operate the mine himself. He just closed it down. Joey Smallwood listened to my advice, whereas I guess Premier Smith didn't. I don't mean to say that I'm infallible. I'm not, but in that case I was right.

When the Government of Nova Scotia bought the plant, when they took it over from DOSCO, they paid the total. If my memory serves me right, of the $25 million, $10 million to $15 million of that was inventory, steel inventory that could be sold. The other part, $10 million to $12 million, was for the plant itself, which they shouldn't have paid anything for. DOSCO should have paid them to take it over. If DOSCO had shut the plant down, it would easily have cost them $10 million to dismantle it and clean up the mess. So they really got a good deal from the Government of Nova Scotia.

I was on the board of SYSCO for a short period. I was received very well on the board. I've forgotten how long I was on, a year, a year and a half, something like that. I've almost forgotten why I resigned. I was familiar with what a director's responsibilities are and I refreshed my memory. And it was rather frightening what can happen to a director. I was not happy with what was going on at Sydney Steel. The minutes didn't reflect my views as well as I thought they should. Unfortunately I was the only one on the board who really knew the steel business. Therefore, in the event of being taken to account, the others could say they didn't know any better. People like Frank Sobey, a very nice old gentleman, was on the board but he doesn't know anything about the steel business so he could plead ignorance, but I couldn't. I was the only one who couldn't plead ignorance and I resigned because I didn't approve of what was going on, of what they were doing.

Not only are political egos a drawback — all egos are a drawback — but politicians are generally said to have a fair amount of ego. When situations like this come up, that ego gets used to handling and deciding on situations, whether they are really knowledgeable on the subject or not. I find it surprising. I've associated with a lot of politicians but they do assume expertise that they don't have. And when a thing like the shutting down of Sydney Steel comes to pass, when they're faced with the facts, they're mea culpa. It takes a great man to be able to change his view based on the facts being presented to him. Politicians' egos will not often let them do that. Politicians don't have little egos, let's put it that way.

I have worried for years about why the politicians don't listen to the experts. I've wondered about it and I've tried to think of solutions to it and why it happens. Votes are obviously a factor, but there's much more to it than that. People would not have supported SYSCO with large sums of their own money, but they'll give your money and my money because it doesn't really cost them anything. They have a vested interest. They're going to get more votes because of the largesse.

How do you protect the public money by preventing these kinds of decisions from being made? It's very, very difficult. All these people are now out of work and you get all the hardship stories. You're a human being, so the easiest decision is to take it over. But when you think of the amount of money that's been spent on SYSCO since the day it was taken over, if that money had been properly used in Nova Scotia, what a difference that would have made. I calculated we could send every employee of Sydney to Florida, give them $20,000, and we'd still save money.

Mr. MacEachen very much had a role in all this. The grey eminence, the representative of Nova Scotia in Cabinet, obviously had a very great involvement. He encouraged it because you don't see politicians not encouraging things going on in their riding, do you? But they shouldn't be involved in the decision making of moneys going into their riding, particularly helping industry. You look around and try to find a very good example of an industry that has been considerably helped by major injections of funds from the government. I don't think you'll find one. It might be an interesting idea never to allow politicians to have anything to do with money that's spent in their own riding. I would agree with that. If you were a councillor in a municipality, or held a high position in a company, you would have to bow out of a conflict of interest. You would have to bow out. Why shouldn't you have to bow out in the government?

The problem is that if Ottawa gives money to a thing like this, it gives encouragement to the provincial government to do the same. It encourages the local people, it enhances their feeling that this after all is a worthwhile, justified project, or else the Government of Canada wouldn't be giving them $10 million, $20 million, $30 million. You see, it encourages a false belief, a false confidence. That's another reason why the Government of Canada should be more careful in the granting of moneys. But they go ahead and do it against the advice of the experts. And you know, it goes on all the time.

JAY GORDON

Cape Breton, Nova Scotia and Northern Ontario: Steel

I'm afraid subsidies play a part in the steel industry — rather a significant one. The most egregious example is Sydney Steel (SYSCO) in
Sydney, Nova Scotia. We've also had DOSCO in Quebec, which until
recently was still government-owned. We have others, not quite as obvious, but nevertheless they're subsidized steel operations in various ways.
Essentially what SYSCO proves is that you cannot save jobs that don't
have an economic raison d'être. It's that simple.

The Canadian steel industry, because of its relatively small size, is at
a major disadvantage compared to something like, for example, the
American or the Russian, until five years ago, and especially the
Japanese steel industry. This year the Canadian steel industry will ship
over 13 million tons of steel, the Americans over 80 million tons, the
Japanese over 100 million tons. We're just not in the same league. We
haven't got the scale over which we can spread the costs of research and
development. So since the 1950s most new innovations in the steel business have come from the Japanese or have been developed by the
Japanese even though somebody else invented them somewhere else. To

its credit, Stelco has actually patented and licensed for a long time now several meaningful innovations in the steel business, but they've been the exception rather than the rule. Essentially the Canadian in the street has been quite content, and, I think, in terms of the economies of scale, justifiably so, to try to buy the latest technology from the Japanese or whoever and not to invent it here.

In the case of SYSCO subsidies were very simple, the government simply gave SYSCO money — period. In the early 1990s the facilities at SYSCO were upgraded and the company switched to an electric furnace operation at a cost of more than $200 million. The government also subsidized SYSCO's so-called sales. In fact, a major portion of the company's sales over the years have been to countries like Bangladesh which never had any hope in hell of ever paying money back. Every time Bangladesh would get hit by another typhoon or hurricane or what have you, Mr. Clark, when he was minister for external affairs, would stand up in Ottawa and say something like, "Our poor friends in Bangladesh have been hit by another natural disaster, so we're going to forget we shipped them 25,000 tons of rails last week, and we're not going to make them pay for them." And I really don't feel obliged to subsidize Mexico City's wonderful new subway. That's what we've been doing. Who's subsidizing my subway? We're building an extension in Toronto and it's going to cost hundreds of millions of dollars, but we're not getting any rails from Bangladesh or Mexico or anywhere else. We're going to have to pay for them.

SYSCO is not the only example. Sidbec is the next in line in terms of size. The Quebec government, when the Grits walked away from what was then Dominion Steel and Coal in Montreal, threw up their hands and said, "Oh my gosh, we can't lose all these jobs, we've got to save it." And over the years they have poured many, many hundreds of millions of dollars into it in their efforts to save it. Of course, not only hasn't it worked, but also the number of people who work for Sidbec today is a fraction of what it used to be.

The amounts of money thrown away are incredible. There was, for example, the Fire Lake iron ore mining project in northern Quebec. It alone cost at least $450 million and was shut down. It just doesn't work when you build an entire iron ore mining complex, a mine, a palletizing plant and railroads to bring those iron ore pellets to a dock somewhere, and then a few years later just shut it down and walk away from it.

But Sidbec has slowly but surely, under very difficult industry conditions, been making its way back to profitability. Of course as soon as it began making a few dollars, the government sold it to a group of Indian steel men who have interests all over the world. We can now only sit back and see what they do with it.

I have a number of theories on why governments make these decisions. Most of our so-called leaders are lawyers. They know how to dot the i's and cross the t's in every last word in the acts of Parliament they pass, but they have no clue as to the economic ramifications of the bills they're passing. Secondly, they're trying to buy votes with the voters' money and at that they are extremely good.

One of the flaws of our democratic system is we elect people for four years. They don't give a damn what's going to happen in five years, it's going to be somebody else's problem. If they're still around because they got re-elected, they just pour some more money in it. One of our greatest problems is that the people we elect to govern us have no conception whatsoever of what they're doing from an economic point of view, or for that matter from a social point of view, because after all, if you screw up the economy, you're screwing up the society.

I had this revelation a few years ago. It's not something like a light snapped on and I all of a sudden saw it. You begin to understand things over time, and one day you wake up and you put it all together and you realize that's what you've got. And that's when you start screaming. Nobody listens, but you scream anyway. In the case of SYSCO I've been screaming for 15 years. Screaming to the world at large, through the press, through the media. It has had tremendous impact: it's been totally ignored!

There are no tripwires. There is no way of stopping it, not under our system. For example, we had a situation where the Conservative Party was all but wiped out in the election. The first thing that happens is that Mr. Chrétien says, "I'm tearing up the piece of paper called this airport deal." Mr. Chrétien's a lawyer. He should know that what he's done is told the whole world, "Don't bother signing a contract with the Canadian government because we'll tear it up if we decide we don't like it. And even if we don't tear it up, the next government's going to do it for us."

Now the Liberals have decided to try to pass an act of Parliament that will protect them from any responsibility for their actions. In other words, they can do whatever the hell they want. They're immune from prosecution. Our country's lawyers just decided last week, I believe, that it would be against the Constitution to pass such legislation. But hey, Lord Acton said it a couple of hundred years ago: "Power corrupts, absolute power corrupts absolutely." The Liberals have too big a majority. They don't have to worry about being challenged. They do whatever they want and there is nothing except a few old fogies in the Senate to even try to stop them.

In the case of SYSCO the impact of the subsidies has been fairly nominal. The reason primarily is that SYSCO is limited to one product, rails. There really hasn't been any substantial demand for that product in North America for a long time. One of the more obscene things I've been witness to in the last 20 years in following the steel industry is the picture of Sydney Steel and Algoma Steel, in Sault Ste. Marie, competing in the press. They were competing over who was entitled to a larger share of what little rail business was available through CN because as a government-owned corporation, each was entitled to its fair share. Fortunately that's over because Algoma is just about out of the rail business.

In 1974, after many years of study and hesitation, Stelco finally decided to start the Lake Erie project. The Lake Erie project was going to be the most modern and the largest greenfields steel mill in North America — 12 million tons. For what it's worth, it's operating at a capacity of about 1.75 million tons today.

One of the major reasons that they finally made up their minds to go ahead with this huge project was that 1973 and 1974 were the biggest boom years in the history of the steel industry. Stelco found itself in the most unusual position of making rather a lot of money. If you make a lot of money, you tend to incur income tax liabilities. So steel companies like Stelco figure out that if they pay tens of millions of dollars in corporate income taxes, the government is just going to blow the money on subsidies to some other industry or on welfare or God knows what. If, on the other hand, they invest that money and build a nice new steel mill, they're going to be able to generate revenues, make money and maybe even create a few jobs. So they started Lake Erie. A year and a half later the entire steel industry was on its knees. The same thing happened with Algoma. In their effort to avoid major tax bills they began to build their Number Two seamless steel mill back in 1980. It destroyed the company.

So you have a situation here where some lawyer politician passes a law saying that if you are going to be a nice guy and invest money in new facilities so as to create jobs, we're going to give you a tax break. The trouble is that the greater your ability to take advantage of that tax break, the less the chances that you're going to create a significant number of jobs. If you want to create jobs, you should buy people sewing machines in the Eastern Townships of Quebec. You'll have thousands of women working. Politicians don't understand that. Do you? If not, you're in bad company.

The collapse of the steel industry at the time had everything to do with OPEC. When OPEC first reared its ugly head in September of 1974, very few people understood the implications of it. I was one of the many millions. Within the year the economy of Europe and North America was hit badly. Virtually every industry was flat on its back. It wasn't unique to the steel industry. The problem was that Stelco had committed itself to spend what it thought was going to be $450 million — the biggest capital expenditure program in its history. No sooner did they start than their earnings and cash flow began to head south. They began to borrow while they still could, and the thing just began to feed itself. It wasn't till the mid-1980s that they began coming out of it.

Tax incentives are counterproductive. You're persuading people to do things that they wouldn't otherwise do. A plant that's put up simply to take advantage of a tax gimmick is probably not economically viable on its own two feet. Once the advantage of the tax gimmick runs out, the plant is in trouble. A tax break is a subsidy. Capital cost allowances on investments, which are available to anybody in Canada who invests money in a new plant and equipment, are counterproductive. They tend to be used by industries that are capital intensive not labour intensive. So the first thing that happens is you create relatively few jobs for huge amounts of money. When a plant was put up because the final factor that was decided in its favour was a tax break, the minute that tax benefit expires the plant can't stand on its own two feet. The whole thing blows up in our faces.

The businessmen involved are simply taking advantage of the system. They just act in a way they honestly believe is in the best interests of their shareholders. As a captain of industry, would you say to your shareholders, "We decided the best thing to do was to write a cheque for

$100 million to the receiver general of Canada"? Or instead, "We're going to build a plant with that $100 million. And not only that, but because we built that plant, we're not going to pay taxes for the next five years either." I would suggest that if you took only the big three Canadian steel mills, Stelco, Algoma, Dofasco, and calculated the negative impact of these tax advantages on them over the last 20 years, say, roughly the same period as SYSCO, I think you'll find the amount of money wasted is not far off from the $2 billion granted to SYSCO.

Nobody's pure in all this. Our American friends scream bloody murder about it but they're just as guilty as we are. They just do it more cleverly. The Japanese are cleverer than the Americans, that's all. But everybody does it. And if you think steel is a problem, look at agriculture. That's the worst example imaginable. It's as if farmers have a God-given right to get money from government.

The first reason for the self-destruction that exists with subsidies, certainly in agriculture, is that farmers have a disproportionately large amount of votes. Rural areas tend to have relatively few people, so it doesn't take very many farmers to elect somebody to represent them in Parliament or Congress or whatever. Virtually every democratic country in the world has the same problem. The problem in the U.S. and Canada is vastly overshadowed by what's going on in Europe and has been for decades. Basically it's nothing more than politicians trying to buy votes. That's how they acquire power.

Why do you think that the government is finally giving SYSCO away to the Chinese?[1] Because they no longer have any clout. What's even more important is that Mr. MacEachen no longer represents them — it's another party. They had the clout for 25 years. They were in a position to elect an MP in Cape Breton who happened to be a very powerful person in the Liberal Party in Ottawa. The Liberal Party was gone for nine years but so what? What the Liberals did 20 and 30 years ago is being paid for today. They're not getting rid of SYSCO because somebody in Halifax finally saw the light and has become a convert to pure capitalism or something like that. It's just not in their political interest to go on throwing money at the thing.

Today SYSCO doesn't use either iron ore or coal; it's based on scrap, which comes from quite a distance, but which can be brought in by water, which makes it reasonably cheap. Let's face it, when you're only producing a quarter of a million tons of rails a year you don't need a hell of a lot of scrap. They could probably tear down the old facilities and have enough to keep them going for a year. The big problem is that they can only make one product, rails. Today CP and CN are trying to consolidate, precisely to cut the number of railroad lines in Canada. They don't need more rails. They want to get rid of the ones they've got.

SYSCO can't ship to the States because the Americans succeeded in convicting them of dumping a few years ago, so it has got to go offshore. They can't ship to Europe because the Europeans have their own problems with rail makers. They can't ship to Japan, they've got problems. So you ship to what few countries are left in the world that are still poor enough not to have their own rail mill. Of course the reason these countries haven't got a rail mill is they can't afford to buy it and they can't afford to buy the rails either. So you give them away.

If we're going to solve all our economic problems on the basis of $2 billion every 25 years or so, plus what the medical benefits and God knows what else cost, hey, we're going to be bankrupt in six months. But the biggest cost of SYSCO is not the money that was quite literally thrown away to keep a handful of people working in the steel business in Sydney, Nova Scotia. The biggest cost is that in the process they created the centrepiece of downtown Sydney — the tar ponds! In Toronto we have Nathan Phillips Square and the skating rinks. In Sydney they have the tar ponds. These people have literally been killing themselves and their children by drinking water contaminated by the tar ponds, by breathing contaminated air. The real costs of the SYSCO experiment are just beginning to be felt as people wind up in hospital with emphysema, lung cancer — all sorts of wonderful and incurable diseases. People who are today 10, 15, 20 years old are going to be deathly sick by the time they're 40 and they're going to be in a hospital. To me that's not only counterproductive, it's the ultimate form of stupidity.

You can quantify what was paid to a company like SYSCO with a fair degree of accuracy, particularly if you go to the trouble of getting all the information, which is surprisingly difficult. But if you're talking about the subsidies that go to an entire region, then the whole thing becomes not quantitatively different but qualitatively different.

A while ago a government minister announced that he was going to stop the system of paying subsidies in the form of grants to individual companies. Henceforth this man has gotten religion. Companies would be required to pay back these subsidies. How you pay back the subsidy, I don't know. If you're going to pay it back, it's a loan — it's not a subsidy. They finally figured out that the grants they were giving to companies in the Maritimes were simply not working. Somebody would say, "Oh boy, if I do such and such, I can get $1 million from the federal government, another $500,000 from the provincial," and they do it. When the money runs out, "You're all fired, goodbye, go collect your unemployment insurance, I'm going back to Texas." That's not that much of an exaggeration. The big problem with this system of equalization we've been trying to run in Canada is that we have prevented the market from imposing discipline on people throughout the Maritime provinces.

The real problem isn't merely that we're spending incalculable amounts of money. The real problem isn't that the money we're throwing down the tubes in the Maritimes could be used for something more worthwhile in another part of the country. The real problem is that we're creating a problem that is growing, and the longer these people are rendered immune from the market discipline, the worse it becomes.

The whole world steel industry would be quite different without subsidies — it's not just the Canadian steel industry. I don't think there's a steel producer in North America that hasn't had its hand in the pot to at least some degree. It's just a question of how much. What is interesting in the Canadian experience is that the companies that have been the greatest recipients, the greatest beneficiaries of government largesse, have been the greatest flops. You start with SYSCO, you work your way down to Sidbec, and then you've got Algoma.[2]

I would argue most strenuously that Algoma is the most successful today because of the steel pricing structure in North America. It has little or nothing to do with what is being done at Algoma itself. And when the market for steel turns around, which it will probably do just as quickly and as suddenly as it turned up a couple of years ago, Algoma, instead of making $30 million a quarter, will start losing huge amounts of money. I suggest to you that the worst possible thing that could have happened to Algoma was the boom it's enjoying now. Algoma exists today not to make steel and certainly not to make money. Algoma exists to save jobs in the Sault because the provincial and federal governments hired accountants who figured out that even Victoria, B.C., would be adversely affected if poor Algoma were allowed to go down.

One of the most interesting aspects of this whole thing is that these damn lawyers don't understand bankruptcy law. They seem to think that if a company is allowed to go bankrupt, its facilities just disappear off the face of the earth and the jobs are all gone. Algoma's new seamless tube mill has concrete walls that are 10- and 12-feet thick. It would take an atomic bomb to wipe them off the face of the earth. When a company goes bankrupt it doesn't disappear. What happens is somebody buys it for a fraction of what it cost to build in the first place and if they don't do too many stupid things, they have a chance to be economic. We don't allow that to happen in Canada.

If it was difficult to lay people off permanently three years ago when the company was still flat on its back, what do you think the situation is today when it's making $30 million a quarter? Are you crazy? You're making $30 million a quarter, $120 million a year, and you want to fire some poor bastard who's making $35,000? You've got to be out of your mind. So when the cycle drops dead again, and I guarantee you it will, it's a question of how long and how bad. They're still going to have too many people making too much money.

Today Algoma, and this is a replay of 1988, is on the verge of spending $500 million on its facilities. Capital expenditures are necessary. There hasn't been any significant amount of money spent on Algoma's facilities, except for that cursed Number Two seamless tube mill, since the early 1980s. But now they're going to start spending huge amounts of money. A lot of that money is going to be borrowed. When the market drops dead again, a year and a half, two years, you're going to have creditors getting wiped out. The whole thing is going to be a replay.

Algoma will wake up one morning, find out it's losing huge amounts of money and make an announcement in the press: "We're going into CCAA again, so you can't get your money back, Mr. Creditor." And the government will be in the same place it was last time when this happened. "Don't worry folks," they'll say, "you're not going to lose your jobs. Mr. Taxpayer and his deep pockets are still here to help you. You've got an inalienable right — to borrow an expression from our American friends — to live and work in the Sault and to make 20 bucks an hour, come hell or high water."

These projects are not allowed to fail because the people have votes. This is the flaw in the democratic idea that Americans were worried about back in 1776 and they were right. It is a flaw. People have votes. That doesn't necessarily mean the votes are used intelligently. They can be used selfishly. So you tell the MP from Sault Ste. Marie, "Hey, either you make sure I keep my job at 20 bucks an hour or I'm going to vote for somebody else." "Oh my goodness," they say. "Don't worry. You've got your job." That's what politics is all about. The rest of the politicians don't say that these expenditures drain money from them. It works the other way around. You grease my palm, I'll grease yours. You slap my back, I'll slap yours. "Tell you what, Joe, you need $100 million for the Sault, no problem. Just make sure you don't forget to vote in favour of my project when I want a piddly $50 million for my town." One hand wipes the other. That's what politics is all about. They're all in the same boat. They all have to get re-elected in four years.

One of the intelligent things about Algoma was that the subsidies were handed out in such a way that it would be very difficult for our American friends to prove in a court of law that they had gotten the subsidies. Neither the federal nor the provincial government gave a penny directly to Algoma Steel Corporation, but they spent tens of millions on manpower retraining, on all sorts of peripheral programs. The Algoma Central Railway gets paid by the provincial government to haul ore from Wawa, Ontario, the last deep-shaft iron ore mine in North America, to Sault Ste. Marie. The railway gets the money, not Algoma Steel. Money's being paid out to keep Algoma going. Money's paid out to keep Wawa alive.

Mind you, Wawa may turn into a boomtown because they might find diamonds there, I don't know, but as an iron ore mining town it should have been shut down 25 years ago. But these people have a right to live in Wawa and no place else in Canada. I mean, God forbid somebody from Wawa should have to move to Thunder Bay. That would be a fate worse than death!

NOTES

1. A half interest in SYSCO was sold to the Chinese company, Minmetals, in 1994. Three years later Minmetals, which never invested any money in the plant, declined its option to buy. Other deals to sell the plant fell through and SYSCO was closed in 2001 and the assets auctioned off.

2. Algoma Steel Inc. has been operating under bankruptcy protection since April 2001, for the second time in 10 years. Employees of the insolvent company accepted a 15 percent pay cut at the end of December 2001.

VIEWS FROM CENTRAL CANADA

LARRY SOLOMON

Ontario Hydro: A Government Monopoly in Action

Ontario Hydro was initiated when Ontarians felt gouged by monopolists in the United States. People who were selling coal to Ontario felt gouged by various monopolists in municipalities who were passing on high prices. So the idea was to bring cheap power from Niagara to the municipalities in Ontario. Ontario Hydro was going to be strictly a vehicle for carrying that power through the transmission lines. It wasn't supposed to be a generator of power itself. This was at the turn of the century.

Over time Ontario Hydro became much more than it intended to be. Instead of being the friendly co-op servicing the various municipalities, bringing in power from Niagara that was generated by private sources, it decided to take over those private sources. Then it started taking over the municipal utilities. Over time it just grew and grew. It grew often through manipulative means, by misleading municipalities in plebiscites promising them cheaper power that was viable. The way they delivered the cheap power, temporarily, was by gouging citizens in neighbouring municipalities. Eventually the

Ontario monopoly grew and made sure that nobody else really could generate power in Ontario.

A visionary called Adam Beck created this monopoly. He was a politician and he saw an opportunity to create an empire for himself. He wanted his empire to be completely unaccountable and he was very clear about this. He felt that it should be free from any provincial control. He said he wanted to create an iron band around his utilities so that politicians couldn't interfere — of course, it's a good thing not to have political interference because politicians can do a lot of damage. But the problem was that there were no checks and balances. There weren't shareholders. There weren't customers who had any choices. There were no competitors. It was the Adam Beck empire. Something that started off being a benign democracy in the end became very pernicious.

It wasn't a good thing for Adam Beck to rob Ontarians of choices as to where they could get their power. It wasn't a good thing to impose on Ontarians Ontario Hydro's own elite view of the technologies that were needed. Initially they went around trying to dam every river. And then they decided that mega–coal plants should be built everywhere. Then they decided that mega–nuclear plants should be built everywhere. In fact, they made a lot of very expensive and serious and poor choices about the technologies that would be viable. Today coal and nuclear technologies, which are the basis of the Ontario Hydro system, are outdated technologies. What is viable is being shut out of this province.

Again, poor choices were made because there were no checks and balances on them. The reason that the Ontario Hydro elite made the poor choices had nothing to do with ill will on their part. I think they were probably very sincere. But there was nobody to challenge them, nobody to question them. And their customers had no place to turn if they disagreed with what was being imposed on them. Also, as Hydro grew, its bureaucracy grew. As its bureaucracy grew, they needed to build larger and larger plants because it's hard to control many small plants with a large bureaucratic structure.

Part of the problem that they had was that they inherited a lot of small plants from all the little municipalities that they took over. So Hydro went on a program of destroying, dismantling, in some cases dynamiting, some 500 small hydro dams across the province simply because they couldn't be managed from head office in Toronto. And they didn't want to have a decentralized structure that would allow all these perfectly fine hydro facilities to be managed in Peterborough and in all the other little municipalities.

The Hydro bureaucrats benefit from the destruction of all these dams. They're able to tighten their control over the generation of power. They're able to impose their view of the kinds of technologies that Ontario should be heading toward. The municipalities had some say in the fact that this bureaucracy was wiping out their dams, but by then it was too late. They had surrendered their powers to Ontario Hydro. Ontario Hydro had set up a system where it controlled some 300 small municipal utilities that really were there to do Ontario Hydro's bidding. They had no ability to make decisions for themselves: their rates were set by Ontario Hydro. They were allowed to buy their power from nobody but Ontario Hydro. Hydro even put commissioners on their boards.

In the early 1960s Ontario Hydro went nuclear. Initially Hydro was skeptical about the nuclear technology. They had to have their arms twisted by the federal bureaucrats, who felt that this really was the wise choice because at the time there was a widespread view that nuclear power was the fuel of the future. So Hydro had its arms twisted. By receiving cash promises from the federal government, it agreed to build the first Pickering nuclear plants. Over time Ontario Hydro developed its own nuclear elite, its own nuclear bureaucrats, who of course thought that nuclear generating stations would be the answer to all of Hydro's problems. At that point they went about with a program that was pretty well exclusively one of building nuclear plants.

The federal bureaucrats wrenched the arms of the provincial bureaucrats because they felt the future was nuclear. People in the boonies couldn't always be trusted to make the right decisions, so they wanted to make sure that those less perceptive than themselves didn't make a mistake. But it was a very serious mistake. The nuclear industry has been a catastrophe for the country, especially Ontario. But also the rest of the country is paying for those mistakes.

The nuclear industry is the largest boondoggle in Canadian corporate history. Plants are built that are worth less than the construction cost. The Darlington complex, which was initially estimated to cost some $3 billion or $3.5 billion, ultimately cost $15 billion. Those $15 billion are ephemeral. They show up on Hydro's books but there isn't anybody in the business world that would pay a dime for the nuclear plants if they also had to assume the liabilities that went along with them.

Nuclear power is not economical. Nobody in the world is building nuclear plants except for Third World countries, which either have them given to them or who want them for bomb-making purposes. Canada has only been able to sell plants to people who will take them for free or who will accept bribes. Nuclear technology is a debt technology anywhere there are viable markets.

In fact, Ontario Hydro was the last company to abandon nuclear power in the Western world. The last reactors to be ordered which were completed were ordered in 1976 by Ontario Hydro. It took until the 1990s for those plants to be completed. But Ontario Hydro has also learned its mistake. It's not planning to build any more nuclear plants. The problem is that it's learned that mistake after it accumulated a $35-billion debt. Canada has actually been giving away some of these CANDU reactors to Third World countries. Recently South Korean officials were indicted and convicted of having accepted bribes, including bribes from agents of Atomic Energy of Canada Ltd, in order to purchase a CANDU reactor. Bribes were also associated with the sale of CANDU reactors to Argentina. It's not a pleasant episode in Canadian corporate life. It's rather sordid.

Ontario Hydro borrows with government guarantees. As a result it has piled up an immense debt, $35 billion, backed up by assets, many of which have very little value. If Ontario Hydro had to borrow on its own nickel, if it had to go to the bond market and tell bondholders that it would be paying back those bonds without any government assurance, Hydro would find that it couldn't borrow any money at all.

They're not playing with their own money. They're playing with taxpayers' moneys and they're playing with rate-holders' moneys. Hydro doesn't have any credit rating. And I've talked to Standard and Poor's and to Moody's in New York, they're the ones who lend the money that Hydro ultimately uses, and they said Hydro doesn't have a credit rating. It's the Ontario government that has a credit rating. We lend the money to the Ontario government; they turn around and lend it to Ontario Hydro. That's their business. "As far as we're concerned we think that Ontario taxpayers can still cough up more if necessary." That's why we're lending the money. We haven't looked at all at whether Ontario Hydro is a viable operation.

Hydro is also certainly speculating with taxpayers' moneys. There is no downside for Hydro if its projects go belly-up. Hydro built

Darlington and cost overruns were something in the order of $12 billion. Nobody lost his job. Nobody was demoted. There's an upside if it happens to work. And every now and then some of these projects do work. But most of the time they don't work. Most of the time they're boondoggles and it's the taxpayer that ends up holding the bag.

Darlington, which cost $15 billion to make, isn't a worthy asset to have. It's an asset nobody would buy; it's a worthless asset. In fact it may have negative value because if Hydro ever tried to sell it, it might find the same thing here as Margaret Thatcher found in the U.K. — that even if they offered bribes of billions of dollars to take it off their hands, people would stay away because the potential liabilities of taking on a nuclear plant are just too great. Private investors do not like to risk bankruptcy. They're not like government. They have people who care about the money that they own. Governments don't own money of their own. They use other people's money, and it's easy when you're going to Las Vegas and gambling with other people's funds to be a big shot. On Ontario Hydro's books Darlington shows up as a $15-billion asset. Had they built it for only $3 billion as they had initially intended, it would have been a $3-billion asset, but because there have been $12 billion in cost overruns on Hydro's books, the $15-billion figure looks more solid.

Because Hydro is so large and powerful, it has often sought preferential treatment and it has often received that preferential treatment. All of Hydro's nuclear plants were exempted from environmental assessments. Smaller projects had to undergo those assessments but not Hydro's nuclear plants. The nuclear establishment in many ways is a black box. They control the access to the technology. It's a very dangerous technology. It's a technology that is not easily subject to scrutiny.

When Ontario Hydro, the largest builder of nuclear plants, goes to the politicians at Queen's Park and tells them, "We must have this plant. If this plant is not built, the lights are going to go out in this province," those politicians are not in a position to assess whether that's true or not. They have no one else to turn to. There are no competing providers of power who can offer a sober second thought. They are captive to Ontario Hydro's claims and the simplest thing for them to do is to throw up their hands and say, "I guess that's what we must do."

The politicians are then sort of held hostage by their own creation, this beast called Ontario Hydro. Politicians have often been quite explicit about the fact that Hydro rules the roost, that the Hydro bureaucracy is able to dictate the policies of the Ministry of Energy instead of the other way around. The Darlington nuclear plant was exempted from environmental assessments. The Pickering nuclear plant was exempted. The Bruce nuclear plant was exempted. In fact, in the first few years since the Environmental Assessment Act was first passed, Hydro had received numerous exemptions. It just felt it was above the law and didn't have to go through the same procedures that those mortal folks had to.

They feel they're unaccountable or above the law because they, well, they make the laws. They are able to draft the laws for politicians. When they have problems they have a very receptive ear. As part of Hydro's mission in building nuclear plants they needed to receive supplies from various nuclear suppliers, like Westinghouse, General Electric and Babcock & Wilcox, who were providing the turbines and various components. But these companies realized that the nuclear technology was far too dangerous for them to stand behind their product. They went to Hydro and they said, "Look, if we have to be liable for the parts we produce for you, we'll refuse to supply you." And Hydro said, "Don't worry, we can take care of that problem."

They went to the federal government and asked them to pass a law, which the federal government passed, called the Nuclear Liability Act. The act states that if there is an accident at a nuclear plant in Canada and if that accident is caused by a faulty part supplied by GE or Westinghouse, or anyone else for whatever reason, no matter how much damage that accident causes — it can even wipe out the City of Toronto — GE shareholders wouldn't have to put up a nickel in compensation. So GE has to stand behind its toaster ovens but they don't have to stand behind the nuclear parts that they provide.

Politicians passed such an act because they were convinced of the need to have a nuclear industry. Governments everywhere were developing nuclear industries. Canadians thought that they had special insight. After all, we created the CANDU and we told ourselves that the CANDU was the best technology in the world. There had to be federal support, they felt, for the CANDU technology. Canada had to be a technological leader going into the next century. Any support that was required was provided. The government stopped at nothing. They passed laws removing the rights of citizens to compensation. They provided subsidies of all kinds. They facilitated trades. It was government's mission to act as salesman for nuclear technology.

The Nuclear Liability Act was passed in 1976 and proclaimed in 1980. When it was passed it was not a contentious issue. Nuclear technology was not questioned by anyone. There really were very few people to question the technology, apart from some citizens' groups, because industry saw a cash cow.

It had guaranteed profits. It would be selling to governments. There was no one there to question the wisdom of removing liability for the most dangerous technology that has been developed. Private companies have invested in the nuclear industry but only when they've had government guarantees. The technology itself is too risky for the private sector to accept.

When Margaret Thatcher decided to privatize the U.K.'s entire electricity industry, there was a widespread view that nuclear power was the way of the future. Business believed it. The government believed it. A good part of the public believed it. But when the assets were finally put on the sales market and prospective purchasers of those assets had a chance to look at the books, they realized that they could not afford to buy the nuclear assets. They were keen to buy the fossil-fuel assets. They were keen to buy the hydraulic assets. They were keen to buy the distribution companies and transmission companies, but they balked at buying the nuclear plants. They felt that the risk was just too high. And Thatcher, who was determinedly pro-nuclear as well as pro–free market, insisted that those companies would buy the nuclear plants.

Thatcher tried to twist their arm and they said, "I'm sorry, we'd like to help you out, we just can't." She tried to sweeten the pot by offering $5 billion in subsidies to purchasers of the nuclear plants. And they said they couldn't afford to take them off her hands even for $5 billion. The result was that the rest of the system was privatized. There is now a competitive system in the U.K. but those nuclear plants could not be sold. They're now in a separate Crown corporation called Nuclear Electric. And that company is going to be running those nuclear plants until they die.

Consumers have to have choices, yet they can't have choices if monopolies restrict the technologies that they can choose, restrict the companies that they can purchase power from. What needs to happen is the hydro monopoly needs to be broken up. Various components of it have to be sold off, those that can be sold off. The ones that can't be sold off, such as the nuclear plants, should be put into a separate Crown corporation where the plants can be run until they're no longer safe to run and then shut down permanently. If we had had a competitive system, we'd find that these boondoggles did not occur.

The problem is that the structure in a Crown corporation is not an accountable structure. There aren't shareholders who feel they've directly lost some money and who want to make sure that those losses don't occur again. Everything is buffeted. Ontario Hydro built a plant that cost too much. The result of that is higher rates that are spread throughout the economy. The cost to any individual is not very high. The cost to the provincial debt is all incremental, so the pain is felt very slowly.

Nobody has a direct say. Nobody can bail out of the Hydro system except by leaving the province. If you want to bail out of your General Motors stock, you can sell it and that will send a message. It's very hard to send a message. The politicians don't have great control over Ontario Hydro. In fact they probably have very little control over Ontario Hydro. It's very hard to get direct reaction even when such a serious blunder can occur.

Hydro has been out of control for most of its history. Every now and then it is tamed temporarily. Right now there's a chairman at Ontario Hydro who has worked wonders in trying to tame Hydro. It has cut its staff by about 10,000. It has chopped $24 billion in unneeded projects. It has taken on the unions. It has been really quite a remarkable display. But even this Herculean effort really has not been enough. Even after doing all this, Chairman Strong has not been getting support from the provincial government, which really fears a lot of what he's doing. Although for a while they were endorsing it. It's a situation where it's very easy to backslide again because a system does not tend to work efficiently under normal circumstances. It requires heroes to do things well. There really are very few heroes in this world. And any society that structures itself on the basis of being rescued every now and then by heroes is fundamentally going to have problems and really cannot function well as a democracy.

ELIZABETH BRUBAKER

Ontario Hydro: Regulating the Regulator

I'm the executive director of Environment Probe, one of the divisions of the Energy Probe Research Foundation. Energy Probe is a large public-interest research foundation. We started exclusively with energy issues, such as nuclear power, but we've since branched off into a number of other issues as well.

We've looked at international environmental issues and local and national resource issues. We also have a division that's working on consumer issues. My division, Environment Probe, works on a variety of environmental issues in Canada, particularly resource issues dealing with forestry and fisheries. I personally have been working on property rights for the last couple of years, looking at how they can be used to protect the environment.

I've been investigating Ontario Hydro. A lot of my work has been in water resources, looking at the damage that Ontario Hydro has done to the northern environment through its dams on the northern rivers. There has been terrible destruction. By damming rivers, Ontario Hydro has flooded lands, destroyed fisheries and eroded riverbanks and lakeshores. It has destroyed the way of life for many Aboriginal communities that depend on the rivers. It has really done a tremendous amount of damage. And unfortunately a lot of these Aboriginal communities are still suffering from dams that were built decades ago.

For example, there's the Matagami River up near James Bay in Northern Ontario. Ontario Hydro built three dams on the river back in the 1960s, and apparently their construction crews actually chased the Native people off their land, then burned down their campsites to ensure that they wouldn't return. Now, that was a different era, but I think it's symbolic of what has been happening through Hydro, and there are a number of other horror stories.

There's a terrible story from the 1940s involving the Ogoki diversion. Ontario Hydro wanted to generate more power at Niagara Falls. In order to do that it needed to find more water to put through its turbines. It decided to divert the Ogoki River up in northwestern Ontario. That river would normally flow north into the Albany River and ultimately into James Bay. But Ontario Hydro built some dams and channels and diverted the river southwards, so that it flowed down the Little Jackfish River into Lake Nipigon, and down the Nipigon River into Lake Superior. Then from Lake Superior it flowed through Lake Huron and Lake Erie, and finally through Ontario Hydro's turbines.

That just wreaked havoc on the environment. They flooded 89 square miles. They caused a tremendous amount of erosion. The flooding contaminated the fish with mercury. The Native people living in the area suffered terribly. A dozen families were flooded off their lands without any prior consultation. The fisheries were destroyed. The traditional hunting grounds were flooded. There were terrible, terrible consequences.

As I mentioned, Hydro didn't consult these people. They didn't compensate them. In some cases they simply denied their requests for assistance. One reserve along Lake Nipigon asked Hydro for assistance in relocating a cemetery that had been eroded by fluctuating water levels, and Hydro refused. It wasn't until the 1970s that they finally agreed to put some riprap along the shoreline. And people today say that they're still paying a terrible price for this diversion.

Obviously Ontario Hydro has done a tremendous amount of damage to all of these northern Aboriginal communities. And often the affected public extends even further. With the Ogoki diversion all of the property owners along the Great Lakes suffered from higher water levels. The damages might not have been as serious as those to the Native people, but they meant shortened beaches, flooded docks, water in basements and erosion which was sometimes very serious.

In a monopoly situation, ultimately politicians and bureaucrats have complete control. Monopolies like Ontario Hydro can get away with more than private companies can, and I don't think that's as it should be. It's hard to tell in Ontario because we don't have a lot of private companies generating power, but if you look at some recent experiences with private power companies, you'll see that they're far more accountable than Ontario Hydro is, far more interested in working out a mutually agreeable solution with the people who might be affected by their projects.

For example, in the 1980s a company called Conwest wanted to dam the Black River up in Northern Ontario, north of Lake Superior. They contacted the Pic River First Nation, who had a reserve by the site that they wanted to use. They knew that they couldn't go ahead without the permission of the people on the reserve. They negotiated a deal that would be beneficial to both parties, which is as it should be. They agreed to build a run-of-the-river station that wouldn't require a dam. They agreed to put fish spawning areas and nursery habitat below the outfall. They had a low intake so that it wouldn't affect the river's flow. They offered the band a 10 percent interest in the project, which amounted to about $150,000 a year for 50 years, so it was a good financial investment for the band. They also trained band members in the operation and maintenance of the plant; they employed band members in its construction. Everybody benefited and the Pic River band found the whole process so successful that now it has decided to develop another small hydro project on its own.

Similarly the people who live around a power plant should control the air quality around that plant, and at one time that was how things operated. There's a system of common law that has operated for the last 600 years. Under the common law no property owner has the right to harm any other property owner. Certainly emissions from power plants harm other property owners. If a plant wants to harm another property owner, it has to get that owner's permission and negotiate a compromise that will be agreeable to both parties.

That's not the way it works now, though. The common law only applies when the government hasn't passed laws and regulations of its own, and there are myriad laws and regulations governing air quality in Ontario. Under the common law there's no such thing as automatically authorized pollution. You cannot pollute unless you have the permission of the people you'll harm. But if the government gets involved and passes a law, then it overrides the common law and grants statutory authority to the polluter. The polluter is then immune from the provisions of the common law, and the people he's harming can no longer sue him.

For instance, a nuclear accident is covered by the Nuclear Liability Act, a federal law that was passed by the government back in the 1970s. It exempts nuclear manufacturers and operators from responsibility in case of a nuclear accident. If there's an accident with costs over $75 million, Ontario Hydro isn't responsible, nor are its suppliers, even if they manufactured something negligently. That's not at all reassuring. It's very unfortunate, but in the event of a nuclear accident, ultimately it's the people who suffer damages who are held accountable, and perhaps the taxpayer. The government has the authority to set up a commission, and that commission could grant damages to people who have been affected. But we don't know if it would do so. We don't know how much it would be able to raise, and any money that it did raise would of course come from the taxpayer, while people who weren't compensated would simply have to bear the cost themselves. So the taxpayer and the people affected by the accident would bear the costs, but it should be the people who are producing the energy.

The Nuclear Liability Act was passed because no insurance company wanted to take on the responsibility for a nuclear accident, which is a pretty good sign that such accidents might have costs that are simply unacceptable to society. If no insurer will take on the responsibility, then perhaps we shouldn't be building nuclear plants in the first place. They're extremely expensive, far more than anybody ever dreamed. They're also proving to be much shorter-lived than anybody thought, with lives of just a fraction of what they were supposed to be.

We're well aware now of the environmental hazards associated with nuclear power plants, from the very beginning of the cycle, with the uranium mining and milling, through the uranium processing, to the operation of the nuclear plant itself, which in addition to threatening people with an accident, also eliminates wastes on a regular basis. Tritium is often emitted into the air or the water from Ontario Hydro's nuclear plants. Then there's the problem of waste disposal, which people still haven't figured out how to solve.

One very interesting story is that of Eugene Bourgeois. He raises sheep on the Bruce Peninsula, near the Bruce nuclear complex. One of the facilities in that complex is a heavy-water plant that periodically releases hydrogen sulphide into the air. Bourgeois suggests that Ontario Hydro's hydrogen sulphide is responsible for some very serious problems on his farm. He has had sheep dying. Lambs have been born without the instinct to nurse. At one time much of his flock went blind for no apparent reason. He himself has suffered terribly. He has had headaches and spells where he has been unable to concentrate and has felt dizzy. He may have even passed out on occasion, I'm not sure. He has gone to scientists and doctors, asking them where these problems could be coming from, and they all agree that the symptoms are consistent with hydrogen sulphide poisoning.

If Eugene Bourgeois had common-law property rights, then he would be able to prevent Ontario Hydro from releasing hydrogen sulphide, or he could work out some sort of a deal with them whereby they would release it at a certain time of year or a certain time of day so that it would wreak less damage on his sheep. But Ontario Hydro denies any responsibility. It says that it's working within the limits set by government regulations. And that's really the end of the story. It's operating under statutory authority.

Governments have long tried to protect their monopolies, their Crown corporations. They don't just protect them; they also promote them. And that's because governments can gain a lot politically from these active organizations. Ontario Hydro is a perfect example because it creates jobs for the government. A hydro construction project employs a lot of people, and the government gets credit for that. Jobs mean votes. A monopoly like Ontario Hydro is a perfect short-term political tool, but the long-term effects can be so contrary to the short-term goal.

The Ontario government isn't interested in the fact that we don't need any power right now, or that nine utility generators can produce power more cheaply than can Hydro. It's also not concerned that these are very expensive, short-term jobs and that, perhaps worse, in raising power rates for the rest of the province, they're actually destroying other people's jobs. If business is paying higher power bills, then it doesn't have as much money to hire people. If consumers are paying higher power bills, then they don't have as much money to spend on other goods that would be manufactured by people working. So these aren't just foolish jobs that are being created: they're actually counterproductive jobs.

Our foundation has been working for years now to privatize Hydro. The province would be a lot better off if people had a choice as to what kind of power ran their homes and their plants. Nobody would pick nuclear power because it's way too expensive and it's the most potentially dangerous power, which makes it even more expensive because one should incorporate the costs of any accident into the costs of power. No private company would invest in nuclear power. It's so expensive and the risks are so high. It's such an archaic monolith. In fact, in Britain when the electricity system was privatized, nobody wanted the nuclear power plants.

WILLIAM TERON

CMHC and Government-Subsidized Housing

Before my involvement with the Canada Mortgage and Housing Corporation I had been a builder and developer for 20 to 25 years, doing design/build work. The prime minister at the time, Trudeau, asked if I would come into government as chairman and president of CMHC. He said that they wanted to put in some rather bold new policies. I spent seven years in government there, and at the same time became the deputy minister of urban affairs, so it broadened into other issues. Since then, for the last 15 years, I have turned that into international policy and developments in international technology. My work is in the same field, but in places like South Africa, Russia and Malaysia.

Programs and policies that were put into legislation during my time with CMHC included non-profit legislation, co-op legislation, rural and Native housing, the AHOP (Assisted Home Ownership Program) and the neighbourhood improvement program. Those programs and policies worked then, and they're still being employed today. But I think those programs addressed issues of the 1970s that were quite different than the issues today. Notwithstanding that I was one of the authors of those programs, I would have to say that the policies currently being used are ready for a total review; and I don't mean just putting Band-Aids on old programs.

The whole debt issue that we have right now was not an issue in those days. In 1973 the Cabinet and ministers were after us to come up with creative, innovative programs, and they had a $3-billion to $5-billion discretionary budget. They had money to work with, and therefore we were able to deal with other issues. At that time public housing was a stigma. Nobody wanted it in their backyards. People who lived in public housing also felt stigmatized by it. So our total focus back then was the integration of the community. Debt was not a problem.

We came up with a deep subsidy that had quite a shocking impact. We would put up a dollar to build non-profit housing, but only 25 percent of the occupants were going to be the poorer people, the "hard-core poor," and 75 percent would be regular citizens. So in order to get integration of people in the same building, we said that no more than 25 percent of the occupants of a single building should be the people who were eligible by not having the means, and the other 75 percent would pay their own way. But that meant that only 25 percent of a program that was funded, supported or subsidized by the government was reaching the hard-core poor. You were getting a 25¢ bang for your dollar.

Those same programs are still being used, and I think, with the debt being such a crippling issue (not only to governments; it eventually gets down to the people because we pay the taxes), that a more efficient use of the mortgage instrument is appropriate today. I think a total review is much overdue. The integration question is not an issue anymore. We don't have that type of situation; not to the same degree. Today we have a debt issue, and if I were crafting a policy now, it would be directed at using precious taxpayers' funds more carefully. I believe that the government can get a bigger bang for the buck.

Today we have the condominium legislation. The government could be buying individual units in all of the buildings, including existing buildings, still getting integration, but using a buck for a buck. That would be using the taxpayers' money more carefully.

Nationally rent controls also came into being during my days at CMHC and made for a very, very difficult period. Barnie Danson was the minister, and I remember the housing ministers from across Canada getting together. At the beginning every one of them was against rent controls because they said we needed more production of rental properties, not less, and this would be counterproductive. But then it became a very unusual situation. I have a great regard for politics and politicians, but in that particular case the politicians came to the conclusion that there were more tenants than landlords, and when they came back to the next meeting there was unanimous approval of the rent controls. I had heard their entire deliberations and it was a difficult, difficult decision. I think it was a bad one.

In these decisions sometimes the political aspects are front and centre. Sometimes there's an economic motivation; sometimes it's social. In that particular case, while the initial instinct of every minister was correct, the final decision was a very political one.

A more complex model has to come forward that deals with the genuine concerns of the renters but also deals with, "How do we get productivity? How do we get more of that kind of housing?" Such a model has not been developed. If there were a new housing review today, hopefully that would be one of the issues on the table, to come up with a good answer rather than a convenient one.

I believe that today there are proper examples and techniques of dealing with affordability without subsidy. I believe that subsidization is a very short-term fix, limited by the capacity of your dollars. And what I found when I was at CMHC was that as much as we managed the governmental funds of subsidies, we were limited by them. If they gave us half a billion dollars, we could help X number of people, and then "too bad" for the others. It almost became an elite system of who would get in and who wouldn't.

We should be developing techniques of a self-reliant and self-sustaining system where basically on their good wages people can look after themselves. I'm very much behind the program of affordability without subsidy. We're working with the Inuit up north, where until now there was a 100 percent subsidy for houses, which were twice the cost due to transportation, etc. We're working with Nunavut right now to develop their own methods of construction, their own architecture to build within their own means so that they're not reliant on subsidy. The old inefficiencies were in bringing in southern techniques, like taking wood up north and building houses which the high winds would strip. We had a very inappropriate, extremely expensive type of construction. We also had, unfortunately, the situation that these were government-sponsored, so there were lots of bucks around. Consequently a lot of creative entrepreneurs took advantage of the situation, happy to provide those services.

As we come up with new methods, there are a lot of vested interests that are not happy. They'd like the old ways to continue. There are a lot of people in all of the governmental programs; a lot of people who made their livelihoods from these subsidies that will find they're going to be cut off. They'll have to adapt. There's no doubt this debt situation is not an arbitrary thing that you can elect to follow or not. We have to cure it or others will cure it for us. I think there's a determination that we will cure it. But there's going to be a lot of yelling and shouting, and all vested groups will come forward.

I believe that Minister Axworthy probably understands that and has the will. He knows that whatever he recommends cutting, there is a constituency that's going to be affected, and he has to expect that people are going to be against it. But he's going to have to be a good politician and know that 29 million of us are going to suffer if 1,000 people of vested interests benefit. So I think he's going to have to take the high road and do the right thing.

I believe that subsidies cut innovation and creativity. They make us fat and lazy. I think we can come up with enormous creativity. Up north housing was costing $200,000 to $250,000. We've set a goal that we will create more relevant housing of top quality for $50,000, 20 percent of the current cost. Necessity is the mother of invention.

I believe that the process of renewal we're going through is a healthy one. It might be painful in the short run, but it will be for the benefit of all of us, particularly our children.

CMHC basically has two roles. Its first is that of the mortgage insurance business. In an orderly marketplace there is sufficient money, sufficient product and quality control. CMHC does that through the mortgage insurance instrument, as a self-sustaining corporation that has nothing to do with any funds from the government. In fact, it makes money each year. CMHC's second role is that when the Government of Canada passes legislation in which there is a housing program of any subsidization, it looks to CMHC to manage those funds on behalf of the government. So CMHC acts as a manager for the governmental account.

The annual subsidy increases go to the ministerial account or the government account. The reason they're increasing is that they're past accounts, the aggregate of all the subsidies that we have committed to poor people, senior citizens, etc. And that account is inching up just by sheer inflation, etc. My understanding — and I haven't been that close to it — is that the federal government is not increasing that. That's a provincial responsibility now. But the past is there and will be with us basically forever; that is, the accumulative subsidies of the past.

CMHC is really not in subsidies today, other than those they've accumulated in the past. The provincial governments are putting up the funds right now, by their own request. They said, "Feds, get out," and now they've got the problem.

As a mortgage insurer, CMHC makes money. But whenever I hear about the privatization of, or getting rid of, CMHC, I think this would have enormous repercussions. When it was created back in 1945, at the end of World War II, there were no mortgage funds. Investors were not putting money into housing because houses were shoddily built, etc. The policies of the Government of Canada and the mortgage insurance work of CMHC made the mortgage instrument an attractive place for investors to put money.

Canada and the United States are two of the very few places in the world where there is a lot of money invested into mortgages, which means money for housing. In all the other countries I know of they don't have such an instrument; they don't have any mortgage funds. So CMHC is the custodian of the mortgage instrument to ensure that mortgages get their fair share of the capital. Instead of people putting money into bonds or equities, we need money put into mortgages. If CMHC was not there today, mortgages could dry up and we'd have a housing crisis.

The government does not back these securities. CMHC is a Crown corporation and charges a mortgage insurance fee, no different than what you pay when buying life insurance. The bankers therefore feel much more comfortable with it. The mortgage insurance program does not cost the people of Canada or the Government of Canada a single penny.

The provinces wanted the responsibility for social housing. It was just a matter of the classic Canadian intergovernmental debate, the federal government versus the provincial governments. I was an instrument of the federal government at that time. I went in knowing very well that I wanted to agree, so I had to be the "reluctant bride," but I was anxious that they do it. But now that the provinces have it on their own necks, I think they would love to see somebody come back in, including the federal government, because housing is such a megaproject.

As far as which government it is, I don't think it matters. The Canadian public is paying some 40 percent of their resources into taxes. I don't think Canadians can be taxed any more. You can shuffle it around between the municipalities, provinces and feds, but that 40 percent is the pie that's got to be cut up. So I don't think that it matters to the public which government pays for it. It's the big pie.

I do believe that the municipal and provincial levels are really the better ones to serve the public in retail matters of housing, when you have to deal one to one. They should be managing it. But my main concern is that the current policies are not as capital-efficient as they can be. We could do the existing job and increase that job over time using less money. I believe the government can do more in housing with less money, with new policies. There is a cushion in the system. We can do things more efficiently today and meet our objectives. So with this review that's being done by Mr. Axworthy, which should follow on to housing, I believe that we can meet our Canadian sense of caring and thoughtfulness and do it for less money. There's that much cushion.

If we don't produce low-cost rental units — and there are a lot of people in rentals because of their inability to buy a house, not because of a desire to be in rentals — then we're pushing these people into public housing of one kind or another. If the government wants to be the nation's landlord, then rental controls are helping them. But that doesn't mean that I don't understand the plight of the renters.

We need a rather complex model that will achieve two or three objectives. The solution that I advocate is inflation and increased salaries: subsidies will decrease and people can step out of their subsidies. Then there are your senior citizens, etc. You can't do anything about those. I believe that the role of governmental subsidies should be confined to the hard-core poor. Unfortunately our safety net in the past grew to the point where, for instance, we heard of a situation involving a Toronto politician where he and his wife were making $120,000 or so and were in non-profit housing. Clearly the program was never intended to include that type of thing. We can't afford that inefficiency any longer. There's a lot of it in the system, and I believe we can bring it into order and not abandon the hard-core poor.

It's a simple economic situation. People go out and they do comparative shopping. And they see a new non-profit apartment go up, and it's available for $650 or $700 a month, when something equal in the normal, private market is available at $900, and they make a simple economic decision. But somebody is paying that spread: the taxpayer. And while it might have been nice until now, I believe that we've got to use those resources to give it back to the hard-core poor.

The environment in the mid-1970s was that the government had a lot of good intentions and thought they could do great things. They felt that if they found a solution, it was up to them to do it. Ministers and Cabinet were eager for ideas: "Please come up with creative ideas to deal with this problem, and this problem." If a good idea came forward, the government virtually jumped at the great opportunity to do good. And at that time they honestly felt that they were doing good. And they were, in the short run. I don't think any of them actually projected themselves and saw that there was an end to the rainbow. Then, of course, as the deficit started to grow they started to try to tighten things up. But unfortunately what then fuelled the demands weren't the politicians that ran the thing; all of a sudden the public started to have these great expectations for the non-profit, the co-op and all the rest. It was a demand pool. I guess the first time we heard of it was way back in Pearson's days, when he said, "We're living beyond our means." Trudeau kept on repeating that, and we started to hear those signs coming in, and now we've got a near-catastrophic situation. We're very much at the end of the rainbow.

I left CMHC because in 1978–79 the opposition said, "You've overdone it. You've overbuilt. Now stop it." But we did see that continue for the next 10 years or so, where the demand was insatiable and they just wanted more and more and more. The recent rash of non-profit in Ontario was just uncalled for. I mean, there were other solutions. We saw a great deal of it, and it was only a matter of time before somebody had to blow the whistle. I'm surprised that the whistle wasn't blown earlier.

I knew of other solutions. I was asked to join a task force on housing and found that a new low-cost house cost $60,000 to build, and yet the newspapers in 1985 were full of used housing available at $30,000. Now, this existing housing being offered at $30,000 was being occupied by taxpaying citizens; but they weren't the hard-core poor. These were good houses. Yet the public purse wasn't buying the $30,000 solution that was available, but was chasing $60,000 solutions. When we made our report for Ottawa after investigating, we recommended a best-buy policy; that is, that to buy housing for our hard-core poor, or even for those of modest means, it should be on a best-buy basis. If you're using public funds, and if you could buy a reasonably good apartment or house on the marketplace for $30,000, then you should not be building a new house for $60,000. Just as if a person needed transportation you wouldn't have to buy him a new car. Nothing happened. I did get feedback: some cynicism that there wasn't much depth to that $30,000 used market. But in fact their study showed the enormous amount of trading per month that happened at that level.

Now, you might say, "That's 1985." But today we have another phenomenon and that is that since the recession a lot of apartment buildings are on the market under duress. Every day I've been watching the ads. Look at *The Globe and Mail* or the *Financial Post*, you'll see picture after picture of apartment buildings being offered, even by CMHC in repossessions. There's one being offered today, in 1994, in *The Globe and Mail* at $37,500 per unit. Something is wrong. These kinds of savings are right there, staring at us. Tenders are out to get new housing built for probably $70,000 to $100,000, and there's a $37,000 solution begging. Is the public purse buying it? No. Why not?

As a deputy minister, when I was a student of my political masters and watching them, I would think that in just the sheer creation of new things, the building of a new house, they could identify that "I did something." To buy a used house down the street to help poor people wouldn't have as much visibility. I think it would be unconscious, but it would be there. When we did the task force report in 1985, the aftermath was that people said, "Oh no, there might be a few, but you couldn't get many." Then they started to get reports of the enormous quantity of housing that went through the registry office every month under $30,000. They agreed with me that there was a vast inventory of low-cost product available to the public purse at half the price. But the report died. Now, was it because reports die or was it because for the politicians that kind of initiative just wasn't sexy enough?

Building the product has a high political visibility, and politicians want to be perceived as doing things. Therefore they drive by these projects and cut the ribbons, etc. While sending rent supplement cheques isn't as sexy. Maybe that's a pretty cynical view. But that's what I think.

I'm working in places like South Africa, Russia and Malaysia on these very issues, trying to come up with housing policies that are not dependent on subsidies and charity. Places like Singapore and Malaysia have progressive ideas that Canada could learn from. The housing board in Singapore, which has their pension fund, imposed that people put 20 percent of their salaries into a mortgage pension fund at two percent, and they become eligible to borrow money at two percent to build their own houses. The Singapore housing authority has more money than product required, so there is an imaginative idea. In Malaysia they force the builders to create three low-cost houses for every seven permits they can get for housing.

There are a lot of good examples around the world, and Canada, I think, is ready for a new commission on housing. We need to rewrite the book. We're ready.

BRUCE LEGGE

Ontario: Workers' Compensation Then and Now

I was chairman of the Workers' Compensation Board for nine years, from 1965 to 1973. I was appointed to the job because I'd spent the previous 14 years of my practice dealing with disabled soldiers from the war, and I knew the medical side of the legal world.

It was a very challenging public appointment. What attracted me was the fact that the board existed to restore the injured worker to health, and to find him a job. And while he was, for example, learning how to do a new job, they would pay him an allowance, which was the employer's money. So it was not a tax-founded thing. It was efficient, and it was run like a business. The first priority was to assure that the workman was being paid for the injury or the disability that was caused by his work.

The board was originally set up as an independent Crown corporation to ensure that it would be free from politics and would deal not only with the law but with equity, the business of fairness. How can you pay a man for losing his sight, losing his leg, breaking his back or any of the dreadful things that happen in industry? You can never really do it, so you must be scrupulously fair to give him as much by way of service and a pension as you can. And that has always been the doctrine of workers' compensation, since 1915 when it was inaugurated in this province.

I was involved personally by making three members of the board the final court of adjudication. In that way the members could see the hard cases that, after appeals and appeals, finally got to the board.

I think that the board has to be concerned with the decision making. That's the most accountable way. If you don't know what's going on, you can't really worry about it. If you see the hard cases, you wonder how a benevolent system that you're working hard to make even more benevolent can fail. And it does, in the odd hard case.

Being a public board, it was controlled by the legislature of Ontario, so the legislation would change the benefits. And the board would change the assessments, or the tax imposed on each worker, based on the risks in that trade. Some jobs, like mining, are dangerous; some other jobs, like running a bakeshop, are not dangerous. When benefits were increased we would increase the imposition on the employer, the money that the employer had to pay.

We had 50 doctors at all times. We had a hospital and rehabilitation centre with 600 beds, so we had ample medical facilities to know the true extent of the disabilities, and we had a way of getting people better. In my day we tried to keep administration costs under 10 percent of our total budget. Seven, eight and nine percent would be the figures per annum. We had in the order of 1,700 to 1,800 people in our administration for the nine years I was chairman. Today I believe it's closer to 9,000, but I'm not sure. I haven't seen any public data, but that's what I hear.

Being a board that deals with human misery which is paid for by somebody else, we'd get complaints about the amount of money that it was costing the employer to pay for his insurance policy. We'd also have complaints from the injured workman because he'd been a highly paid employee before, but he was now only getting three-quarters of his salary, up to a maximum on which he found it difficult to live. So there was the question from the workman: "How do I live on this amount of tax-free money?" And from the employer: "How do I pay?" Those were the chronic complaints that would come to the board. They'd come to the legislature, too, because it changes the benefits. Benefits are changed by statute. When they're changed the board has to find a way of getting enough money to pay for the change. And the government doesn't give them money. At least it didn't in my day.

The principle on which the board operated then was that this was public money, being the employers' money, which existed for the good of the injured workmen, and therefore there was to be no waste and no debt. If you have debts, you pay interest on the money you borrow, which detracts from the money available to rehabilitate the workmen. It was that simple. I don't know what they're doing today, but we did not run debts.

There are very few people who are as stingy with public money as I am because I'm from the old school. You cannot have a lavish bureaucracy and save money. Every additional person that you give a signature to, to spend money, is costing you and your employers. So you have to be very tight-fisted in the administration of all social services, I think.

Today the board has a sizeable unfunded liability. I think that if the board ran out of money to pay the statutory benefits that the legislature said should be paid to an injured workman, there would be dreadful trouble because you would have people in hardships, through no fault of their own, without money to pay for them.

I think that maybe they spent more money than they should have, and perhaps they hired more staff than they should have, and I'm not saying they did, but those are the only explanations that jump to mind. I've never discussed it with anybody. But if you spend too much money, you're going to have too much debt, which reduces the amount of money that you have for your victim, the injured workman. The government is quiet about it. But do you think any government would like to come forward and say, "Yeah, we know about that, there's another $12 billion we have to pay"? I don't think so. I don't think anybody's willing to say that. They're more likely to say it was somebody else's fault, "before we came to power."

I would be very much against deficit financing for injured workmen, just as I would be for injured veterans, who are a responsibility of the federal government and still get pensions for their war injuries. If the board was insolvent, well, in our present social democracy it is government that picks up the tab for everything that goes wrong, isn't it? So I think the poor old taxpayer would have to do it. But I pray that it never happens because it would be a disaster of enormous proportion.

I'm not going to say when the board went off the rails. But I say that any board that adjudicates and spends public money goes off the rails

— willingly or unwillingly, for good reasons or for bad reasons — when it spends more than it takes in, when it gives more to someone than it can provide. You're not doing somebody a favour by borrowing the money from somebody, to pay Peter from Paul, are you?

I think the worker has always rightly felt that he was entitled to be compensated for the loss in health, strength or skills because of his injuries. He should certainly be compensated, I believe; compensated for life, as long as the disability is a disability. That's what compensation is all about: paying for something that was beyond the control of the injured workman. I think the board is doing that. It may even be doing it with more money than it has. That's the problem, I think.

If they think that they're following the principles of just and equitable public management, then they're probably trying to do that. But if they're spending more money than they're getting by a sizeable amount, they're probably failing in that principle. And nobody knows it better than the person doing it. The easiest thing, if you're a public administrator, is to give in to complaints by establishing a new department or service that you tell the public won't cost very much but will solve the problem. It invariably does two things: it costs a great deal and it doesn't solve the problem.

I think that the Government of Ontario, no matter what happens to the Workers' Compensation Board, has to stand behind the legislation that it has approved, and if there is a financial crisis with payments for the board, the government would have to stand behind it. The government has to recognize that the board only administers the legislation that the government of the day provides for it. Politicians have to look very carefully at Crown corporations that indirectly collect and spend money.

I don't know if there's too much politics in the board today. I think that members of the legislature, members of Parliament, aldermen and mayors have always known somebody who is a friend of theirs who was injured, and they would write to us, saying, "Would you mind having a look at this case? Because he's having a hard time." And I don't think that is wrong. If the administrators paid attention to it as an evidentiary matter, it would be wrong. I never did. I'd always write back and say, "We'll give it the closest attention," and we did. And that's all you can say. You couldn't promise a deal because somebody knew the mayor or the member of Parliament or the Cabinet minister. You just couldn't do it, and I don't think anybody seriously wanted you to. But they wanted to be able to say to their constituent, "I spoke to them and they said that they'd look at it very seriously."

There's always pressure on the board from politicians, organizations of employers, governments, labour unions, all sorts of people, and also from their own elected people. You know, doctors elect presidents of the Ontario Medical Association and so on. There's all sorts of pressure, and a lot of it is legitimate. You can't have too much good advice.

In my day the board only had consulting actuaries. Today it also has in-house actuaries. If you look at insurance companies, they all have actuaries on their payrolls. And those actuaries all have access to consulting actuaries because there are really complicated mathematical problems in this work. I see the board as a casualty and life insurance company, so I think that it can have in-house actuaries. But I think it has to have consulting actuaries because it must be satisfied that, as in dealing with disease, it has the very best actuarial advice that's available; and as in disease, that the very best consultants are available to find ways of curing it. They've got to have the best advice.

Without being judgmental I think that you can't promise more politically than you have the money to pay for. And that goes not only for a taxpayer and directly given government services, but also for the indirectly funded and indirectly serviced organizations, like the Workers' Compensation Board. Unless you provide the money you cannot provide generous benefits by legislation, can you?

As for pinpointing the causes of current problems, you could do it by a royal commission, which would cost a mint of money. They can go over the operations since the war of the Workers' Compensation Board and see what went wrong and so on, but think of what that would cost to uncover that. Mind you, I believe they're doing that now. I suppose the government has accepted the responsibility of "fixing" the board by appointing a commission of inquiry. If they knew how to solve it, they wouldn't have appointed the commission.

The debt situation in Canada is the same as in a family: if a family spends much more than they can earn, they're going to be in dreadful trouble. Somebody will foreclose on the mortgage and they'll lose their house. They'll have to give up their car and take the TTC. There are terrible consequences to living beyond your means. Now, the people of Canada are saddled with an enormous load of debt federally, provincially, municipally, at every level of government, and you can almost call it "the Canadian disease." We have to stop spending more than we have because it's going to wreck the economy. We started because the voters will take anything that's given to them, won't they? Isn't that the idea, to seduce the voters to support you by promising something good, hoping that you can pay for it? But when you can't you don't hear politicians saying, "We promised too much." They'll say, "You got too much." But politicians have to be elected, you know. They're not politicians if they ain't elected.

The Canada Pension Plan has a $500-billion debt. I can't even think in terms of that astronomical sum, it's just too much. I don't think any Canadian can; we're all numbed by these astronomical figures. But as far as the idea of the government diminishing our debt goes, I wouldn't say that I'm hopeful. But I would say I think that it's inevitable, or even inexorable, that they will have to do it because even that socialist oasis of power New Zealand had to do it. There's an accounting for everybody. If your bookmaker says you have to pay up, you have to pay up.

If I were asked to help the board again, the first thing I'd say is, "Thanks a lot, but no thanks." The second thing I'd say is, "If you want me to give evidence before a commission inquiry, I'll do it." But that's about all I'd say because I don't think you can second-guess anybody's administration. My advice to the board would be, "Do your best. Work hard. Be honest. Stay away from politicians."

DAVID FRAME

Ontario: Workers' Compensation Policies and Industries

The Workers' Compensation Board is a huge bureaucracy. It has over 4,000 employees, and their responsibilities under the legislation are multifaceted. It's a much-criticized organization, so you've got people over there that feel they have to cover themselves and are afraid to make decisions. They're often afraid to go out on a limb and take a leadership role. Because of that, you have an embattled organization that doesn't like to make decisions and for the most part is forced down the path to change.

Our relations with the board are fairly complex. We have to deal with it at many different levels. There's the WCB itself, as the administrator of the act. There's its corporate board of directors, which is constantly reviewing policies, programs and how they deliver policy; you have to deal with them first, usually before you can deal with the administration. The administration tends just to try to follow the policy. Above and beyond that, most important is probably the government, which dictates legislation and regulations. We have a responsibility to work at all of those levels, and to work with the employer community to try to get all employers to agree with the direction we want policy to go. And we find it's most effective to work with the labour community to get agreement on policy changes. You start to make it easier for the board to agree with you when you can tell them there isn't going to be conflict on an issue, that you've resolved how changes should happen because you have agreement with the labour community.

Who sits on the corporate board of directors and how they're appointed are very topical questions. There are some fundamental changes in Bill 165. The government is formally recognizing the board of directors as being a bipartite board, with equal representation from labour and management. The legislation in the past hasn't defined it that way, but often the board of directors has included people from the general community. You may get technical people who are seen as being on both sides of the fence, like a doctor, for instance.

The major problem is that there isn't even a fundamental agreement on what the WCB is supposed to be. There are essentially two views. One is that it provides a social safety net and is a major part of our government's social fabric. The other is that it's an insurance program. And those are completely different points of view.

The employer community is told, and we believe, that it's a mandatory insurance program. All employers have to pay into that program. In return their employees' salaries are covered if they have workplace-related accidents, and the employers are protected from being sued by their employees. That's the basis of that insurance contract that we believe we have. The other side will tell you that it's a social program. UIC, CPP and WCB all fit together, and it's the responsibility of those programs to make sure there are no holes in the coverage and nobody's falling through the safety net. So there's a fundamental difference of opinion of what we have.

Part of our problem is that the government has been unwilling to define in legislation exactly what it's trying to do and what its approach is. The repercussions are evident in its new legislation. The government has come forward and said that about $2,000 worth of new payments will be made for those who are already receiving pensions. That's $2 billion which wasn't paid for, in an insurance sense, by the employers of the day whose employees had accidents. No other insurance program that I know of — no private insurance, anyway — says, "If you're not

193

covered, don't worry, come back to us and maybe we'll cover you," which is in a sense what they're doing for that $2 billion.

But on the other hand the government is saying that this is not a government-backed insurance system. The stakeholders, labour and management, and the board of directors have the responsibility to decide how it's going to be paid for, and government doesn't have anything to do with that. They're backing away from any association with it. So on one hand they're saying it's like private insurance. On the other hand they're mandating all sorts of new costs from old accidents. They're sending two very different messages.

We've asked the government what will happen if the debt overruns the board, and they haven't answered. Indirectly they've said that the board of directors has to decide how they are going to deliver their mandate. That mandate is to pay injured workers for workplace-related accidents and disease. If they stop doing that, that would be a failure not of the government, in their mind, but of the board of directors. What they're saying to the board of directors is, "If current rates don't cover the costs, increase the rates."

One implication of higher premiums is that some people will avoid the system. The burden's already fairly high. In our industry the average employer pays about $3,000 per worker to the WCB, so it adds up. Ours is a very competitive industry. We recently had some research done which showed that the profit margin in the construction industry is less than one percent. So companies are looking for an edge on their competition to get work.

A survey was done by an independent organization about seven or eight years ago, and they came to us with their information. It said there was about a 25 percent difference between those people who were working in the construction industry without paying premiums and those who paid their premiums. We went to the board and said, "Apparently 25 percent of the industry isn't paying." They looked at it and said they could account for about half of that. But they agreed with us that about 12 percent weren't paying. That 12 percent means about $25 million a year. The board tried to decide what they could do to collect it, but in the end they threw their hands up and said, "We don't know how to collect that money," and they gave up.

There's been fairly substantial growth of an underground economy in the construction industry. Let me give you a scenario. Two contractors are looking to do the same job, and they both charge, let's say, $20 an hour. One says, "Here's my price," at that $20 an hour, "plus I have to charge you the cost of WCB, Employer Health Tax, CPP, UIC." Suddenly there's a 20–30 percent cost on top. The other employer says, "Look, I'll just charge you my costs, and I won't charge you any of those taxes, if we do it for cash." We know who's getting most of that business in certain small sectors; it's the cash market. There's just too much of a burden being placed on the employer to collect on behalf of the government.

The message is clear for some companies that they can get around their payroll taxes. The board's processes are such that it regularly audits the larger companies, so they pay every nickel that's due, but a lot of the smaller companies are never audited, and they know that. Sometimes the board doesn't even know about them. They find that they can be more competitive simply by not paying their WCB premiums, and maybe other fees as well. We suspect there are employees out there without coverage, but I don't have any numbers on that.

We would like to see governments move away as much as possible from payroll taxes. It's not just the WCB at $3,000 per employee. In Ontario there's also the Employer Health Tax, which is in the neighbourhood of $1,000 per employee. There are CPP costs and UIC costs. You add them all up and suddenly there's a tax burden of $5,000 or $6,000 to employ somebody for a year. That's a tax on employment, when the stated goal of government is to encourage employers to do more hiring. You're going to be able to hire more people if you can lower that burden, and I think that should be a goal of any government.

If I were running a construction business, I'd pay the WCB because of the inherent fairness that's in the basic system of providing the coverage that employees deserve, and for my own protection from being sued by my employees, should they have an accident. The basic premise is still there and it's still right. I think employers recognize that they have a responsibility to make sure their workers are properly covered. In theory it's an insurance system, so if you stop paying, your workers aren't covered, and I don't think employers want to do that. They're put in a Catch-22 situation. They recognize the essential justice of the system, but the government takes advantage of them and says, "You will pay and pay and pay."

The ultimate solution is to have a government that will accept these essential premises: that employers need a certain amount of control;

that costs need to be controlled; that there should be certainty in the system; and that when you say you're going to pay off the unfunded liability, there's dedication to do it. Part of that dedication is choosing not to increase the costs, and we've had government say it's going to do that. But it's government much more than the WCB itself that has increased the new costs.

There is an unfunded liability of $11.7 billion today. The unfunded liability is the amount of money that hasn't been paid for by the Ontario employers, but has been promised to workers in the form of pensions to be paid over their lifetime. There are about $16 billion worth of commitments in the system right now and only about $4.3 billion of funding. So that remaining money hasn't been paid for, although workers are counting on that income. The problem is that $11.7-billion debt was accumulated under the employers from 1915 through 1994, but it's going to be paid for by employers after that. It's not necessarily the same group of people; employers come and go. But all future employers will face the burden of having to pay off that debt somehow.

What does it mean? To workers, because the amount of the unfunded liability goes up at a huge rate of $300 million to $500 million a year, it means those payments to workers aren't as secure as they may believe they are. There are scenarios that the reform process came to which said the unfunded liability could go all the way to $52 billion. But what they didn't say is, before it hits $52 billion, the system would go broke and workers would stop receiving their benefit payments. That's where the real stress and tension are in the system: how to guarantee the legitimate payments to workers and at the same time fund the pensions at levels that are sustainable by our employer community. It's a delicate balancing act.

The construction industry has, in "per worker" terms, a higher than average unfunded liability. Last time we looked, the unfunded liability per worker was about $29,000. If the board had to call that unfunded liability today, a small employer with 10 employees would have to go out and find $290,000 to pay for that. That's a big bill, and a frightening thought.

There are a number of things that need to be done. First of all the legislation has to be simplified. It's overly complicated and often doesn't give the board the room to do good, proper administration. The wording of the legislation also has become more complicated. It requires the board to do certain things by a certain deadline, rather than giving them the freedom to go out and work to see that what needs to be done is done. Let me give you a simple example. The wording is quite specific about how the board is to determine the average wage an employee has been earning, and based upon that average wage it determines what rate they'll be compensated at. In the construction industry we've gone through four years of recession. Our workers used to work an average of about 1,700 to 1,800 hours a year, but now they're working 1,100 to 1,200 hours a year. They're working a few weeks here and nothing there. But often when those workers are injured they've worked a full week. The board takes that information and says that based on those 40 hours they're working 2,000 hours a year, not 1,100, and will give them 90 percent net of that. It pays them at that rate.

The problem is, it should be 75 percent net, not 90 percent net. We've shown time after time that with 90 percent net for somebody that's off work four, five or six weeks, because of the net effect and the lower taxation effect, they actually take home more than 100 percent. They bring in 30 percent or 40 percent more than what they would have made if they hadn't been injured. Now not only are those workers over-compensated, but they're also not motivated to go back to work. We've talked to the board about this, and they said, "We'd love to fix this, but the legislation says this is how we're to determine average wage." What can they do? They need the legislation fixed.

I think the whole act needs to be rewritten. The current act is based upon the original writing of about 80 years ago. A lot of it isn't relevant, a lot of it isn't used and a lot of it needs to be loosened up for proper interpretation.

I think worker representatives have a reasonable understanding of the unfunded liability situation, but I don't think a lot of people really understand it. Some people think that the WCB has to go to the bond market and sell bonds or something like that to finance it, but that's not the situation at all. But it's not a make-believe debt either, like some worker representatives have said. It's real money that has been promised to real people and it will be paid. The question is, who's going to be left there holding the bag to pay it when the bill comes due?

Who's going to be an employer in 2014 when they say it's all going to be paid off? It's hard to say. Employers come and go very quickly in these modern ages. The nature of business is changing very quickly.

A lot of the older, resource-based industries that the board was based on are disappearing, and more technology- and service-based industries are emerging. So it means some fundamental changes for the board and who its clients are as well.

In the last recession the board lost a lot of employers, there's no question about that, and lost a lot of its payroll base. Now the economy's coming back, but the WCB revenues don't seem to be coming back as fast as the economy. That reflects the new economy; some of it isn't captured under the WCB, as opposed to the economy we had in the 1980s.

The provincial auditor has said that the unfunded liability is not a debt of the government, but a liability of the employers. I think he's primarily right, but I would like government to answer the question: if employers fail on that debt, who pays? And we've never had the answer to that question. I think the workers should be asking that question too. The law doesn't state that employers are responsible for the unfunded liability. The law states that the employers will pay assessments based upon the needs of the system.

The government has stated that the new system and the new board of directors will be given that responsibility. In fact the government goes further; it says we asked for the responsibility to take care of this debt. That's simply not true. The fact is, the bond rating companies have gone to the province of Ontario and warned them that they're coming to the end of the line, as far as being able to get money at the rates that they've been used to. In fact their rates have been going up.

And so Ontario is doing a number of things. You saw what happened with the social contract a couple of years ago, trying to show they're responsible with their money. They're trying to move the WCB away from looking like it's dependent on the government, should it default. It's part of that program. The government's purpose in this is to float its bonds and to keep its credit rating where it is, or maybe even improve its credit rating.

Now the board of directors is going to be defined primarily as bipartite, and in theory both sides, labour and management, are supposed to reach consensus agreements that they can both buy into. That's part of the package where government says, "We're handing over certain responsibilities to the stakeholders, labour and management." And they have a responsibility to handle the issues, develop the policy and then hand over the policy to the administration to administer.

There are some problems with this. First and foremost, the major causes of the unfunded liabilities aren't the board's decisions; they're the government's decisions. The board had very small unfunded liabilities back in the early 1980s when they decided to index the act. And suddenly about $2 billion of new unfunded liability came on the board, which had not been foreseen in the financing. The board said, "We need a way to pay this off," and after a long consultation there was agreement: the bill would be paid off 100 percent by the year 2014. So there were 30 years to pay it off.

Governments have come forward again in Bill 162 and passed new laws, and they brought in some fundamental change, future economic loss, which in fact has almost doubled the cost of new pensions. They've brought in most of the new costs. And now again, in Bill 165, we see government coming in and adding about $2 billion to new supplements and pensions.

So while we can criticize the board, and they do deserve some criticism, government has driven all the new costs and has said, "Over to you, board. You've got to decide how to pay for them." So now we have new costs, and the reason we're not paying off the unfunded liability at the rate we need to for 2014 is primarily because legislation keeps piling on new costs after new costs.

What we have to do is say, "That's it. These are the costs we're going to pay for. Any new things that come in, we have to decide." We have to recognize what those costs are. The board of directors has to decide, "This is how we're going to pay for them and this is how we're going to stay on track to pay off the unfunded liability by 2014."

And so that new board of directors, when it comes in early next year, is going to have to get to work and get that fundamental agreement between labour and management; no new costs without knowing how we're going to pay for them. And it will have to develop a plan that says, "This is when we're going to pay off the unfunded liability. This is how we're going to do it. And we're going to stick to that plan no matter what."

LES LIVERSIDGE

Ontario: Workers' Compensation — Unfunded Liability, Mismanagement and Waste

We're a management consulting firm specializing exclusively in workers' compensation issues. We work for businesses, trying to hold their hand and lead them through the maze of regulations that an individual company has to deal with on a day-to-day basis. We help them with claims management issues. We help them determine their proper assessment rates and whether or not they are in compliance with the almost endless list of regulatory exposures that Ontario business has to deal with. We help them with appeals and applications for reconsiderations of decisions from the WCB which they believe are incorrect and unjust. And we educate them about how to ensure that their financial and legal interests are protected in Ontario.

It's almost impossible for a company in Ontario, regardless of size, to keep pace with the rapid change of regulations dealing with the WCB. The program, originally designed over 80 years ago to replace a court litigation system, has grown into this complex maze of rules, regulations, processes and procedures that frankly are well and beyond the individual businessperson. They simply cannot cope with the massive regulations, exposures and rules that are thrust upon them. They need some help to get through there, to make sure that, one, they don't fall delinquent of rules and regulations they don't understand and, two, they don't pay more than their fair share. The employers are really the taxpayers in this case, as workers' compensation is a payroll tax.

It can never be forgotten that Ontario business supports the development and the delivery of a workers' compensation program as much as workers do. They want it for the very same reasons, to make sure that workers injured on the job get a just, equitable entitlement. Everybody wants that; that's very important to understand.

But overall there's an awful lot of waste within the Ontario workers' compensation system. The assessment rates, the amount that a company contributes to the WCB, are among the highest in the country. Right now, in 1994, there are approximately 5,800 people employed by the WCB, give or take a few hundred. In the early 1980s there was probably a little more than half of that. So it's an organization that has ballooned in size over a decade and a half. I don't know if that's part of the problem. More staffing doesn't appear to have fixed the problem. More staffing doesn't appear to have given the board the tools to find out what's wrong. More staffing doesn't appear to have assisted in getting people back into the workplace. There have been additional administrative costs. More government staffing tends to create more regulatory exposures, more red tape and more officiousness, so I don't know if it's part of the problem, but it's certainly not part of the solution.

The Workers' Compensation Board is teetering under the weight of a humongous debt of well over $11.5 billion, increasing astonishingly at $2 million a day. Businesses want to see costs down to make sure that they remain competitive, both within the Ontario marketplace and on the international scene.

The Ontario workers' compensation program has an obligation to disabled workers to make sure that somebody who is dependent on this system has their money guaranteed for as long as they're going to need it as a result of the disability. That's only fair. The board is supposed to have in the bank basically the same amount of money that they expect they're going to need to pay for the future costs of worker benefits. The shortfall, or the difference between what they have in the bank and what their future payments are going to be, is the unfunded liability. This problem started at the very least in the early 1980s.

Interestingly, at that time business first began to become really involved in workers' compensation. Before the early 1980s it was probably a relatively inexpensive form of insurance to provide benefits for on-the-job injury. There were other problems as well, first noticed in the 1970s. I think that the system, the benefit-delivery model, was somewhat unfair. The system was not very responsive to the needs of disabled workers. The bureaucracy was somewhat unbending and rigid. The processes and procedures weren't very open or fair. It wasn't until the late 1970s, for example, that the board first started publishing its rules. It didn't even tell people what case they'd have to make.

In response to those pressures a movement started in the late 1970s and early 1980s, bringing much-needed changes and reforms on the benefit-delivery side of things. One of the unattractive results was that the debt load began to increase. Now, the response from business was interesting at that time. Around 1984 Ontario businesses realized that the WCB was approaching a state of crisis, and they said, "This system must be properly funded." The businesses took this rather opportune moment to work for the very first time with the WCB and the government to develop a long-term funding strategy so that this unfunded liability would be controlled. Business voluntarily put forward massive increases in their assessment rates of 15 percent per year, each and every year for three years, followed by 10 percent increases per year for three more years, all over and above the rate of inflation. So that was a huge financial commitment for Ontario business to get on track with this unfunded liability. And as early as 1987 the WCB stated in its annual report that this was having some effect. They said that the contribution was working, and the unfunded liability, if everything held true, would in fact be paid off by the year 2014, an important date.

Two years later, in 1989, the WCB said that actually everything was working well ahead of schedule. They said that the WCB would pay off the unfunded liability not in the year 2014, but in the year 2007, if business did but one thing: hold accident rates at the same level from 1989 until 2014. Well, business did better than that; it held accident rates down. They continued to drop each and every single year from 1989 on. But a couple of years ago the board admitted that you could just forget 2007, you could forget 2014; the unfunded liability would continue to grow. And about a year and a half ago some projections indicated that the unfunded liability could actually hit over $50 billion by the year 2014, when it was supposed to hit zero.

This is a debt for employers and for workers. It's a real concern, and probably the best barometer of the financial health of the system. Let's just look at this with some perspective. The Ontario unfunded liability, in relation to all of the unfunded liabilities in every jurisdiction in Canada, absolutely towers above them. Other jurisdictions are treating this seriously, and they understand that there is an obligation to ensure that workers can expect a guarantee in their payments. And that's really what we're talking about: can a disabled worker who is dependent on this system, who looks to the Workers' Compensation Board for his or her livelihood, depend on the money being there in the future when he or she needs it? If you have an ever-expanding economy, job base and assessment base for employers, then people who say that the unfunded liability isn't a real concern are probably right. But if you don't have an expanding job base, if you have a declining job base, then you have a debt spread over a smaller number of companies. It becomes a real, significant and important issue of workers' compensation and the competitiveness of Ontario business.

I'm sure the Ontario government would love to say that the unfunded liability doesn't exist, "Don't worry about it," but the people who are considering investment in the province of Ontario are worried about it. Other jurisdictions are worried about it. It's becoming a competitive issue now between provinces. That's not helpful. The province of New Brunswick has made some tremendous efforts to try to reduce its unfunded liability, and I think there's a recognition of the relationship between the financial health of a program like workers' compensation and the ability for the jurisdiction to attract employment. A press release issued by the premier of New Brunswick on August 31, 1994, says, "This province will have among the lowest assessment rates in Canada, and that will help create jobs for New Brunswickers." And it also means that people in Ontario won't get those jobs. Right now, for a new company coming into Ontario, automatically 20 percent to 25 percent of their assessment contribution insures, not the cost of accidents that they're going to be responsible for, but the cost of accidents somebody else was responsible for.

It's clearly wrong for a government to improperly pass on costs incurred to a future generation. It really flies in the face of what an insurance program like the Workers' Compensation Board is designed to do, where you expect to take the costs of doing business today and pass them through to today's generation of businesses and consumers. That was the initial design upon which this program was based. To take the easy door out and to say, "Well, we'll pay you over and beyond what we can afford today because somebody else has to worry about paying that tomorrow," is clearly wrong.

And if tomorrow there's no money for that, who has to pay? Well, people have to pay for that through increased taxes when they can least afford it, and jobs will be lost. People will have to pay for that through reduced benefits when they've been disabled through no fault of their own, and their income will be lost. And that is wrong and cowardly. This happens in spite of the fact that Ontario has one of the highest assessment rates. It's not an issue of Ontario businesses somehow getting a free ride and not paying their fair share. In fact Ontario businesses have been paying far more than their fair share. If you look at the assessment rate by province for this year, Ontario is the second highest and is way up there. It has been a growing expenditure each and every year. And if you look at the assessment contribution per worker, in Ontario it is the highest. So you have the most assessment being paid per worker, the highest unfunded liability and a declining accident rate. Something has gone seriously wrong within the system, and somebody investing money is going to be worried about that.

I was talking to a company the other day, and they told me that a year or so ago they were thinking of expanding in Ontario, but they decided against it and instead went to New Brunswick. One of the reasons they went was the cost of workers' compensation. That was part of their decision-making process. So it's already having an effect. And what's going to happen is, if Ontario is not competitive, Ontario won't get the jobs; somebody else will.

There's a lot that has gone wrong. And there have been a lot of good intentions. I think that everybody has wanted to try to fix this program, to make sure that we had an equitable program. There's probably no specific answer as to when the program started to go out of control, but it was sometime in the 1970s. There are a lot of issues at play here. There have been a lot of changes, some right, some not so right. There's been a lot of effort, a lot of will from a lot of people, to try to ensure that Ontario has the most productive, fairest and most equitable workers' compensation program. And I think what we have here are a couple of decades' worth of good intentions gone sour.

In the 1960s and 1970s the system was not very equitable. I don't think it was particularly fair to disabled workers. You would have a lot of workers, as a result of their injuries, being left at poverty levels, and that was clearly wrong and it had to be fixed. On the other side of the coin, though, you had a lot of workers who were getting $400- to $700-a-month pensions that had a cash value of between $50,000 and $100,000 returning to their pre-injury jobs at their pre-injury wages. So the WCB was overcompensating the majority of Ontario disabled workers and undercompensating the minority of them, and that was wrong. And those people who were undercompensated were often very tragic cases. That problem was fixed in 1990 when the law was changed. I think it was a little late and should have happened much earlier than that. The actual initial blueprints for those changes were issued 10 years earlier, and we really had a debate over a decade about how to design a fairer benefit-delivery model.

From the 1970s through the 1980s the system was sensitive to the fact that some people were dealt with unfairly. And the only way to resolve that was to try to compensate by opening up the entitlements further, by opening up the purse strings even more. A lot more people got overcompensation, and that's the legacy we have today in Ontario. I don't think there's any politician who set out to do the wrong thing. On workers' compensation every politician wanted to do the right thing. I think that they earnestly responded to the problems as they saw them.

Unfortunately there was never a lot of in-depth research and analysis of what really were the problems and how they ought to be fixed. Workers' compensation became a political football. It became a case where legislative reform wasn't based on "Let's design the best, most effective program," but "Let's respond to some of the immediate political problems that we have. Let's look at some of the anecdotal evidence that's being presented and let's respond to that." And I think that political expediency has a lot of responsibility for the current shape of the system. Eventually that will have to change.

It hasn't been a situation of either politicians giving more or workers demanding more. I think there's been a bit of both. Politicians respond to pressures placed on them. Throughout the 1970s and 1980s people became more aware of their rights. They became more interested in ensuring that they were fairly treated. There were literally dozens and dozens and dozens of worker advocacy groups created throughout the province. Every local jurisdiction had an advocacy group of one form or another trying to fight on behalf of injured workers, with the mindset being that the board must pay out more in benefits. I think the politicians simply responded to that growing pressure.

But not only is it in the interest of workers to make sure they're getting a proper, fair, just entitlement, it's also in their interest to make sure they're in a program that has the ability to survive and sustain itself. And there's a real risk that we have crossed that line. There's no conflict between providing fair, proper levels of compensation and the system sustaining itself. Those two ideas are not at all mutually exclusive. In fact, they are absolutely inclusive of one another. A fair system will provide a proper level of benefits. Nobody, because of an injury on the job, should be left in any level of poverty. Nobody, because of an injury on the job, should be placed in any hardship as a result of that injury. So I don't think that the unfunded liability is a recognition that, "Well, we have to compensate somehow for something, and in order to compensate fairly, we have to run up a debt." That's not the case at all. The problem is there is a lot of waste, mismanagement and overcompensation within the system. I'll give you a few overreaching examples.

About a year and a half ago, in the spring of 1993, the current government began to recognize that there were some serious problems within the system. The government before this one recognized that. And the government before that also recognized that. At this most recent instance, though, the premier pulled together a blue-chip committee of senior people representing business and labour, a real blue-ribbon panel of people with an immediate and vested concern about workers' compensation. The business group brought together five CEOs from major corporations, formed focus groups around the province and for the first time undertook some real in-depth analysis. They discovered that the system was bankrupt. In a report issued to the premier in the fall of 1993 they said precisely that: the system is bankrupt and things have to be fixed. There was initially some sense of optimism that we would get to some of the root problems. Then politics took over and that fell apart.

But as for some of the things we have to address, I've got a couple of examples of simple overcompensation and waste. These are real cases for real people, things that have actually happened. They're quite legal;

nobody's doing anything illegal here. Nobody is fraudulently obtaining benefits in these examples.

Here's one case of an individual who had an injury in 1992 and returned to work in September 1993. So it was a fairly serious injury. There was a period of recuperation and rehabilitation, and while they were off on workers' compensation benefits they got $2,100 a month tax-free, which was their lawful, proper entitlement. Then they returned to work. The problem is, under the current law that individual, even though they no longer had any wage loss and even though they no longer had any continuing problem with that disability, received $800 a month tax-free until June of the following year: an overpayment of over $6,000. It wasn't an illegal overpayment; the person was properly entitled to that. Well, that's waste. That's wrong. That money should be given to somebody who needs it to compensate for a wage loss.

Another example, a similar type of situation, involved an injury in 1993, a return to work and a continuation of a benefit of $1,000 a month tax-free for a period of 17 months after this person returned to work. This person got $16,000 tax-free over and beyond any wage loss. That's wrong. That's not what this system is designed to do. Workers' compensation should not be a windfall for anybody.

Here's one more example of an individual who had an injury. During the course of recovery he decided that he wasn't going to go back to work. He voluntarily retired from his workplace. That individual, before the injury, was receiving $2,240 a month income. After the injury he was receiving $4,579 a month. That's wrong. Workers' compensation should not be benefiting over and beyond the actual loss. That's not what the program was designed to do.

I don't think there are any innocents, and I don't think there are any people who are totally culpable. I don't think that anybody set out to destroy the workers' compensation program. In fact just the opposite. I think everybody has been well intentioned, trying to do their best, but nobody has really understood the nature of the problem. That understanding is becoming clearer now. So a more relevant question than "Who is to blame?" is "Who has the responsibility now to fix this problem?"

I think it rests with everybody. Government, business and workers have a responsibility to fix it. All three parties are guilty of contributing to this problem, and all three parties have to come together with some real, sustainable, realistic and long-lasting solutions. I think the repairs have taken so long to come because there is such a political sensitivity. There's a real concern about any politician appearing to cut benefits, even if it's recognized that the program is too benefit-rich. There's a real nervousness about going in and cutting benefits unless and until a crisis is put before them. Well, I think we now have that crisis.

It may well take a crisis to have political action. This seems to be true if you look at what's going on in Canada overall: it's not until a program reaches a crisis point that people respond. And I think people will have to accept the changes. They have to understand that if you have a truck stalled on a railway crossing and a freight train looming toward that at 50 miles an hour, and it's 500 feet off, you know it's going to hit it. You don't have to wait for the crash to try and get the people out of the truck.

Well, the government is waiting for the crash. If that crash happens, if the system is unable to sustain itself, then the people who are hurt are not just businesspeople, not just people who are trying to invest money. Disabled workers who have a dependency on the system will be hurt because the benefits that they expect won't be there. Everybody in the province will be hurt because there will be fewer jobs. People will understand that. I think they're beginning to appreciate that you cannot have a system that is unfair by overcompensating individuals. At the same time you cannot have a system that does not give a disabled worker a fair and proper level of compensation for an on-the-job injury.

If I were a worker or if I were a businessperson, I certainly would be concerned today. I'd be concerned that the system is falling apart and the tough decisions aren't being made. Leadership is what is needed on this issue. There are no simple answers. There's no answer that's going to be to the satisfaction of everyone. There are tough decisions. What we need right now, in 1994, are strong leadership and a will to get to the root problems.

I think there has to be a realization that technically the system is bankrupt today. Cheques aren't bouncing yet, but that may be a matter of time. And what has to happen is that the very thought of the Ontario Workers' Compensation Board actually collapsing and ceasing to exist should be unfathomable by anybody. It cannot happen. It simply cannot be allowed to occur. So you have to get to the core solutions.

Ultimately the government is going to be responsible if a cheque bounces. And the reality is, if the cheques start to bounce and business doesn't have the money to pay, then either you stop paying the benefits or you increase taxes to the businesspeople or you start increasing taxes to the Ontario taxpayer. None of those alternatives is attractive at all.

There are a few key solutions, things that must be done right away. First and foremost, cut the waste out of the system. There's so much mismanagement, unnecessary regulation and red tape. Cut that out of the system and you do a lot to promote more business in Ontario. Bring assessment rates down. Don't start increasing them again. Bring the level of taxation down. Let it be known that Ontario is open for business. Get the political hacks and appointees out of the WCB. This is not some playground to deposit old political hacks and to get them into the bureaucracy of the civil service. You need first-calibre insurance executives to run the board as a business. That's absolutely needed at this point in time. Look at entitlements in a responsible manner. Make sure that every worker who has a just entitlement to benefits receives his or her proper entitlement, but don't try to compensate for things the system really can't deal with, such as stress.

Other jurisdictions have already developed these solutions, have already put them in place and are already getting results. That's all that's needed. It's not that complicated. The design of the solutions really isn't the problem. The problem is the will to get these solutions in place in Ontario.

VIEWS FROM THE WEST

CLAY GILSON

Western Canada: Government and Agriculture

The government's hand has been fairly deep in agriculture. As in several other sectors, government support and regulatory activity have been extensive. But because of the realities of reduced fiscal capacity, trade agreements and so on, there is no question that it'll be less so as time goes on.

We have to go back and set the stage. You have to go back to 1935, when the Wheat Board was set up and provided with what was called "dual marketing" at that time. Farmers had a choice. They could market through the board or they could use the open market. And to a degree that's what happened. Farmers voted with their feet, if you like.

During the war, of course, they closed down many things and regulation came into place. The board handled marketing through that stage, but right after the war they decided they wanted a plebiscite as to whether they were going to have, among farmers in the Prairies, open market or complete board monopoly marketing. The farmers at that time agreed that they wanted the board to be the central selling agency. It was the central selling agency for a good number of years, working internationally as well as nationally in the marketing of grains. I should point out that even while the board was operating there were crops not on the board. For example, canola and flax were open-market operations. So it's a mixed economy.

Canada never really subsidized farmers the way the United States did for a long time. It was only in about the 1960s that we started to get into the subsidy game. In the meantime south of the border, in the United States, they had a parity price program for the farmers that had operated out of the Depression for nearly two or three decades before Canada got involved. And even when we got involved we resisted the formula type of approach. It was more ad hoc, for emergencies, drought and so on. As time went on the farmers more and more pressed for formula pricing, price supports and so on.

I think the biggest and the most dramatic pressures in terms of the grain industry came when the Common Market in Europe developed some strength in about 1980 and started to challenge the United States and world markets. They met head-on in terms of subsidy; who had the biggest treasury, in other words. On both sides enormous sums of money poured into export subsidies. It was hurting the smaller countries such as Australia and Canada. By 1986, 1987, there was absolute chaos. Our farmers in Canada began to say they were badly sideswiped by this subsidy war, and therefore they wanted the government to help. And government did move in with fairly major subsidies.

They were trying to offset the U.S.–European Community war. But the budgetary claims became larger and larger. It was just impossible, when one looks back, for a small country such as Canada to compete in that game. It just wasn't possible; we're not a big enough country.

I think the Organization for Economic Co-operation and Development (OECD) estimated that Canada, for the whole industry, was up to about $6 billion to $8 billion in terms of income, transfers from consumers, direct government payments and so on. That has dropped drastically in the last few years, and there are two reasons for it. First, whether in agriculture, forestry or anywhere else, it was becoming increasingly evident that the country's fiscal capacity to handle those sorts of programs was declining. Secondly, from 1986 on, it was clear that there was going to be major agriculture trade reform under the General Agreement on Tariffs and Trade (GATT) and under the North American Free Trade Agreement, and agriculture trade reform meant pretty fundamental reform in internal policies. So for those two reasons you began to see increasing difficulty in coping with support programs to the industry.

Look at the trade war, where I think there was over $1 billion put in two years in a row. Was that beneficial? Well, when prices started to take a beating domestically because of the trade war, the farmers didn't like a $1-billion offset. They wanted their income from the marketplace. They didn't like the handouts, and governments didn't like it, but the fact was that there was this $1 billion-plus going into the industry. So it was a temporary, short-gap reaction. Then we had the major North American drought. Again there was over $1 billion in the Prairies, and in Ontario as well, that went out to try to take off some of the effect of this massive drought. It was obviously a short-run measure, ad hoc in many ways, not even budgeted. It was an emergency measure. But in terms of the long run, one has to stand back and say, "What is the best approach?" And that's going on right now. Massive change is coming.

I think the two major forces at work that are going to transform a lot of things are the trade agreements and reform of trade. Every country has to think about how they're going to change their policies. Australia and New Zealand sort of anticipated this, and they deregulated. Other countries are now facing this reality. We're signing GATT and it's going into effect in July 1995, and major changes have to be made, including subsidies. What went on in New Zealand and Australia has been watched very carefully.

In Canada, and I suspect in other countries too, the public capacity to deal with support of this type has to be re-examined, refocused and consolidated. We can't have the proliferation of separate commodity price support programs. You're probably going to see a major consolidation of those policies back into a more focused program and less support. That's the reality.

But I doubt if that will happen tomorrow. It's not just farmers. Rail companies and grain elevators and the whole infrastructure were based on past policies. What you will see, and what you are seeing, is change. I was out to a rural community program just three or four days ago, in the western part of the province, and the attitude of the rural communities now is that they have to look at less and less government support. They're now rethinking at the grassroots level. You're going to see a major grassroots-up attitude that they're going to be more innovative.

When you go out in rural communities now, you see amazing changes happening. Small entrepreneurs, small steps, but they're doing things now they wouldn't have done, wouldn't even have thought of, 10 years ago. They're saying, "We have to find ways to become more self-sufficient. We know the reality out there that we're facing in terms of public support, and so help us, we're going to see what we can do at the rural community level."

So you're going to see change, but it'll cause some adjustment pains and difficulties. It'll take some courage for the leaders to try to introduce the types of changes that are needed to lead to the emerging realities. It won't be easy, but it'll be coming down. We deregulated our trucking industry two years ago, and it was very traumatic at the beginning. But now they're saying, "Leave us alone," and they've finally adjusted. They want to feel that they're earning the income from the marketplace. But there was some pain in there, sure there was.

The average taxpayer has also been the recipient of many subsidies. Three or four years ago I walked with farmer parades in the cities of Regina and Winnipeg. I was trying to listen to the urban side of it, even as the farmers were marching in the streets saying that we've got problems with international trade, etc. As I listened carefully I realized that, yes, there was support there, and there was going to be more because of the drought and so on. But I also was picking up that urban people too were recipients of public support of many types, whether social programs or economic programs. And what I was hearing was, "Maybe we're coming to a change."

That was three, four, five years ago when these marches were taking place. So it wasn't just in the rural community, and it wasn't just urban people pointing fingers. It was urban people saying, "Yeah, we too have been the recipients of many programs, and maybe we're coming to an age now where we have to rethink what we're doing."

There are a few questions here that put the subsidy issue into perspective.

How important are subsidies in agriculture relative to income? It's a question that's been looked at under the trade negotiations very carefully. I would say in a practical sense, from 1986 through to probably 1990, in Saskatchewan, for example, the government payments into the grain industry were equivalent to what they took home by way of net income. In other words, without the government payments

216

there would have been no net farm income in that province. So that sort of puts into perspective the importance of the subsidy. Associated with that, for two years in a row there was about $1.2 billion put out into the grain industry. And this is another big question: who benefited?

Farmers will be quick to tell you, and I think it's to some degree true, that they didn't derive the full benefit of those subsidies — the $1.2 billion didn't all come to them directly. It was passed on in the form of money to transportation and servicing of input industries, so the subsidies have been of benefit to, if you like, the whole system, not just the farmers. So when we think about looking ahead, when we see limited government capacity to cope here, and the need and the pressures under the trade agreement to cut those subsidies, make no mistake that it won't be only farmers that will feel the impact of it. It will be the infrastructure industries such as transportation and so on. In fact, that's the debate right now.

If the government decides it has some limited income available, how are they going to provide it by way of safety net or minimum income support into the industry? That's another big question because every commodity group had a price support. Now, under the trade agreement they're supposed to get out of this. Instead of pork subsidies and wheat subsidies and transport subsidies, if they consolidate it into a smaller package, how is it to be packaged in a way that's of most value to the farm community and associated industries? That's the big question at the moment.

I think the message that is coming out this way is, if we're to support a sector such as agriculture, then keep it highly focused. Focus on the family, for example, or the farm business. Don't try to support commodities as such because what happens is that when you have supports under wheat and hogs and commodities, it doesn't allow for the market. Government policies are dictating how resources are to be used, and there's a bypassing of the marketplace. Sooner or later that's going to cause real problems. The key issue is how to focus whatever support is left, with reduced government budgets and so on, in a way that protects and does whatever it's supposed to do for the family, while at the same time allowing that family to respond (and I think I see this more and more) to the realities of a global marketplace.

JOHN DUVENAUD

Manitoba: Grain Marketing

One of the things that we do is publish a market advisory for Prairie grain farmers. It's called *Wild Oats* and we gather information for it from hundreds of sources. We monitor the newswires, we talk to the trade, we talk to individual farmers, so we know what's going on. We work with professional agriculture commodity market analysts to figure out what is happening in the market, and what could affect supply or demand and therefore price. We get grain prices from a large number of bidders and we monitor the action in the grains futures markets. We give grain farmers an analysis of what to be watching for and we recommend when to make sales. I'm not the only person supplying market information to Prairie grain farmers. There are already other people moving into this industry.

It's still a minority of farmers, certainly, that uses any kind of information service, but the number is growing. Tough times make good managers, and the grain business has been through some tough times in the last 10 years. Farmers are getting more sophisticated, knowing more about marketing, understanding the process. As that happens, more and more of them are able to use market information services.

The Crow Rate is the most poisonous program in Western Canada.[1] We borrow $700 million a year, give it to the railroads and use that money to pay foreigners to take our best raw product out of the country and process it somewhere else. It's a subsidy that, de facto, exports our secondary processing.

It's your money. The government is borrowing it on your behalf. Half of it is wasted or siphoned off by non-farmers and you're going to have to pay all of it back, plus interest. If we wanted to have a more rational system, we would just simply get rid of it. Initially the price of export grain might drop by 30¢ a bushel, but over time the price of food is the price of food, and how we handle grain transportation in Western Canada is probably not going to affect the price of food. The biggest effect will be that more of it will be processed here and we'll have more economic development on the Prairies where the grain is grown.

Three and four years ago the pool was short in a big-time way, and the federal government did in fact put a lot of money into grain farmers' pockets, and the government programs saved a lot of grain farms. But the days of government putting a lot of money into grain farmers' pockets are over. Who in Canada is going to be subsidizing grain farmers anymore? Farmers have hard assets. They've got property. They've got machinery. They produce real commodities: food. I think that farmers subsidizing other Canadians is more likely going to be the story over the next while.

I wouldn't classify the Canadian Wheat Board as government. The way it's structured now, it reports to the federal minister of agriculture, but that's by no means a requirement for an effective operating Canadian Wheat Board. The board could just as easily be operating under the direction of a board of farmers. Then it would have a far clearer mandate as to what it should be doing.

The Canadian Wheat Board doesn't provide subsidies to Canadian farmers. The Wheat Board sells Canadian wheat. The Canadian Wheat Board is the sales agent for the export of wheat and barley in Western Canada, and for domestic use of wheat. It's a bunch of guys that are about a block and a half from here, a lot of whom I know, good, professional wheat salesmen. The Wheat Board has done a lot of good for a lot of farmers over a long period. But we're coming to a turning point in the industry, and there's an awareness among farmers now that there is such a thing as marketing export grain on one's own. We've come through a period here where we had, specifically in southern Manitoba, a kind of grain that the board couldn't handle last year, but for which there was a real market just across the line in the States. A lot of farmers took their own grain and sold it down there, and found out that in fact they could sell export grain just as easily as they can sell export canola or export flax or any other product that they produce.

The question of having a Wheat Board monopoly was not an issue a few years ago because not many farmers thought that there was any other way of running it. Now farmers know that there is another way. They can drive their trucks across the border. Some of them, at least, can make the sales. And a lot of them are doing a better job than people who sell through the board. So now we've got a situation where a structure that served well for many years doesn't appear to be tenable anymore.

Grain marketing is different in Western Canada. We grew up while our dads were farming. It was all small trucks, so you hauled to the local elevator, wherever it was. It was mostly pool elevators or United Grain Growers, so any extra profit at the end of the year came back to you in dividends. It was mostly wheat, oats and barley, all of them handled by the board, so everybody got the same price. It didn't matter whom you sold to or when you sold it. Farmers in Western Canada are really behind the eight ball when it comes to marketing. We just didn't grow up with the idea. Most Prairie farmers were out doing summer fallow when they were 11 and setting the combine when they were 18, but we've been protected in this country from having to do our own marketing. When you have an agency doing all your marketing for you, then you don't need to go out and find information on your own. And if you don't need to go out to find it, you probably don't bother. And you're less aware that you have other options.

But now more than half of the grain, by value, is sold on the open market. The value of canola approaches that of wheat. Canola, flax, rye, oats, peas and lentils, all of that is completely open market, and there are not very many farmers left that haven't grown one of those things. The prices are changing by the day, and farmers are figuring out (quite effectively, I'd say) how to handle that marketing. Once you've learned that you can market your own lentils, canola and flax, when the idea comes up that you can market your own wheat too, well, it's a different idea, but really not that strange when you think about it.

The Wheat Board is a treasure for Canadian grain farmers. There is no talk of abolishing the board. But do we make it against the law for a farmer to sell his wheat to the highest bidder? That's really what the question is here.

I know a fair number of farmers who have sold wheat outside of the CWB, and a lot more that have gotten someone else to do it for them. There are two reactions from other farmers. One is resentment and the other more and more is, "How do I get in on it?" There's a sense of confusion because we've been told for years that the board does the best job. Now guys are seeing with their own eyes and their own receipts that it isn't necessarily the case.

There was really no enforcement mechanism to stop farmers or anyone from hauling wheat or barley south. And of course all kinds of other grains go down routinely. Nothing happened to virtually all of them until recently. At that point the Wheat Board asked Agriculture Canada to ask Canada Customs to crack down on farmers exporting without a permit. The board, having no mechanism to enforce its monopoly, had to get Canada Customs to enforce it for them. They instituted a system of fines for farmers shipping wheat south without an export permit. They charged one farmer, Dave Sawatzky, and then they seized a truck here, taking it one step further. They subsequently searched Sawatzky's house and that of another farmer, Andy McMechan, for any of those kinds of records.

It's one thing to put roving squads of customs inspectors at the borders across the Prairies to stop farmers from selling wheat, and they've effectively done that now. But to maintain the kind of surveillance that would be needed to stop any kind of non-board exports, I just don't see it being practical. There are too many border crossings and it's like water behind a leaky dam: you have to have everything stopped all the time for it to be effective. There are too many jobs for customs inspectors to do. It's unsustainable over time to use the force of law to stop guys going down. It's just not in the cards to do that over time.

A private company commissioned Angus Reid to do a survey here. They did a couple of them this year. The one they did about six months ago was narrow: on barley, farmers narrowly favoured dual marketing;

and on wheat, farmers narrowly favoured the Wheat Board monopoly. They did another survey here about a month ago and the majority of farmers (though a narrow majority) favoured open marketing for both wheat and barley.

For a farmer that wants the board to market for him, I would say, "Fine, market through the board." The board will presumably retain its ability to market wheat, and if people want to use them, they should be absolutely free to do so. The question is, who gives anyone the right to tell another farmer whom he can or can't sell his wheat to? He grew it. It's his.

Change is always the cause of some nervousness, I guess, but I would say that most of the farmers that I know believe strongly one way or the other. The ones that think about it, most of them get their heads around the fact that this is their own wheat and it's ludicrous that you haven't got the right to sell it to whomever you want to sell it to. You can see that there's momentum building now. In the last little while here there have been three things that have really focused broad attention by farmers on this issue.

When the Canadian government agreed to caps on the amount of wheat that we can export to the United States, they really raised the issue that there is an American market that gives pretty good returns. Secondly, when the Wheat Board got Canada Customs to start imposing those fines on farmers exporting, another awareness came about then. "This is our sales agent. Why is our sales agent getting the Government of Canada to make it difficult to sell wheat?" And thirdly, when the RCMP and Customs raided those farms, again farmers thought the same thing: "These guys are supposed to be working for us, not getting the government legal system to come in here and search people's houses for records of wheat sales."

It's gone too far. The only scenario that will work is for farmers to have the right to market any of their grain to whatever buyer in the world wants to buy it. We've come to a place in this country now where Canada Customs controls three kinds of exports out of this country: endangered species, toxic waste and wheat. That's ludicrous.

NOTES

---

1. The Crow Rate, under the name (after 1982) of the Western Grain Transportation Act, was finally abolished in 1995. Everyone who talked about farming in Western Canada cited the Crow Rate as a major reason for the problems facing agriculture.

    The Crow Rate resulted, in the 1880s, from a deal between the CPR and the government to put a rail line into southern British Columbia to maintain the sovereignty of the country against the threat of U.S. railways coming in. This deal was a special rate for settlers' effects coming to the West and for grain going out. It was an agreed statutory rate in perpetuity and included all the sites this railway had at that time.

    The problem was that as the Prairies continued to develop, there were additional railways and more elevators and there was inequity between those that ran the original elevators and those that ran the new ones. In the 1920s the government made it a statutory rate for all elevators and all railways to all points. This worked for a long time because productivity increased and there wasn't much inflation, so the farmers' price to ship their wheat to port was kept low. But in the late 1950s costs to the railways were no longer sustained by the revenues of this fixed rate, and they started to lose money. As a result, the price the farmers had to pay to transport their grain began to increase.

TED ALLEN

Manitoba: Soviet-Style Grain Transportation

Grain transportation is a hugely regulated part of our industry. You have a Soviet-style czar, so to speak, who allocates out this resource among the competing companies. It's not market-driven at all. We need a market-driven kind of system rather than a Soviet-style, top-down allocation of resources. It's been very inefficient and a lot of mistakes have been made. The "czar" agency is called the Grain Transportation Agency, and is part of the Department of Transport. From time to time they devise new rules as to how freight cars get allocated out among the competing interests, but they don't have any bottom line. It doesn't cost them any money if they make a mistake and they don't get rewarded if they do it right.

This system hasn't been around all that long. It was put in place because of a series of crises in transportation management. That alone says something about our industry because other industries, which don't rely on this unique kind of organization, don't have these periodic crises. It's because the transportation side of the business is much more market-driven, rather than a resource allocated out by an agency of the Crown.

There's a law called the Western Grain Transportation Act[1] which is also very detrimental to our industry. It's a subsidy paid to the railways for hauling farmers' grain to market. It's very dysfunctional from a number of perspectives. For one thing, it's a very inefficient way to deliver a subsidy to farmers, presuming you want to deliver a subsidy to farmers. It's very wasteful. In effect it says to a farmer, "If you want to haul your grain in a wheelbarrow, we'll subsidize it. But if you want to be very competitive and efficient, we can't work with that." The act itself works against the grain farmers that it is supposed to aid. In addition, Canada's the only country I know of that subsidizes the export of raw materials and penalizes secondary processing and value-adding. That seems to me to be an insane situation. If you want to collect the subsidy on your grain, you can't process and move it in any other way than under the rules of the Western Grain Transportation Act. That drives the overdevelopment of the rail system. Also, all the costs get averaged, so that the most efficient producer pays the same rate as the guy on the very expensive line. There's no incentive to become efficient.

United Grain Growers acts as agents for the Canadian Wheat Board for wheat and barley that is marketed outside of the borders of Canada. We're more able to have some control over the market side of it in products like canola, peas and some of the new crops. However, we are very frustrated because again the transportation impediment comes into place. It does you no good if you've found tremendous markets overseas for a product like canola (and we have) when you have adequate supplies produced domestically and you can offer farmers very attractive returns, if you can't move it from A to B because of transportation impediments.

In October we discovered, after making our sales commitments, that the GTA put in some new rules, and we can only source 57 percent of the transportation we need to meet sales we've already made. It's tremendously frustrating also when you're trying to attract young, bright new people into the industry to renew and regenerate your staffing. The current system is very security-oriented, so everyone knows where they fit in. Everybody's comfortable in their little boxes, as long as you don't look at it from an international perspective. If Canada creates this insular kind of attitude, many countries will pass us by in the international marketplace. And with grains and oil seeds the bulk of these products have to be exported because we produce huge surpluses of them beyond our own domestic needs. Therefore we run a great risk if we stay in the comfortable pew and don't look at the broader world around us and see where it's headed.

There was a tremendous debate over this whole thing when it was first put into place in the early 1980s, and the debate has not gone away with the implementation of the act. It continues to this day, and there are farmers who are very vocal about wanting this system changed. Unfortunately there are a lot of vested interests that try to keep it in place. In an industry that's hugely regulated, all the regulators, like the Grain Transportation Agency, are concerned about their job security.

But there's been a sea change in attitude amongst farmers toward a lot of these regulatory bodies. I've seen more change in the last six months in farmers' attitudes than I had in the previous 30 years. Higher prices have been the driving force, of course. Especially in the last year, farmers have discovered that they can get a much better price in the U.S. for their grain than they could get by selling it to the Canadian Wheat Board. I won't go into all of the reasons for that, but some of them are related to different farm programs in the two countries. The bottom line is, we have a free trade agreement with the U.S., and these fellows discovered that by selling on their own they could get a much better return.

The other day a farmer by the name of Dave Sawatzky found that his home had been invaded by the RCMP and Canada Customs. They came in and seized all kinds of records. He was charged by the RCMP for exporting grain without a Wheat Board permit. What's interesting about it is that they were so concerned about exporting wheat out of Canada. I don't want to beat this Soviet analogy to death, but most countries are concerned about what's coming into the country. Only the old Soviet-style operations were concerned about what was leaving the country. In this case we have a bit of a Berlin Wall concern about exporting wheat. It's not some kind of state secret. It's a food product.

The debate is interesting because there are those who support the Wheat Board and say it must have a monopoly if it's going to survive. But how is it that Australia has a wheat board that has been exposed to competition domestically, and has given up many of the support systems that the government previously offered, and yet it's doing quite nicely?

Our Wheat Board needs to undergo major reforms. If they don't reform themselves, I don't think they'll survive. And if they don't survive, the fault will lie with those who have insisted on the status quo. Of course there would be major winners and losers evolving over a very short period of time. Sometimes people think they have the right to survive in a business but what you have is the right to a decent opportunity at succeeding or failing. So, yes, there would be major changes. I think that would be refreshing in an industry that measures change by a hundredth of a percentage point in market share from year to year.

I've been amused because invariably at farm meetings advocates of the status quo tend to be older farmers who get up and make the pitch that what they're really interested in is a future for the young farmer. But when you look at it objectively, what they're really saying is, "I want an environment where we have inflated land values so that the young farmer can pay me a high price for my land and I can retire more comfortably." Because the system is partly subsidy-driven and partly regulatory-driven, there are all kinds of built-in anomalies that tend to support land values at a higher level than they might otherwise be. Fundamentally land values get supported by a system where there's value ascribed to that land that wouldn't be there in a market-driven system. Lower land prices would work to the advantage of young and new people getting into the industry.

We'd obviously like an opportunity to try to win. I'm sure others feel the same way and those companies that could adapt most quickly to changing conditions would survive. Overall there would be two winners, Canadian farmers and Canadian taxpayers. Taxpayers now fund a system which costs them money and jobs in the economy, so the taxpayer would be a big winner. But farmers would be big winners too because in a competitive environment where much more efficient marketing practices prevailed, farmers would net a higher return for their product.

NOTES

1. See note on the Crow Rate on page 223.

KEITH LEWIS

Saskatchewan: Government Subsidies

Back in the late 1980s I was involved with the Saskatchewan Canola Growers Association. I was president and on the board of directors of that organization for a couple of years. We were part of the larger agricultural infrastructure in Saskatchewan involved in lobbying Ottawa for subsidies for Western farmers. Just about every farm organization was involved in the lobby, particularly the grain-related organizations. At that time we were very much under the influence of subsidies in other countries. What was happening in Western Canada was because of what other governments were doing in Europe and in the United States. The pressure was there to do something.

I was never really convinced that this was the best approach to solving the ills of agriculture, and the organization that I worked with never took that approach either. We always felt that the marketplace was where farmers should derive their income, and the particular commodity that I worked with, canola, was always a market-oriented crop. However, in the politics of farm organizations in Saskatchewan it was important at the time to appear to be unified, to have a clear voice coming from Western Canada.

We went to Ottawa on a number of occasions. One time in particular we met with the prime minister, the minister of agriculture and the deputy ministers. There were probably 30 of us from Western Canada gathered in a room in the Centre Block of the Parliament buildings. The result of that lobbying effort was that Brian Mulroney and his government pumped over $1 billion into the economy of Western Canada. The federal government and provincial governments all came through with very large amounts of money for Western farmers.

The government's stated purpose was to address what was viewed as a short-term problem in agriculture. What they failed to realize was that this problem had been going on for some time, and that it was going to continue, and in fact would get worse over the years. And of course that only resulted in more demands for more money. You could probably tick your calendar off — every fall after harvest farmers made their annual migration to Ottawa to look for some more government support.

But the people who benefited from production-based subsidies were not farmers. The ones who benefited were the banks who needed the money, the grain companies that needed the grain, the railroads that needed the grain to haul to port, and the list goes on. Farmers recognized that the government money was going to flow, and built that into their cash flow. And when they presented those numbers to their lending institution, or when the grain companies looked at those numbers, they knew that it assured cash flow coming in and also production because all of these subsidies were tied to producing grain. Obviously the farm community hasn't benefited very much because we still have the same problem.

Farmers are really quite adept at making the best use of government programs. Everyone understands that. If there's an opportunity to gain from a program, they'll make the best use of it they can. But I think the subsidies over the years have been very detrimental to agriculture in this province. I believe that production subsidies have distorted farmers' planning decisions. They have encouraged the planting of grain on land that might very well have been used for other purposes. It's been detrimental to the lesser-subsidized parts of agriculture, like the livestock industry.

The Gross Revenue Insurance Program was one government program that we had. GRIP basically guaranteed a return from every acre of crop that you grew, based on calculations used in crop insurance and that sort of thing. Because GRIP was based on production, you had to grow the crop to get the money. It basically encouraged you to grow as much crop as you could on your farm. Farmers have been encouraged to grow particular crops that are very lucrative. In 1991 they grew lentils for GRIP, not for the marketplace. So we've certainly seen distorted planting decisions. Farmers didn't respond to market signals, they responded to what they thought were the best returns based on the government programs. It seems pretty obvious that over the years when subsidies were flowing into Western Canada, the farmers were gearing up to maximize their return from those subsidies. That's what happened then, and the consequences, I believe, are still with us today.

The quota system, for example, which allowed farmers to sell grain on the basis of the acres they farmed, encouraged farmers to bring more marginal land into production. This sometimes resulted in land being brought in that was highly erodible, and caused environmental consequences. The land either washed away or it blew away. Nevertheless, the encouragement was there to farm that land to get the money from the subsidy programs.

We've had a subsidy, called the Western Grain Transportation subsidy or Crow Rate,[1] which pays the railroads to haul grain to port. With that in place, why would you divert grain to a flour mill or a pasta plant? It's pretty obvious that there's a problem here because we don't have any of those things in Western Canada and it has cost us jobs. For example, in North Dakota there are four pasta production plants. They are all operating on durum from North Dakota and Canada, but the jobs are all in North Dakota. There isn't one single job produced here in Saskatchewan, even though they're using our grain.

I think the subsidy programs that we've seen in the past are gone forever, and I don't think we'll see any new programs coming along. We just can't afford them. The people of Canada can't afford them. To subsidize any industry is not a good investment. I would like to see subsidies out of agriculture completely. However, I think there's a need for farmers to have some form of insurance. Saskatchewan is a risky place to farm. Our climate is quite variable and we can end up with some pretty bad situations. There should be some way of assuring that farmers can protect themselves in bad years. But I question whether there should be any government involvement. If there is, it should be done in a different way than direct injections of cash. There are other ways we can do it, ways that give us a chance to manage it ourselves, rather than having it managed by some large bureaucratic entity, which we seem to be doing right now.

We've created a tremendous burden on the taxpayers in this country with all of these various programs and institutions in place, and it's cost enormous amounts of money to maintain them and sustain them. I think there's a growing recognition by farmers that there has to be some significant, fundamental change. And while there definitely are farmers that would disagree, I believe there are more and more farmers who are willing to accept that we can do a lot better without subsidies and without government programs.

The Wheat Board has become irrelevant in today's world. The world has changed a lot since the Wheat Board was initiated over 60 years ago. Farmers of today are looking for marketing that suits their own particular needs and business. And they are finding that the Wheat Board just doesn't fulfill that need anymore.

NOTES

1. See note on the Crow Rate on page 223.

FRED RANDLE

Alberta: Government Subsidies

Feeding cattle has become a big industry in Western Canada. It's profitable at times, when the prices are good. It's different, though, in times of oversupply and undersupply.

Feed grain, especially, is an answer to the manipulation of the Canadian Wheat Board. Basically they'll take some of the grain and some they won't. We got into one situation where we couldn't sell all our wheat. The export market wouldn't take it all. So to keep up the efficiencies of our farm, we got into a system of feeding cattle with some of our excess grain. It created very economical secondary processing.

Then the government came out one time and said, "We've got too much wheat. We need a LIFT program," which meant Lower Inventories For Tomorrow. They paid us to seed our land down to grass. Well, it distorted everything so badly that pretty soon we had all this grass but we didn't have any wheat to sell. It hurt us and it hurt our reputation as reliable suppliers in the world marketplace. We weren't able to supply the product when they wanted it. You gear up for certain operations, and then all of a sudden they don't want your grain. It puts you in a severe financial situation.

With the technology that we have today and the marketers that are in the marketplace, if you only have one market to sell your grains to, it restricts you. So the better way is to do your secondary processing, if you can, and try to market as much of your product as you can. It keeps the young people on the farm. It makes better, more efficient use of your land, your machinery and your buildings. And it gives you year-round work.

Nobody else in the world operates a business like we do, where when we market through the Wheat Board we don't know what we're going to get for our product for 18 months. We set up this year, we grow the grain next year, and then 18 months later we know what we are, going to get for that product.

The new generation of farmers have commitments and cash-flow concerns and must market their product as quickly as they can grow it, but they're not calling for subsidies. We want out of the subsidies. We want out of the government. We don't want the government in our business. There are just too many layers and layers of regulations and strings attached when we do take subsidies. It's very discouraging. Maybe it had its place over the years, but today I think that more and more farmers want to run their own business.

And the subsidies basically come with strings attached. The farmer never really gets the subsidy. It goes somewhere else. In my business it goes to the elevator companies or the railway. It really doesn't benefit the farmers, but it keeps those industries going. We have very little control over our product from the farm gate.

Subsidies are bad for the taxpayers, the people that are really paying for them. Why should we be taking their money when they don't even know where it's going or what we're spending it on?

JIM PALLISTER

Manitoba: Canadian Wheat Board

The stated purpose of the Canadian Wheat Board is to maximize the returns of wheat and barley to the Western Canadian farmers, but there are a number of problems with the Canadian Wheat Board as it's structured now. The Wheat Board started off as a voluntary organization. It worked quite well from 1935 to 1943. It was made compulsory as a war measure so that they could bring in cheap food for the war effort, and that compulsory aspect of it has stayed with us long since the war was over.

The main problem is the fact that it's a monopoly. As a monopoly it's unable to adequately service the tremendously changing, dynamic world market that we have out there. This is fragmenting into smaller and smaller markets all the time, demanding more and more products. I feel that farmers should be released from that monopoly control and the Wheat Board should be made voluntary so that the farmers could work in a team approach, a dual marketing system where farmers could be free to merchandise their own products.

Farmers have got technology that they didn't have when the Wheat Board was set up in the horse-and-buggy days, when they needed that marketing agent to help merchandise their products. Now farmers have got phones and a lot of them are well educated and can put deals together quite easily.

I know a fellow, Allan Johnston, who runs a little grain brokerage in his garage selling special crops. He serves about 3,000 farmer clients, marketing their products for them. He knows the opportunities that Western farmers are losing, that all Western Canada's losing because of this Wheat Board monopoly. Contrast that with the big Wheat Board office building, with the commissioners there making $150,000 plus perks and country club fees. These kinds of things happen when you have monopoly control.

The Wheat Board handles all our money and all of the wheat that leaves Western Canada. The money from all the wheat that leaves Western Canada goes into the Wheat Board and then it's distributed out to us after everybody else takes their cut. The railroads work on a cost-plus deal. The Wheat Board itself takes its cut right off the top. The various unions and port facilities along the line take a cut and we just get what's left. The movement in Western Canada is all about liberating us from being welded to this high-cost, inefficient system that doesn't have to compete. If we were free to sell our products ourselves and go around that system, we would then have the leverage with which to make these other players more efficient.

There's an element of risk with the Wheat Board because it has this pooling system where they give you some of your money now and they'll give you the rest later. And you don't really know what you're going to get later. And everyone that wants to export grain is required to participate in this pooling system. With an open market you're able to make a deal in advance for the total price of your grain so that you know what you're going to get before you even deliver that grain. In fact, I can price next year's crop on grains like canola, peas and lentils right now on the open market. In the case of Wheat Board crops, because of this pooling (I call it the Lotto Wheat Board), you don't really know what you're going to get. So it's riskier.

And we've seen in the last two years that the Wheat Board system itself is not risk-free. The Wheat Board refused to market the grain in eastern Manitoba last year because it had a fusarium problem.[1] It had tombstone kernels in it. The Wheat Board came out with a statement in August saying, "We will not be marketing any of this grain." They announced that there would be no payments for it at all. That meant to the farmers, who were dependent on the Wheat Board to be their sole marketing agent, that they were out of luck and that they had no other option. They were able to sell it as salvage or as feed for around $1 a bushel. Meanwhile, some of their neighbours who viewed themselves as more than producers, as marketers as well, and who were a little more skeptical about trusting in what the Wheat Board had said, went out and found markets for their grain and were able to get as much as $4 a bushel for this same product that the Wheat Board had dictated as being virtually valueless. It made a difference to these farmers of hundreds of thousands of dollars in some cases, and it made a difference to the economy of Canada and to the taxpayers of Manitoba.

It was a very good price for grain and it said something to a lot of people about the competitive American system as well, how fast they responded to this problem with tombstone through blending and upgrading and cleaning, and merchandising and seeking out the markets that are down there. I'm not a big advocate of the American system, but a free-market system gives people more choices and it forces people to be more competitive.

The farmers that had trusted in the Wheat Board system lost a lot of trust because of that refusal. This is the type of thing that happens when you have a monopoly. Decisions can't be made because you have no other option.

I think many farmers believe strongly in the Wheat Board itself. And I think some farmers, from a philosophical point of view, believe that the Wheat Board should continue to be a monopoly. They believe in these grand schemes, that somehow the government can look after us all best, better than we know how to look after ourselves.

This is why I think a dual system is best — because there's a number of people that want to continue dealing with the Wheat Board. It has built up trust with people. They like that it stabilizes prices and reduces risk for them. So we're not about taking anything apart. We're about building; building new opportunities and building more of a team approach between the people that want to do their own business and find their own markets. We'd have the Wheat Board as a stabilizing influence and another choice for farmers.

One of the problems with the first Wheat Board was that people were free to opt in and out, and they did it almost to the point where they were abusing the privilege. But what we would propose is that the Wheat Board, through its contracting system, ask people to commit grain at the start of the year, possibly a volume of grain or all their crop, so the Wheat Board knew what volumes it was going to have to work with. And then the farmers would be required to come up with that grain, and not opt in and out and abuse that privilege. Farmers will be better served if they have two choices. It's up to the individual to choose whichever system they prefer. It would become more of a co-operative approach.

Part of the definition of "co-operative" is the word "willingness," and since we're not willing, the Wheat Board system is not co-operative. It's coercive. We're required to deliver our grain there, as illustrated just last week when the RCMP paid a visit to a fellow who wasn't willing to go along with the Wheat Board system. We don't think that's appropriate at all. The RCMP incident brings home to farmers the realization that you're required to participate with the Wheat Board or else. A number of farmers have started to ask, "Or else what?" I guess it helps you realize what'll happen if you don't participate, if you don't choose to co-operate. I think it serves to show the ridiculousness of this situation, the bizarre side of it, hopefully to everybody in Canada. We're talking about wheat here. I mean, is there not enough crime out there? We're not talking about cocaine, we're talking about the ability of someone to grow and merchandise his or her own product, product that was produced on his or her own farm.

And in this case it was product that the Wheat Board didn't even want. They had said, "We don't want this wheat, there's no market for it, it's worthless." And these farmers got together and said, "The Wheat Board doesn't want it. What am I going to do, go broke? Go on welfare lines?" So they took it across to the highest bidder, which happened to be an export market. And now they're getting a knock on the door from the Wheat Board. It's unfathomable, really. The Wheat Board Act itself is being challenged under the Charter of Rights and Freedoms by a number of farmers in Western Canada right now.

Catherine the Great was sitting around her cabinet table with all these cabinet ministers and she asked her minister of finance, "What's going on? We're taking all of this money in taxes and we don't see any of it. Where's it all going?" Her minister of finance took an ice cube from a water jug and handed it to the person next to him.

Then this person handed it to the person next to him and so on, until finally, by the time it got to Catherine the Great, all she got was a wet hand. This is sort of what goes on when you get too many people handling your product.

Right now, if I ship my own grain to an export customer, I'll get the full amount. If I ship to the Wheat Board, which I'm compelled to do by the Wheat Board Act, there'll be a bunch of deductions to pay for the Wheat Board. We'll have to pay an elevator to elevate grain and then load it back on the truck before I can get it out of the country. I'll have to put my grain into this pool, and then I won't know what I'm going to get back out of this price pool for a year and a half. I'll have to pay terminal charges on a terminal 1,000 miles away that I'm not even using. In addition to that, I'm not going to get my share of the freight subsidy because I'm going to ship it myself. So by participating in the legislated system, the regulated system, there's not much left for farmers.

We have a subsidy that goes on the export of raw grain out of Western Canada. In a country where the stated objective is to try to encourage industry, to try to add value to raw products rather than exporting raw products, why would you have a subsidy on the export of raw grain? It has hurt the livestock industry in Western Canada. It's a disincentive toward milling and food processing in Western Canada. It's basically a disincentive toward living in Western Canada. There are other subsidies. There are insurance programs that help to stabilize farm income. The farmers contribute to them as well. I don't think that they're quite as negative because they don't discourage or encourage any particular kind of production, they just help to stabilize the income. It's a volatile industry to be in, so they have a good public policy purpose. They also help in the case of crop failures and so on. But this freight subsidy has really been a negative thing for Western Canada.

There are a number of people that make a good amount of money on the movement and export of grain: the elevator companies, the railways, some of the unions at the terminals and so on. They would like to see the grain continue to go up the elevator and out into a train because they make a good levy or royalty for handling the grain. They are saying that farmers want that subsidy retained, but it's elevator companies masquerading as a farm lobby that really want that subsidy retained in its present form.

I think an open market presents more opportunities for young people because of what's happened with all the special crops in Western Canada. Young people are prepared to venture into these crops. They're prepared to learn how to grow them and how to market them. Young people aren't afraid to use technology, they aren't afraid to phone all over for information and for markets. They seek out opportunity. They need opportunity. A system that stands between you and customers, that restricts you and restrains you, is not for young people. Getting into farming today is a challenge, but I think it's possible if you love doing what you're doing, if you're prepared to seek opportunities and if you're not afraid to ask questions. It's an information world and farming is no different. What we're into now is not a world of property and capital so much as it is a business of information, seeking out opportunity, getting the latest research, the latest varieties, the latest techniques. And that is much more vital to your future as a farmer than whether you had a certain piece of land passed down to you.

The people that were in marketing boards at the start did well and now, as they age, it's like a closed club. The young people are having to pay big money to get into these marketing boards. That is a requirement or obstacle to entering the business that shouldn't be there. It's there because of protection, because of high prices consumers are having to pay, and it does impede the ability of young people to get in. With open-market crops there are no barriers, there's no government intervention, so anybody can get in, anybody can try, anybody with initiative wanting to take a risk. The CWB tell us they're doing a good job, they tell us they're running things efficiently, but there's no access to information there. Even though I'm paying the full bill there, I have no real way of finding out what they're doing. I did see an ad, by the way, in the *Winnipeg Free Press* two months ago, advertising for a lifestyle and fitness co-ordinator at the Wheat Board, so I'm sure they're active there, keeping their energy levels up!

In 50 years there's been a lot of good faith and trust built up between farmers and the Wheat Board, and they have made a lot of pronouncements that they are looking after the best interests of the farmers. But it seems to me that they're somewhat immune and insulated from the tremendous changes that we've all been through in the last 20 years and will continue to go through.

I have a great deal of confidence in the evolution that competition brings out, the changes that competition forces on economic entities. If the Wheat Board had to compete, it would answer a lot of those questions. We wouldn't have to make those decisions collectively. I wouldn't have to write a letter and say to the Wheat Board, "I think you should do without those country club memberships." If we could take our business elsewhere, then you would see the Wheat Board as a co-operative entity, a voluntary entity trying to attract our business, trying to respond to our needs, trying to seek out markets. They will change the day it becomes voluntary. The day we get our dual market there'll be a lot of positive changes for all farmers, big and small.

There's almost an implication that if someone can seek out markets and better themselves economically, somehow that's going to hurt a smaller farmer, or a farmer who doesn't do that. I don't buy that at all. If the marketing board is a good thing, then it must be better for me than it is for the small farmer because I'm going to have more bushels than the small farmer. If it's adding dollars per bushel, then it must be helping me more than it's helping him. If the freight subsidy is a good thing, then it must be a better thing for me than it is for him because it's a subsidy that's based on so many cents a bushel.

A lot of smaller farmers are behind the movement to get things changed too. I know of organic farmers that produce products that the Wheat Board simply can't merchandise for them, wheat and barley that they'd likely get up to $10 a bushel for in the United Kingdom and U.S. markets. Highly specialized and fragmented markets provide opportunities, and I don't think it's necessarily related to farm size. There are a lot of big farmers, for example, some of the people on the Wheat Board advisory committee, some of the people involved in Manitoba Pool Elevators, that feel strongly about maintaining things the way they are. It's something that goes across the lines of farm size. A dual marketing system will still provide small farmers with the opportunity to patronize the Wheat Board and provide them with the stability that they perceive that the Wheat Board has.

If you get a good job and earn a lot of money, it doesn't hurt me. If we're part of the same community and part of the same country, it helps me if other people are willing to try to better themselves economically. And the one problem with the support for the Wheat Board is that a lot of it is based on negative emotions of jealousy ("Someone might get a better price than me") and of fear ("I'm afraid of change"). Now, are those negative emotions the things on which to build a country? Are those negative emotions the things on which to build a strong rural economy? I don't think so. I don't think jealousy and fear should play any part in who you choose to market your grain. If you're jealous of me or if I'm jealous of a farmer who gets a better price than me or does a better job of marketing than me, why should I want to use the government to make sure that he gets the same as me? To bring him down to my level? To make sure that he doesn't even try? To make sure there are rules that keep him from trying to get that good price? The whole country's going to be worse off if we have that attitude.

The world market is huge out there. You won't get a lesser price for your grain just because your neighbour gets a better price for his or her grain. If that neighbour finds a flour mill in Taiwan, or in Vancouver for that matter, that wants to pay big money for some of his wheat, great! Let him do it. Let him serve that customer. This modern economy is about serving markets, servicing customers and providing the products that they want. It's not about making sure that everybody gets the same price for a bushel of grain. God, those are negative things that will hold Western Canada down.

When the Wheat Board was brought in we had 360,000 farms in Western Canada and now we have 125,000. It's not necessarily because of the Wheat Board. Surely we would have lost a lot of farms anyway. But it is because of those attitudes.

Notes

1. The "fusarium problem" was fusarium head blight, a fungal disease.

ALLAN JOHNSTON

Saskatchewan: Canadian Wheat Board

We have clients all over Western Canada and some down through the States. Farmers approach us with their commodities for sale, and we try to market the grain for them to the highest bidders. Some of them just call when they're done with the harvest. They list all the grain they've got and we stick it in the computer. Then, when we're looking for a certain commodity, I know where it is. We have hundreds of companies that call us and thousands of farmers that use our services. We charge the grain companies a small tonnage fee for buying the grain for them. That way the farmer doesn't have any charge to him, other than the phone call.

They also give us an idea of what kind of price range they're looking for. If I can achieve that, I call them back and say, "All right, I've got this put together." If they decide to sell, then I just immediately change hats and act as an agent for the company. I'll say, "I'm buying for Company X from Farmer A." I write it down as a purchase order and fax it through to the company. From that point on I'm out of there. The dealings are between the company and the farmer. It's that simple.

We do it virtually 18 hours a day. We take orders from companies and calls from farmers from 6:00 in the morning until midnight. We prefer that they call at office hours, but sometimes they can't do that. My work is in the office here, on my farm, and in my house, so my whole family's involved. My 10-year-old son sometimes answers the phone and takes the call. We have all the latest technology here. We probably have more here than a lot of grain company personnel would have at their fingertips. We have a satellite system that brings in the grain futures live from Chicago and Winnipeg on what's called DTN. I use that for my market information. A computer keeps track of all this information: our purchase orders, clientele base and grain for sale. It looks high tech, but it's just normal business to us.

Cellular phones are a very big part of the farm base now. They're in combines, tractors, everywhere. It's a great convenience for farmers and for us. I can call right through to the guy in a combine in the middle of his quarter section of 160 acres of land. He can be out in his field, picking his crop up or taking his grain off, and I can call him and talk about marketing that grain. Or he can call me to say, "This is approximately what I'm going to have this year, what's it worth?" And he can make a marketing decision as he's picking the grain up. It has sped the whole thing up. It has revolutionized marketing.

There's a fax coming in right now. This is from Taipei, Taiwan, regarding malt and barley for beer production. I'll just read it to you.

"In our looking for a reliable source for malt and barley, your good company was introduced to us by the Canadian Trade Office here in Taipei. Would like to inform you that we would require 50,000 metric tons of barley per month for beer production in mainland China. Would like you to please send us your best offer to CIF, Nanjing Port. Together, please pass us your detailed specifications for our references. Hoping to have the opportunity to start a long-term co-operation with you. Hereby we look forward to hearing from you."

Fifty thousand metric tons of barley per month, there's no limitation on that. China is kind of a bottomless pit for production. They're big beer drinkers. They want malt for beer; that's an endless thing, year round. If you did 50,000 tons, you might increase that to 100,000 tons. And that would come back to the farmers here. It could just mushroom and grow, and it could be a steady market for them continuously. And they were put on to us by the Canadian Trade Office in Taipei, Taiwan.

That's the Canadian government's office. They put them on to us. But I can't do anything! The employees at the government office don't realize that. It could well have happened that these people have approached the Wheat Board and they're not getting a reply. Maybe they go back and see I'm in the world grain book, so they try Johnson's Grain Market.

The infrastructure here for this is, bar none, the best. We've got some of the best in the world with railroads, terminals, inland ports, elevators and cleaning facilities. We've got it all. We just can't use the damn things. It's all screwed up. It's just one bureaucrat after another, one control after another, one person dipping into the pot after another.

The reason I can't do anything is because I've got to approach the Wheat Board to get a buyback on this barley. And I can't even buy it from the Wheat Board. It has to be bought from an agency of the Wheat Board, one of the larger grain companies. So I can approach the board and they'll give me a buyback, but then I have to go through an agency. The board puts a high buyback on this price, and then one of these companies will put another margin on there, which they should, it's the business they're in. But I can't go to farmers, buy these 50,000 tons, phone this company in Taipei and say, "Send $1 million to a trust fund in Regina, hold in trust until this barley is delivered to the port, and then you release the funds, we release the grain." These farmers might have a net return of $1 to $1.50 per bushel more in their pockets than they can get through the board, but we can't do this. It's all got to go through the board, and they tie this up and they take their costs off it.

So I'm pretty well sure I can't get the grain out of Canada because I won't get a buyback that will work anyway. I'm going to purchase from American firms, possibly get that out of Seattle, and service it. And that's a big deal. That's 50,000 metric tons a month. That is a gigantic deal in the millions and millions of dollars. If it's sourced out of the U.S., it's going to have a very adverse effect on Canadian farmers because that's 50,000 metric tons that didn't come out of Canada. At $2 a bushel, the value will work out to about $5 million per month on an ongoing basis, and I could probably source those 50,000 metric tons out of Saskatchewan from our 5,000 growers and put it together with a letter of credit held in trust. When they deliver their grain to Vancouver, it would all be done.

As far as my going to the States, that's probably what I'm going to try to do with that deal. But these huge deals get so big that you wind up against the multinational grain companies. They have sourcing power, their own facilities, contacts and agents worldwide. I'll give it my best try, but it's hard for me to get in on a gigantic deal like that because I'm such a peon in the industry.

The departments of the government are definitely working against each other. There are just so many bureaucrats, so many people involved in agriculture that don't have any net gain by it. They're just doing a job. They've got their pension and their paycheque. They do nine-to-five and they're out of there. And I'm not here to get rid of the board. The board can do some of this too. But there are thousands of these kinds of things that could be done individually that the board just can't begin to look after.

The Wheat Board has 450 employees in Winnipeg and $22.7 million to staff that operation. That's for the wages alone, per year. That's almost $51,000 per employee. Over three-quarters of them would be secretaries, who would not make $51,000, so that means the cream at the top are making huge wages. I call them up several times and they don't get back to me, or else they call me back three or four days later and they give me a buyback that won't work once you add the freight to it and everything. They keep it all closed up in their little, tight, bottlenecked system. It's corrupt. It's ridiculous. I don't care what anybody says. Also, the Wheat Board is closed to the access to information. We can't find out what their costs are. The whole system is just a bureaucratic chain of command, and they keep it all bottled up there.

They are supposed to be working for our best interests, but there's no farm representation at the Wheat Board. There are farmers that are Wheat Board advisory members, and they're elected, but they don't control it. As far as I'm concerned, they're all puppets to the Wheat Board. Whatever the Wheat Board tells them to say and do, they just go along with it. They don't make any changes. The board was enacted in 1935, and as far as I can see, read, hear and understand from being involved in the business, there have been no changes whatsoever. There haven't been any changes in the Wheat Board for 50 years, so I don't know what a Wheat Board advisory board does, other than give a stamp of approval. "You're doing a good job, keep it up!"

It just gets more bureaucratic and more expensive all the time. Their costs have increased by a dramatic amount, but there are thousands and thousands fewer farmers. Their increase in marketing grain is only a mere four percent, yet their costs have gone up 34 percent in the last six years. That's the kind of thing that happens all the time. I can't really come right out and say there's a cover-up, but there's certainly protectionism with the government, the Wheat Board, the whole union system, the railroads, the dock workers. Each of them takes a little bit out of the farmers' pockets. There are thousands of farmers out there that say the board is the best thing that could ever happen, but when they get some of these facts presented to them, they start to think.

I want to keep the Wheat Board in place, but it should be a free, constitutional right that you can market your commodity wherever you like. You can in every production industry in Canada except wheat, barley and durum in Manitoba, Saskatchewan and Alberta because of the Canadian Wheat Board. They just inhibit marketing. They're always in your face.

For example, last week a guy called me from the U.S. He wants 200,000 bushels of high-quality durum wheat. I've got one customer alone in Penn, Saskatchewan, who's got 85,000 bushels of it. He'll sell it at U.S. $5, picked up in his yard. I can't do that. If I phone the Wheat Board, they would want probably $5 or $6 to buy it back from them. And then I've got the freight and all that, and the company in the States has to have some margin in there. It just won't work. But if the board was out of there, I could pay this gentleman U.S. $5 and pick it up in his yard. He'd be tickled pink to take that and avoid all of the system and the subsidy to get his grain to Thunder Bay and Vancouver, which would then be shipped around the world. This guy could sell it for $5, the freight paid for by the American buyer, the whole thing's a dead issue. There's no more subsidy, no more cost to the taxpayers.

If I want to ship oats out of Wellwyn, Saskatchewan, to Minneapolis, I can't ship it to Winnipeg and then down the BN Railroad to Minneapolis. I can't do that. You know how it's got to go? It's got to go loaded to Thunder Bay to get the Crow subsidy rate,[1] and then they haul it back full to Winnipeg, and then they go to Minneapolis with it. So that process probably ties up that car two, three or four weeks longer than it should be, all because somebody won't sign a piece of paper that says, "Turn that thing south at Winnipeg."

There are lots of good things happening in the Canadian grain industry. But the Wheat Board was set up to protect the farmers back in the early 1930s, when there were very few elevators. They had one or two choices for selling their grain. They were so busy breaking the land and getting rid of the grain in there, and they were getting ripped off by grain companies because the companies could control their bids and the whole situation. So they organized. And I would like to point out only 60 percent voted to have the Wheat Board; 40 percent didn't vote for it. And it was not mandatory that they had to sell to the Wheat Board, but during World War II it became mandatory, and then it just carried on from there.

I don't think anybody enjoys bureaucracy. That's the way of life in the modern world right now. There are bureaucrats in your face no matter where you go, but in Canada it seems to be a huge problem. We have the PST and the GST, and the farmers have the Wheat Board. There's just no end of bureaucrats in your face.

We've been demanding some changes, some restructuring. Ralph Goodale, our agriculture minister, was saying before he was elected that we were going to get this. Now he's been elected, and he's studying it! Studying goes on forever. These study sessions are incredibly wasteful. They're useless. They just spend millions of dollars in all aspects of the country, studying things instead of going out to the people and just saying, "All right, let's have a choice here. Let's have a vote. Let's get the farmers involved."

Dave Sawatzky and Andy McMechan challenged the Wheat Board and hauled their own grain and their neighbours' grain south to the States, and had a large net return on some of it. The Wheat Board wouldn't even buy some of that grain because it was diseased with fusarium last year. These guys just want to open this market up. They want a choice and under the Constitution it should be there. So they challenged the Wheat Board and the government imposed a tariff on the Canadian export of wheat and barley. Not the Americans, but a Canadian! And they brought Canada Customs in. Canada Customs stopped these guys and charged them under the Canada Customs Act, like they were trying to haul drugs across there. These farmers are hauling wheat and barley for God's sake. It's their wheat and barley. They paid for it. They've worked on it. They had the debt on the farm, the debt on the machinery. They needed a certain net return on this grain, especially the fusarium wheat. They needed to get some dollars out of it and the Wheat Board said, "We can't market it." So they did it on their own. Now one of them gets nine police officers moving into his farm. Give me a break.

We're organizing to support these people that were charged. Sixteen police officers spent a whole day at two farms, raiding these guys and searching their buildings for documents that they were offering anyway. The whole thing is just beyond belief. It's a police-state tactic and we just don't agree with it. We're going to organize this rally, and we've been telling people, "Come out and show your support." I think they're going to come out in the thousands. We want Goodale there to answer questions and not come there with some speech, saying that he's going to study the situation. We want some direct action. I'm pushing, as many of the others in this group are pushing, to take some real, militant action. Not guns or anything, but I mean action, where we set a deadline and then we start striking. We'll take some action to get some attention, shut down the economy by using the tractors to shut down the roads, whatever we have to do to get everybody awake.

I've got three or four deals here in the last week that I can't even begin to talk about. Here's one I dug up from Bonner Springs, Idaho. There's a feed lock. They want 250,000 to 300,000 bushels of feed barley and they want that for the winter. Well, I can't take it to them. If we had a continental barley market, I could just go to my local growers, 200,000 bushels of barley is nothing. One farmer could have that, and I could make him a deal. They'd send the trucks in and pay cash up front, bang, it's gone. It's a done deal. But I can't even reply to the guy because if they take the trucks to the border, Canada Customs impounds them and charges $2,700 or $3,500 per truck because of a tariff on Canadian wheat and barley. If it was canola, I could take it down there. Flax, lentils, peas, mustard, oats, rye, I can take all these other grains, but I can't take these holy three: wheat, barley and durum.

Companies call me from the U.S.: "We need some high-quality durum. We need some high-quality, high-protein wheat. We need malt and barley." I say, "According to the laws of the land, you're supposed to do it through the Wheat Board." And these people are saying, "Well, we're Americans. We don't belong to your Wheat Board. We'll buy it. We'll pay for the farmers the freight. You just find it." So I set up the farmers. I told them the rules, that it was two years in jail and a $5,000 fine. Most of the time I was wasting my breath because they just said, "Let's set her up. We'll do it anyway." The only way to make money for the farmer, make the buyer happy and make the whole deal work is to go around the system against the laws of the land.

You don't have to figure anything out for today's farmer. His mind's a calculator. It has to be. He's in his combine or his tractor, and he's got $1 million of debt on his machinery and $1 million on his land. It's big, big business. This is what the urban population of the country doesn't understand, the debt load these guys are carrying. They just think of a farmer as a hayseed with a piece of straw hanging out of his mouth, with bib overalls on. That's not the way it is today. It's a high-cost, intensive, very threatening business. The weather's always against you. The markets are always against you. What we want the urban population to understand is the cost of what's going on here and how they're getting zapped for this because the inefficiency of the government is hurting the agriculture out here.

The argument is that if the Wheat Board disappears, the price of grain will drop. That's totally ridiculous. It won't. Farmers are businesspeople. They can't afford to sell their grain under the market. It's like a car dealer. If he's got 40 cars too many, he might blow off five of them at a cost price so that he can keep operating. And a farmer might blow off some of his barley, 5,000 or 10,000 bushels, at his cost price or a little less because he needs the cash flow, but he's not going to sell his whole crop production. He'll come back to the Wheat Board if they have the best deal, or he'll continue to search for a market, or he'll sit on it until the market improves. We're not talking about hayseeds here, we're talking about businesspeople. They know their cost of production per acre. They know it better than most factories in Canada, by far. They produce it themselves. They store it. They nurture it. They spray it. They do the physical work. They do everything. The farmer and his wife have got this right down to an art.

One of my biggest beefs is that we ship our grain virtually uncleaned to Thunder Bay and Vancouver. We ship it dirty. In 100 railcars, if you have two percent or three percent dockage, two or three railcars out of 100 are going to Vancouver and Thunder Bay with that grain, being again subsidized by the taxpayer.[2] It's cleaned there by union labour at $15 to $28 an hour. And then when a farmer back in Western Canada needs feed grain for his livestock, the freight's got to be paid and that grain is shipped back out here. Generally it's processed. So there are jobs for the processing, the cleaning and everything that should be done here in Western Canada.

As far as value added for grains in Western Canada, there's a multitude of things that could be done. There are all kinds of industries that could be created out here. There should be pasta plants, ethanol plants, pea-splitting plants and other spinoffs. There are all kinds of things that could be done right here in the West, creating employment, dropping our welfare and unemployment structure, and drawing people from the four million that are in Toronto and the one million that are in Saskatchewan. We should have a bigger tax base out here. It would be better for everybody involved. Just get rid of the subsidies.

We're losing our population base all the time because of the economy. The young people are leaving. They're going to Alberta to work in the oil industry. They're going to B.C. They're going to Toronto. They're going to the U.S. They're going abroad. They're leaving by the thousands every year, they just can't stay here. We have a great education system in the University of Saskatchewan and University of Regina. We educate them and then they're just gone. They go because there's no base to keep them here. There aren't enough people to warrant the professionals. We're losing our doctors. The small towns are dying.

The farm economy is struggling and there are more and more regulations coming in. There's always something. But the biggest thing is the price of the grain is just ridiculously low. If the price of bread goes up 10¢ a loaf in Toronto, the taxpayers scream and yell. But with the price of wheat at $1 a bushel, the farmer might get 2¢ or 3¢ out of that, it's all in the system. There's nothing to the farmer. It all goes back into the system, into the unions, the railroads, the fees, the infrastructure, the bureaucrats, and it's all sucked out. It happens every year and it just gets worse. It doesn't get better. It gets worse.

There are answers. We have the infrastructure. We have the people. We have the technology. We have the brains here to do it. But we don't have the government behind us. They're always in here like leeches, taking something out.

NOTES

1. See note on the Crow Rate on page 223.
2. One of the things that caused major problems with the Crow Rate was "backtracking." That is, the railways would only get paid the

Crow Rate if the grain were taken from the Prairies out to one of the ports. Grain that was going straight south to the U.S. would first be taken to Thunder Bay to get the subsidy, then hauled back, and then it would go south. The inefficiency of that movement took up part of the subsidy, and anything above the subsidy cap was paid in full by the farmers.

Jim Harriman

Alberta: Proposed Reforms

We buy grain direct from farmers and take the shortest route possible to get it to the end buyer, and we offer a lot of innovative marketing programs to improve the producer's price. In the Canadian grain industry we're sort of the biggest of the small and the smallest of the big. It's a very regulated industry and there's a small number of large companies that control the market, together with the Wheat Board. They very much work with the regulators to keep things in such a way as to service their vested interests and investments in the country and in the ports. So in certain markets our ability to access the ports is dependent on working with them and their agreeing to do that with us. It's basically a monopoly made up of the pools, another large co-op that just went public, a couple of major private companies and the Wheat Board. They monopolize the industry and try to get the rules structured in their favour to prevent change. They're controlling competition and in some cases eliminating it. Competition typically brings options, choice, innovation and efficiency to the marketplace, whether it's for the farmer, the company or the end user. The status quo tends to "control" that so it doesn't happen.

Subsidies are a big part of the grain industry. The main transportation subsidy is a historical one which is paid to the railroads to cover a portion of the freight rate for grain exported out of the country through the ports. It has basically worked against the milling, crushing and processing industries here, and the servicing of U.S. processors. Transportation subsidies are not good for people like me, or for Canadian society, or for the future of the country.

Historically subsidies may have been a good thing at one time, but in my opinion they've caused a lot of damage to the country and to the farmers. They have basically exported jobs, industry and investment out of the country. They support the status quo infrastructure, all of which is organized for exporting raw material not finished products, and haven't allowed the development of added value in the West. In eastern Canada the development of added value from the farm gate to the process level is about a three-and-a-half-fold increase, $1.00 farm = $3.50 process. In Western Canada for every dollar the farmer gets, there's only about 70¢ of added value in the Prairies. And it's a $10-billion industry here, so if you could just increase that 70¢ to $1.40, you'd have a $20-billion industry in the Prairies, which means a lot of jobs, which means a lot of tax base. It's like adding car manufacturing plants in the West, but instead you're going to make pasta, flour, gluten-free food fibre, these sorts of things. The subsidies are taking opportunities away. Most of the young people in Saskatchewan have left for opportunities in other industries because food processing hasn't developed in Saskatchewan.

Last year, 1993, was probably the best or worst example, depending on your perspective, of the difficulty in accessing railcars. As a result of floods shutting down the Mississippi system, there was a shortage of rail equipment throughout North America. The Canadian industry, including the Wheat Board, made heavy sales to the U.S., and that resulted in about a third of the equipment winding up in the U.S., taking two to three times as long to get back as going to the West Coast. There isn't good access for competition in any of these things, nor good access for a farmer to take another approach. After the floods we had the situation where a farmer couldn't get his grain through Vancouver, and because the cross-structure and the subsidy structure wouldn't pay him if he went through the West Coast U.S. ports, he wasn't able to shift his business.

There was a change in legislation that briefly opened up the market in the U.S. for barley. That continental barley market was open for a period of 40 days, and the farmers, or the companies they chose, could deal directly with U.S. buyers. Doing so put about $30 a ton more into the farmer's pocket than when he was dealing through the board system and the line elevator system. But that innovation was eventually overturned through a court action. The difference of that $30 now goes to the system again, rather than to the farmer. This system captures the money at the expense of the producer. The average farmer would produce maybe 500 tons of barley. So that difference would be a cost to the farmer of $15,000, easily.

But this also resulted in the status quo trying to get control of that at the expense of servicing other markets. The result was that a lot of Canadian Wheat Board export customers had ships waiting in harbour in Vancouver for historic periods of time. And the cost of that delay came out of the farmer's pooled price. For all of the grains marketed by the Canadian Wheat Board, which make up the most tonnage that is exported, it's a pool price system, with the costs also pooled in. So if the system's inefficient and results in large demurrage bills, that comes out of the farmer's price. Our system costs about $75 a ton to get grain from the centre of the Prairies into a ship. It doesn't allow for efficiencies to try to do that better.

In the best of all possible worlds, if we had total efficiency, we would only need about a third of the equipment that we have today. That isn't likely to happen, but that is sort of the utopia. There's a lot of consolidation of new facilities on the Prairies. Some of these are being built by farmer groups who are unhappy with the way the status quo works. There's one that's well established at Weyburn, a farmer-owned Prairie terminal. Under the present situation they don't have a scenario where they can run unit trains to the port on a regular basis. A unit train of grain in Canada has about 112 cars, and you take it from a Prairie point straight through, direct to your port situation, and turn it around.

Typically when organizations utilize unit trains in test markets and test approaches, they can get about a seven- or eight-day turnaround. In other words, it takes seven or eight days to load, go to the port, unload and come back. The average turnaround under the current system is about 27 days. So there's a major efficiency that the structure today will not allow to happen.

With transportation the industry takes the position that it's a finite resource, that there's only so much of it and that it has to be managed. And because it has to be managed and doled out equitably, and because the people who do that have authority but no accountability, a commercial operation like the Weyburn Inland Terminal is not allowed to go out and operate its own unit train. To lease them they have to go into the overall system, and they just get a diluted advantage from them. The Weyburn terminal producers, if they were given the flexibility and allowed to operate that way, would be quite willing to lease or buy their own cars. After all, the farmers built the terminal. They wouldn't have any problem. And a hopper car, I believe, is worth about $90,000. Instead, taxpayers are paying for the bulk of the fleet, which is about 20,000 cars, and they're paying for the replacements. Every year there are some replacements that have to go on. And the reason that the industry doesn't pay for it is because (a) they don't have to and (b) they're not allowed to.

The reason that taxpayers have ended up owning 20,000 railcars is that, well, it's the Canadian way. If you're going to have equality, in Canada that's supposedly the government's role. It flows out of our centralized system of marketing, which is supposed to be for the common good. It's just another step across, therefore, that the cars should be for the common good.

Over the years the rate that the railroads get for hauling grain has slowly changed. Back in the late 1960s and early 1970s they let the boxcar fleet run down. I don't know all the details, but when they got into replacing the boxcars with hopper cars, the federal government, the Saskatchewan government and the Alberta government stepped in and started building these fleets.

Groups asking today for more railcars are still focusing a lot on the problems of last year, when more equipment in the right place would have helped to correct things. But the railroads claim, and I believe them, that they have in the order of 29,000 cars in service for grain, and they advise that any more would just cause congestion, which wouldn't help get the job done. So the problems this year are not with the supply of equipment, they're just the normal problems with the system and the way it's managed.

One of the key problems is that the people with all the authority over whether or not you can get a railcar, or whether or not you can meet a sale, don't have any responsibility. We have to move to a situation where there's a commercial relationship between the railroads and the shippers, and if one doesn't perform, it's financially and legally responsible to the other.

It's difficult to get to that situation in Canada because of the Wheat Board system, where the farmer's paying all the cost. So I foresee a scenario where the system will get divided between the board segment and the non-board segment, the non-board becoming more commercial and the board staying subsidized.

GRAHAM KEDGLEY

British Columbia: Grain Transportation

My involvement in grain goes back to 1970, when I became involved with Neptune Bulk Terminals. They were owned by Federal Grain, a company that is still around as Federal Industries, but whose interest in the grain industry was bought out by the pools in 1972 and 1973.

Currently grain gets on the train in the Prairies and is moved out to the elevators here. The elevators here perform two tasks: they elevate the grain so it can be cleaned and they act as a storage facility for that grain. Then, in the port here, the grain is put on the ships for export to various markets.

Taking the grain from the Prairies and moving it out of Canada takes 20 to 30 days, but it should take a week. The elevators were built many years ago and grain in those days could get out here easily because there wasn't the volume. It could get cleaned fairly quickly and then move offshore. Today, with bigger volumes and congestion, the situation has changed. But unfortunately the system hasn't changed dramatically to cope with the new circumstances.

When grain comes off the field it comes with the screenings, or the chaff, around it, and you've got to remove all of that because you're exporting strictly the grain seed. If you only brought clean grain out here, then you would be leaving a useful product, and people would then, I think, be interested in improving hog farms and such things on the Prairies. It would be more efficient to clean the grain on the Prairies. When I was president of Neptune we worked on the Grain Train, the only bulk clean grain experiment that's been carried out in Canada in recent times. It was a very successful experiment, but it died when Federal Grain was taken over by the pools. In that experiment, carried out in 1972, Federal Grain used a cleaning facility on the Prairies, so the grain was clean prior to coming out to the port here. It came in a unit train with 100 cars, each carrying somewhere in the range of 10,000 tons. The product came through our bottom dumper, fell right onto a conveyor belt and went straight onto the vessel. There was no waiting, and the train was gone in eight hours, back to the Prairies again. It was a tremendous success.

We weren't forced to shut down the cleaning system on the Prairies, but Federal Grain got out of it. It was a public company and didn't have the same tax advantages that the pool companies had. So Federal Grain's directors saw that they were always going to be a little behind the eight ball in terms of grain movement, and elected to get out of the grain trade. The pools, which are a co-operative and the major mover of grains today, offered Federal Grain a very nice price for their whole grain system. The pools drove out the competition. Whether or not they were trying to do that, who knows? But they certainly achieved it.

The reason the grain is still cleaned out here is that the pools have the elevators. These big giants, some people might call them dinosaurs, are well established here. The pools have spent a lot of money on them and continue to do so. Their cleaning facilities are here, so they want to use them. Hence the grain is hauled out here dirty. So what would you do with these elevators if you turned around and decided to clean on the Prairies? You'd leave them empty or you'd convert them to condominiums or something. That's the challenge.

The situation here is that when you get the grain out in Vancouver, you have the congestion of all the railcars, and you don't have anywhere near as much land available, in terms of storing the cars. And it's not that they should be stored; they should be moved back as quickly as they can.

In my opinion we definitely don't need more railcars. It's tragic that people keep talking about more railcars. I remember when Alberta was a very rich province and had all that oil money. They were the North American Arabs, and they spent an enormous amount on railcars in the belief that they would solve it all. The reality is that railcars are still taking 20 to 30 days to turn around and get back to the Prairies. You don't need more railcars; what you need is railcars running properly, never stopping.

The airlines are a great example of what the railways should be. They don't ever stop their planes if they can avoid it. They're too expensive and they've got to keep them moving. The railcars should be doing exactly the same thing, they should be continually moving. A coal train, for example, has a turnaround of seven days from mine and back to mine again. The coal industry and in fact all the other bulk industries, whether sulphur or potash, have gone to unit trains. These move in a block of 100 cars, sometimes 110 cars, each car with 10,000 tons of product. The cars get locked together and never come apart.

So the train comes from the mine or wherever it gets its product and arrives here as a unit; that's why it's called a unit train. It gets unloaded as a unit and it goes back as a unit, and it virtually never stops rolling. Coal is extremely successful like that, against the grain trains, which are all split up and shuffled around like a deck of cards. You'll get a train made up of 20 cars of this and 10 cars of that, and then when it gets out here to the coast, it gets all jumbled up. So the cars stop, sit around for days on end and get muddled up in this whole system. The grain industry is not optimizing the use of the fleet it's got. Please, let's not see more railcars put in the system, all they'll do is clog it more and stop it. The railcars are not what you want to address in terms of solving the problem.

The grading system is part of what slows them down. I guess the people that are marketing grain from Canada believe that they need this enormous spread of grades. We are truly a supermarket in terms of different types of grains. It's my belief, knowledge and understanding that the Americans don't have anywhere near these numbers of grades. Canada does have them, however, and they're complicated. So we get ships wandering all around the port here, making as many as four calls.

That brings us to the congestion in the port here in Vancouver. Demurrage is a charge that's levied by a ship when it arrives in the port, ready to accept product, and the product isn't ready for it. The ship owner says, "Look, my ship's here. I want money for sitting around in the sunshine waiting until you load me." Those rates run somewhere around $8,000 to $10,000 a day for a decent-sized ship in Vancouver. In the 1970s we were running up huge demurrage charges, many millions of dollars. I think in 1972 and 1973 they were about $30 million to $40 million a year. This is money paid to foreign shipping companies for the pleasure of their ships sitting in Vancouver. And this continues to be the case. This year we've had 30 or so ships sit in Vancouver waiting for product, and we are in turn paying offshore ship owners big sums of money, which eventually come out, of course, of the pockets of Canadians. It's a very unfortunate function of a system that really isn't working. Part of the problem right now is that there are no penalties for a railcar sitting out here and the penalty for the ship sitting out in the harbour is hidden, the farmer doesn't really get to see this. I think if the farmer, along with the Canadian taxpayer, really knew the costs that he is in fact currently paying, then it really would dramatically change. But it's slow; it's very slow.

We really had a "fire" going on in the Prairies, as it was called in 1972, with our Grain Train. We had a film called *The Federal Grain Train*, and a song that went with it, and it was shown all over the Prairies as the new, innovative way to go. I think if the pools had not bought Federal Grain out, today you would see a totally different grain system. I do think that was historically unfortunate.

You would see grain cleaned in the Prairies, you would see it coming out here in unit trains to match ships sitting here, ready to take that grain, and you'd see grain leaving the Prairies and moving out of Canada within a matter of a week, versus 20 to 30 days.

The current system just means more costs for the farmer and taxpayer. It probably means more to the farmer than to the taxpayer, in the sense that he isn't getting as much as he should be getting for his grain, and therefore he's more tempted to move into other products. Farmers aren't just growing grain today because they see better returns on their acreage from other things. The system in the States is quite different. You see a lot more trucking of grain to major elevators. We still have a lot of little elevators in the Prairies. In Canada it's still very much a railroad system. I would think it's more efficient to transport by truck. In the United States you see the grain cleaned on the prairies and brought out to facilities such as I've described, where it is stored for a very short period of time and then put on the ships. The Kalama facility in Washington, which is a loading facility, cost $52 million. The facility that was put in Prince Rupert in recent years cost $320 million. That difference is that the Prince Rupert facility does have cleaning capacity, but the cost is quite dramatically different.

I think it's interesting to put in perspective some of the demurrage charges that we've paid on ships here. We've paid in excess of $30 million some years. If that was even just $25 million, and you relate it to that Washington facility across the line, then after two years you've almost paid for a facility like that.

With the high cost of land today, I think port facilities really should be loading facilities, with perhaps some storage holding. The cost of the land here in Vancouver that this elevator is sitting on is in the tens of millions, probably hundreds of millions, of dollars. This prime waterfront land is extremely valuable. So you have a hidden cost in using it for cleaning grain, and a questionable cost because really there could be a high-rise right on the waterfront here. Some people would welcome it, some wouldn't, but I'm sure that's what will come in time because that's the way the system will evolve, without a question in my mind.

There are also some wasteful transfer payments. The Port of Vancouver is a subsidiary of Ports Canada, and just last year we saw $30 million transferred back from the Port of Vancouver's operation to Ottawa. The reason for it remains to be seen, and the arguments can be many. As a Westerner I would say that it went back to subsidize some of the East Coast facilities, which are losing money. And the $30 million could have either gone into better facilities out here at the coast or reduced some of the charges in the port here.

No matter how you carve the cake, I think it is scandalous to see $30 million taken out of our port here and moved back East. I know Eastern people might say, "Here we go again, someone complaining about Eastern Canada," but the reality is that it happened. It's documented. It happened in 1993, and that's not the first time it happened. It's happened before. I like to think that it won't happen again, but I fear it might.

Far be it from me to say what it supports out East. All I can attest to and know is that $30 million left our jeans here in Western Canada in the Port of Vancouver and headed east, never to be seen again. Whether it was productively used or it just went down the cesspit, I don't know, but it went.

JOHN HODGE

British Columbia: Shipping Grain

Grain is the major commodity moving through the Port of Vancouver. When I was in Montreal there was a huge movement of grain out through the St. Lawrence River, but the markets have changed the direction of the grain. Now the big markets are China, the Far East, the Middle East and Russia, if they have any money.

We represent the interests of foreign ship owners. They send ships to this port, we look after them and their crews, and we arrange the tugs and the pilots and make sure the cargo gets onto those ships. We're responsible to the ship owners and to them only, and we have to report to them daily about what's going on with their ships. The ships that we represent load cargo for the Wheat Board. We don't look after a lot of ships working with the private companies.

Ship owners worry about their ships and how quickly they can turn them around. When the ships are moving they're making money. When the ships are sitting around they don't make any money at all. It costs about $6,000 to $8,000 a day just to sit there. In a perfect world the ship comes in from the sea, we get it passed for inspection, it's cleaned, it goes alongside, loads, and then it sails. We can do that in 36 to 48 hours. I can bring a container ship into this port and turn it easily within 36 hours. Logs are usually here, waiting, and we get an excellent turnaround with coal.

But this is a seasonal business, and there are certain times of the year when it's a lot worse. Worst case, we could have a ship sitting around here for six to eight weeks. Others will come in, load and get out again; then you've got a happy ship owner.

With grain what happens, as I understand it, is that the Wheat Board promises to sell X hundreds of thousands of tons to a particular country. They say, "We have a program. We will deliver 400,000 tons a month to your ships," and those ships are then arranged.

But there are all sorts of problems that can delay the delivery of grain to the port. Bad weather in the Prairies can mean that the farmers can't get their grain to the elevators. Derailments happen, and they certainly set things back. There can be a shortage of railcars; for whatever reason, this was very apparent during this past season. We've also been known to have work stoppages in the harbour, which can delay movement of anything for a few days. And meanwhile the ships are coming. You can't stop them; they're not going to anchor in the middle of the ocean. So they just pile up here.

The ship arrives here and once it's clean we're told, "Well, you're going to have to wait," so the ship will go back and wait out there in the harbour, and here it will sit until we get the OK to bring it alongside. The ship could be sitting at anchor for 50 days; it can be as bad as that.

Don't get me wrong, this is not a typical example, but it can happen. And that's the type of thing which is a nightmare for the ship owner. There was a story I heard the other day about one of our ships waiting out here. It was here so long that its speed going back to the Far East was reduced by two knots because of the barnacles that had grown during its stay here.

So it's the Wheat Board's responsibility to have grain at port. But sometimes the grain is not there, ready for loading, because getting the railcars turned around quickly and back to the Prairies is a major problem. If the cargo isn't all ready at one berth, but at two or three berths, then we'll load as far as we can at one, get pilots and tugs, go to the second berth, load there, get pilots and tugs again, go to the third berth and load there. This takes more time, as you can imagine, and it costs a lot of money.

There's no real way to forecast how long a ship is going to wait. When the ship owner makes his calculations, he works on the basis that he's probably going to have to wait 10 days. This is the way you think; you have to write that into your calculations. But when suddenly the ship is going to be waiting three to four weeks or more, then everything changes. The ship owner may be trying to fix cargo when his ship is emptied at the discharge port, trying to fix cargo to another area. When this occurs the freight rate he quotes is going to be higher. If the ship is coming to Vancouver, he's going to have to build in a safety factor, so this is going to cost more. Then, I suppose, the Wheat Board will find that the price for moving the grain could be higher in the Port of Vancouver. This will lower the payment to the Canadian farmer. And if there is a surplus in the world, ship owners are going to quote a higher price to come here than, say, if they go to Australia, and this will be reflected in the final price that the Canadian farmer receives.

No one in Vancouver is accountable for the delays. All that the Vancouver Port Corporation does is provide facilities. We present the bills for demurrage to the Canadian Wheat Board. What happens after that, we don't know, but I have to assume that ultimately that price will be deducted from the final price of wheat received by the farmers.

JOE BEWS

Alberta: Subsidy-Free Beef

I've always considered myself a cowboy because I come from cowboy country, but really I'm a food producer. I produce beef for people to enjoy. I ranch some pretty rough country just west of here. I'm the third generation on the same land and I love what I do.

The beef industry is subsidy-free and I hope it stays that way. It has to be that way, as far as I'm concerned, as an attitude. That's the way my ancestors came, with that attitude. They came out here with a lot of personal pride in what they did and how they settled it, and they didn't want any help. They left it to me and they want me to do the same thing. Governments have tried to offer support and our associations have turned them down flat. They've tried to push a lot of things on us and they haven't done it yet.

The government tempted me once. The provincial government had a drought program. You could invest a certain amount of money, and if you didn't get so many inches of rain between May and June, you could capitalize on it. It worked out that I could invest $4,500, and if I received less than five inches of rain from May to June, I could capitalize on about $70,000. I thought, "Oh boy, this is a pretty good investment here. You know, there's a good chance that I could win."

And I tell you what, the night before it was all over, it rained an inch and a half. I never got a dime. I woke up the next morning and I asked myself, "Huh, what kind of a food producer am I?" I mean, what a bad attitude to have. I'm supposed to be raising food, and here I'm hoping that it won't rain so I can't raise food, so I can make a bundle from the government. That's a bad attitude. I've never filled out another form since. That was it for me.

The government has tempted us, it tempts all groups, and I'm glad it didn't catch us. That's for sure. But we're all paying for subsidies It's just a big merry-go-round. We're all paying to help subsidize other outfits. Cattlemen can resist subsidies because there's a good lobby and we have good people that get involved with government. Our spirit is strong and pretty hard to penetrate. Governments haven't done it yet, and hopefully they never will.

Just recently, at the CCA conference in Kamloops, the whole Canadian Cattlemen's Association turned down any kind of a subsidy at all. So it's fairly unified across Canada now and that's a good sign. We want to do it on our own.

The West was founded on that attitude. People were sick of the attitude down East. They were sick of the government involvement, so they came out on their own and wanted to do it on their own. There was a real sense of personal responsibility, and they've passed that on to us. That's an attitude that everyone should have. You can't go wrong with it.

I always think of a hockey team that's been losing, and they ask the coach, "What am I going to do here? We've been losing." And the coach says, "Well, we've got to go back to the arena and get back to basics, get back to the things that got us here." And I think that's what Canadians have got to do. They've got to get back and rethink the whole attitude that made us great. Personal responsibility, which we've lost, was what made us great.

STAN WILSON

Alberta: Keep Government Out

Cattle ranchers have opposed marketing boards and government intervention since day one in this country. We've been able to keep government out primarily because we've organized associations which lobby against that sort of thing. We're honestly quite amazed at how much influence we do have, considering the number of us, but we've been successful in stopping that sort of policy from being applied in our industry. I remember that when Eugene Whelan was the minister of agriculture, he sent out a questionnaire to all the beef producers in Canada. The question was whether or not we wanted to have a marketing board. I called it the "questionable questionnaire" because the dairy people in the country, who liked that sort of policy, got two forms to fill out, and many beef producers didn't get one at all. So he had to abandon that.

Frankly we know that government can't run things as well as we can, especially in cattle. It's been proven time after time that whenever they get involved it becomes too inefficient. I think we can do it more efficiently through the open market. Marketing boards require supply management to make them work properly. They can't possibly predict what the market is going to be in the future for cattle. They might for chickens because the biological nature of the two beasts is quite different. If we wanted to predict what the market for our product would be, we'd have to look about three years into the future. We have never found anyone in the cattle business that could predict that, and we know for damn sure that nobody in the government could.

We've always had what we call a beef cycle, and I'm sure other countries have it as well, where we underproduce for the market for a while, then people become optimistic and retain breeding stock, and within 10 years we go through that cycle again of having too much. That's been there for a long time. I think the producers are becoming more aware that you have to look far enough ahead not to oversupply the market. We call it "supply management on a volunteer basis." We're quite happy this way.

One thing about our industry is that we're not confined to Canada. It's always been a continental market or an international market. In order to be competitive we have to have the flexibility to market our product as we want to. Meanwhile other subsidies have inflated the price of our feed grains.

Feed freight assistance was put in place during the Second World War in order to encourage the production of meat on each coast to supply our armies and our allies with pork and beef. That feed freight assistance allowed, for instance, Western grain to be moved to the Maritimes much more cheaply than the actual cost of freight. That program was never removed after the war. And it actually created a distortion with the grain producers in the Maritimes, who in turn felt that they needed help, so they got a subsidy too. This is an example of why we have these debts in the country. It's a very foolish policy. We have to compete against subsidized freight in order to acquire the same product for our business.

A strange thing happened once, regarding that policy and the Crow Rate on grain for export. The Alberta government felt that the livestock industry in this province was very important, so they put in an offsetting subsidy to offset the detrimental effect of the Crow Rate and feed freight assistance. In other words, the Alberta taxpayer was subsidizing the beef producer in Alberta to counteract the federal government's subsidy for the grain producer in the Prairies!

We always use the term "natural comparative advantage" in producing. We have the climate, the land and the expertise to do things like producing grain in the Prairies and producing cattle in the foothills of the Rocky Mountains. That's where all this stuff should happen, logically, but when government intervenes, they move that production away from where it's natural and comparatively advantaged.

The dairy industry produces beef as well. We've always been fairly quiet about this, but everyone has felt in our industry that we're competing against unfair policies when they have their cost-of-production formulas, protection against competition and so on. They use the same inputs that we do. They buy hay and grain and they borrow money at the bank, and we have to compete with them on kind of an uneven playing field.

It's very difficult for a country like Canada to have two diametrically opposed systems of production in agriculture, and that's what we've had for many years. It's awkward for the government, when negotiating free trade in Brussels, to defend a commodity group that doesn't allow any imports. The dairy industry's quota system is a perfect example of what happens when government becomes involved in trying to influence production. It always becomes capitalized into asset values.

Unless he's got an established business behind him — or a very friendly and foolish banker — I just don't see how a young farmer today could enter dairy farming under the quota system. The price is so far above the actual producing value that it just isn't feasible. So keep government out of our business because it always costs us.

TOM LIVINGSTON

Alberta: Government Distorting the Market

We don't want government involvement. We've seen some classic examples of governments farming inefficiently. The Russian government has tried to farm since 1917 and they've consistently starved to death. The American government has tried to farm since about 1934, with the advent of Roosevelt, and they've had a surplus. So the point is that governments do not know how to farm.

I've dealt with the government. In 1980 the livestock industry in Canada was supposed to go metric. The manager of the Canadian Cattlemen's Association told us there was a stockholders' meeting in Lethbridge, and that there was no use in complaining about metrication because we would be metric within a year. Well, some of us didn't particularly like the metric system, so we decided that we wanted to stay with the imperial system until such time as the Americans went metric. I had occasion to go to Ottawa and I had a meeting with the minister of consumer affairs. The Clark government had been elected in the meantime. After we explained the ramifications on the livestock business of going metric, the government put a moratorium on all metrication, not only in the livestock business. After that the Trudeau administration never had enough nerve to try to force the cattlemen into metrication. We're still measuring cattle with the imperial system, on the hoof. We're just about the only primary industry that has stayed with the imperial measure of our products. And the reason we've stayed with it was because we refused to go metric when the feds said, "Roll over and play dead; you are going metric."

The government has also tried to get marketing boards involved in the livestock industry. Bud Olson was a member from my federal riding, Medicine Hat, and he was elected to the federal government on the Social Credit ticket. He became somewhat enamoured with the Trudeau administration, and they became somewhat enamoured with him. He crossed the floor and joined the Liberals. The reward was the agriculture portfolio, with the idea that he would deliver the livestock industry to the marketing board. But the livestock association consistently refused to have anything to do with single-desk selling. You look at the grain situation and you can see what happens.

When governments in Canada were more affluent and there was a little more money floating around, there were several instances of provincial governments subsidizing the cow/calf industry in their own provinces; in other words, trying to buy an industry. But they always ran out of money, and the natural advantage always took precedence. You produce the cows where they can be produced the best, unless governments are willing to subsidize the livestock industry in their own provinces.

Saskatchewan tried this. In the late 1960s and early 1970s there was a glut of grain in Saskatchewan. I bought oats and grain for 1¢ a pound, 34¢ a bushel. Saskatchewan was drowning in grain. So in 1971 the Saskatchewan government, in their wisdom, decided they should have a livestock industry. They granted the Saskatchewan producers $250 a head for any cow that could walk down the gangplank off a truck. Immediately there wasn't a cow in Alberta that wasn't worth $250. Albertans rounded up all their cows from 12 years old up and sent them to Saskatchewan. They were worth about $62 a head in Alberta but $250 a head in Saskatchewan. Neighbours of mine became wealthy selling cows into Saskatchewan. But the Saskatchewan producers, the people that bought the cattle, were in many cases not fixed up to handle beef cattle. As a result, a large number of cows got into the wheat piles sitting around in the field, with disastrous results. The cows died. If a cow over-loads on wheat, she'll die.

They tried to buy an industry and distort the natural advantage of the industry, and it didn't work. The Saskatchewan government finally ran out of money. They lost a large share of their cow/calf industry, and they lost quite a large share of their feeding industry. This is an example of government getting involved in someplace where they have no business being involved.

Another example is the quota system in the dairy sector. I'm not a dairy man and I hate to comment on somebody else's business, but there are some dairy producers in our area that have paid as high as $8,000 per animal unit for the quota. The quota's worth far more than the cow or the land. What the quota system means is, I couldn't buy a dairy farm today. I could buy cows, but I'd have to sell milk on the open market because I can't afford a quota. I understand that with the GATT agreements and the free trade agreement, quotas will be worth nothing. But people paid between $5,000 and $8,000 per cow for a quota, which certainly restricted entry into the dairy business. It was a closed shop. There was only so much quota available and the quota was worth more than either the place to produce the milk or the cow that produced it. If the quota hadn't existed, I guess the milk producers would be selling milk for what it's worth, instead of what some government agency decided it was worth. Milk is about half the price in the U.S. than it is in Canada, the reason being that Canadian dairy farmers had a closed shop for quite a long time.

And one reason that the beef business consistently avoided single-desk selling and marketing boards is, if your marketing board is going to be a success, you have to have a quota system. You have to have a limit on production and you have to have closed borders, such as Alberta's had in milk. You can't send milk from Saskatchewan to Alberta or from Montana to Alberta because the border's closed. It can't be imported into the province. But the livestock industry has consistently said, "We don't want quotas. We don't want limits on our production." When cattle are worth a lot of money, we're going to produce a lot of cattle, and when they're worth nothing, we'll cut the numbers back to suit our-selves, but we don't want the government telling us how to do this.

If we're going to have a country that works, we'll have to get rid of provincial boundaries. There are more provincial barriers to trade in

Canada than there are to international trade. The United States, when the country was put together, decided in their wisdom that no state could erect a barrier against products from another state. So there's been free trade between states in the United States ever since the country was put together. But we decided in this country, in our wisdom, that each provincial government would be its own little fiefdom, and we'd keep products from other provinces out, such as B.C. beer or, for instance, grain going into B.C. There was a time in Alberta when if you owned a farm in Alberta and a ranch in B.C., you couldn't put your own grain in your own truck and haul it to B.C. to feed your own cattle because there was a provincial boundary. And we wonder why the country's in trouble and why the country won't work. Well, that's one of the reasons.

The West, meaning Western Canada and also the western United States, was settled primarily by livestock people. Farmers didn't come out here first. Cowboys came out here, livestock producers came out to the West. They moved west to escape government domination and the restrictions that were taking place on the eastern seaboard. The West was populated by independent people who wanted to manage their own affairs.

I'd say the cowards never started and the wheat died on the way.

MOIRA WRIGHT

Saskatchewan: Losing Oil Ventures

The Husky upgrader here in Lloydminster was a joint project of Husky Oil, the Alberta government, the federal government in Ottawa and the Saskatchewan government. The deal was signed in about 1987 and altogether about $1.7 billion has been invested into the upgrader. The Saskatchewan government and Husky Oil are the only remaining investors in it, with a 50/50 share. Over the course of the investment in this deal since 1987, Ottawa has lost about $500 million, Alberta taxpayers have lost about $400 million and Saskatchewan taxpayers have probably lost over $200 million. So it's well over $1 billion that's been lost to date in this venture, and many analysts and independent assessors say that there isn't a hope of recovering any of the other investment that's been put into the project.

Husky Oil produces quite a bit of heavy crude in this area and in Cold Lake. For years they've been trying to attract private investment for an upgrader to take the heavy crude and upgrade it into a synthetic crude, which is then sent to refineries to be refined into what we put into our cars as gas and motor oil. They didn't have any luck. They couldn't get a private investor to put a dollar into it, so of course they turned to government. Part of the reason for that, perhaps, is the oil industry is better qualified to make those kinds of investment decisions and it just wasn't seen as a viable option. It seems that their judgment is turning out to be correct.

Somewhere in the process, between the provincial 1986 election here and the federal 1988 election, a deal was signed which brought in all three levels of government. It seemed in the end that it was easier to convince people to invest money when it was other people's money and that's the unfortunate case, as it often is with government. There are a couple of things about the timing and the location of this project, too, that raised eyebrows. First of all, as I said, it was signed right between a provincial election and a federal election. It's also geographically right between Don Mazankowski's home and Bill McKnight's home, two former federal PC Cabinet ministers. So there still is a question about the location of it.

The upgrader has the capacity to produce 46,000 barrels of oil daily and I think it's operating at or near capacity now. The only thing is that it's operating at a loss. It's losing $2, I think, on every barrel it's producing. We're finding that the difference between the price of heavy crude and synthetic crude, the input and the output of this upgrader, is not enough to pay for the cost of upgrading the oil, partly because the increased demand here at Lloydminster has created a higher price for heavy crude. It's also because upgraders are losing some of their business to refineries because refineries are retooling to take heavier forms of crude to refine it.

Now heavy crude is in higher demand from a lot of other refineries that formerly were taking synthetic crude and refining it, so there's a shift in the industry that some oil industry experts are saying has permanently narrowed the price differential, and these kinds of upgraders will never be able to turn a profit with the existing facility. Of course, if they're going to retool, it's going to cost a lot more money and there just isn't the kind of investment around to do it. There have already been indications that more money will have to be invested to update this facility to be able to lower the costs of the upgrading and refining, if any refining is to be done. Obviously that indicates an initial investment that was not well thought out. It had a cost overrun of $400 million. The taxpayers had to kick in $400 million to complete the construction of the project. In all phases of it there seems to be a lack of insight and judgment because there was a political push in the timing, in the elections, in the jobs they wanted to lay claim to.

The Government of Saskatchewan claims that they made a good investment decision sticking with the project because Husky stuck with the project and they must have a good reason for sticking with it. That makes us wonder, "Why would Husky sink more money into a losing project? What kind of vested interest do they have in keeping this upgrader operating?" There's more to that story than meets the eye. Husky are big producers of heavy oil in this area, so they've got a permanent customer for their product here. As well, even if they aren't supplying the other heavy oil, they own most of the pipelines that feed the upgrader, so they're making money there, I'm sure. This project has created a bigger demand for heavy crude, so that of course has upped the price of heavy crude that Husky produces. Finally, Husky can write off the losses here against other parts of their investments in other areas of the oil industry.

But many think that Husky's staying in is not a justification to keep more tax dollars in. I'm not sure what Husky's whole reasoning is. They may have reason to believe that this project will make a profit down the road but they're looking at it with a different set of factors than the taxpayer.

The promise of jobs, economic development and diversification was a very hot topic during the 1980s. Governments wanted to lay claim to that job creation and that economic development and they still want to lay claim to the 300 or 400 jobs that are dependent on this upgrader. So that's partly why governments are involved in these kinds of ventures. They're expected to create jobs these days. Also, the local economy here has received a boost from the spinoff jobs from it, but whenever you're talking about investment, you've always got to look at the opportunity costs. How much in tax dollars was taken out of taxpayers' pockets, out of existing industries and households to put into this losing venture?

You've got to weigh that against the jobs here. Governments do not use the same rationale and common sense in investment that individual taxpayers do if they're left with those dollars themselves. In terms of the other profitable Saskatchewan businesses and industries and households that have suffered, if you spread it all over the province it doesn't seem like a lot but it adds up. I would wager that the economic opportunity and jobs lost to this investment far outweigh the jobs here today.

The enormous waste of money is the whole problem in Saskatchewan right now. Because of these investments that were made over the 1980s, we've got a $20-billion gross provincial debt now and the debt servicing costs on that in a year are about $1.4 billion, which works out per family of four to about $5,600 dollars a year. That money doesn't go to health care and it doesn't go to education. It simply leaves the province with interest payments. I would wager that the jobs lost through the excess taxation and debt incurred by the project would far outweigh the economic benefits that this project can claim. Even if you take the basic numbers and you look at losing almost $3 million a month and put that off against the 300 jobs that are here, that's $10,000 per job per month. Of course all of that imposes a tax burden that makes Saskatchewan not very competitive compared to its neighbours, particularly Alberta to the west and the American states to the south. Saskatchewan businesses are finding it tough sledding these days.

Just recently both Ottawa and Alberta walked away from the oil upgrader project for 7¢ on the dollar. So just think about that as a personal investment. In 1987 you invested $100 and you got $7 today. That's what they did. And some say they actually got a good deal. The Saskatchewan government stepped in and went from owning 17 percent to owning 50 percent, and Husky went from owning 36 percent to owning 50 percent. So now they're 50/50 partners in it and they will share in any losses down the road.

The common question is, why did Saskatchewan purchase it if it's losing money every day on it? Why would the Government of Saskatchewan want to own 50 percent of a venture that's currently losing millions of dollars a month? The politicians have claimed that in 25 years they'll maybe hope to make a return on their investment. But if it was government's role to make investments, to get a return on their investment, they could put the money in a bank and earn a great profit in a couple of years. I think the history of the province is one where we have a wealth of natural resources yet there hasn't been the same development as in, say, Alberta. So they're putting themselves further into debt to make sure that the short-term gain is achieved, but, I mean, the loss is there. Anybody will tell you that an asset is only worth what you could sell it for in the current market conditions.

Currently the Husky Oil upgrader is losing about $2.8 million a month. While we're making moves to balance the budget, we don't have extra money to put into these kinds of losing ventures, so why would the government want to own 50 percent of a venture that's so risky? I think that's a question that's not sitting well with a lot of Saskatchewan taxpayers right now.

There are other projects in Saskatchewan that have been similarly problematic throughout the 1980s and even before that. There's a government lending agency called SEDCO that is currently losing over $40 million a year and a lot of that's in interest payments on bad debts that were incurred. Governments were throwing money at all kinds of different business ventures, trying to jumpstart the economy without having that faith in the economy where if you just can provide a competitive tax environment and provide a competitive way of life, business will set up on its own. You don't need tax dollars to subsidize it.

You're not seeing a lot of opposition politically to this investment. The Opposition right now is the PC Party, the bunch that threw the money into it in the first place, and the new government's throwing more money into it. I think we've been paying for Lloydminster upgraders all over the place. In Saskatchewan we've got a history here of creating an unhealthy business environment by expropriating private property in the past and then trying to encourage private investment by throwing tax dollars into businesses that weren't viable.

If you just sit down and think about it, most families and small businesses would agree that they manage their money more efficiently and make much wiser decisions than government. We have a long history of cases where governments feel they have a moral justification to take tax dollars out of families' budgets to invest in businesses because they think they know what's best for the province. The private sector is very frustrated with it. We have a very non-competitive tax environment here compared to Alberta, which is really making it frustrating for business opportunities here.

The most important natural resource we lose in Saskatchewan every year is our young people who are educated and raised here. A very high proportion of university graduates from Saskatchewan leave the province because there simply aren't the economic opportunities here to stay. That's one of the real tragedies and it's dimming some of the hope for the future.

RON OLSON

Alberta: Magnesium

In late 1987, when I was vice president of Citibank, Alberta Natural Gas approached Citibank and a number of other banks to put together financing proposals for the construction of a magnesium plant. Magnesium is a product that's superior to aluminum in terms of strength and weight, and it has better manufacturing capabilities when used in industry. Alberta Natural Gas believed they had the ability to produce magnesium and make money selling it at the same price as aluminum. So we put in our proposal and, along with the Royal Bank of Canada, we were selected to lend the money for this plant. ANG was part of the private sector. They had looked at it and decided they'd only pay one-quarter of the capital costs.

What banks do is they analyze risks. Now, banks are in the business of obtaining money from people who have surplus funds and lending that money out to people who require funds. They try to find investments that are risk-free. Whenever a bank makes a loan, it tries to make sure that it has at least two ways out of the loan. In this case there were two ways out of the loan. If the plant worked, the banks would get their money back from operations and profits made by the operation of the plant. If it didn't, the bank had a government guarantee from the province of Alberta. So since there were relatively few financial risks, the loan was judged to be acceptable from a banker's perspective.

Banks lend money to other businesses without government guarantees, but as I said, generally they will look for at least two ways out of any transaction. For example, if I'm going to lend you money to buy a car, I have two ways out. One, I can take the car and I can sell it and get most of my money back. The second way out is you will have a job, presumably, and you'll be able to repay the loan from money you make from your job. In this case, to put it in perspective, if the plant didn't work, you can't get your money back by selling a plant. If these people couldn't make it profitable and couldn't operate it correctly, there's no way the banks or any other entity could make it profitable. So that was not a clear way out of the loan.

Government involvement in these sorts of things could be a hangover from the days of high oil prices and surplus revenues, a time when there was an attitude, possibly within various levels of government, that they should be more involved in managing the capital in the industry of the country, as opposed to allowing the private sector to take care of these matters.

The rate of return should be a function of the risk. In this case what we have here is a very large-scale pilot plant. This type of a venture should have been funded entirely by equity. Given the risks, you should achieve a 30 to 40 percent rate of return on the initial equity. With normal projects without this type of risk, a return to equity holders should be in the 15 to 18 percent rate of return.

From the initial start-up the plant probably operated about a year to a year and a half. I am not sure how much of the final product they ended up selling. I don't think there was a lot of revenue generated through the process. From start-up they eventually achieved maybe 50 to 60 percent capacity utilization.

The plant cost approximately $130 million to $135 million, up until it started operations. From that time on there was probably another $40 million put into the plant and its mothballing by Alberta Natural Gas. So we have a total of in the area of $175 million, of which the province guaranteed the first $102 million. In addition, the province has been funding interest on the loan since 1990, in the neighbourhood of $10 million a year. So taxpayers are on the hook for close to $1 million a month. The $175 million that was invested in this plant has essentially been lost. Without government guarantee this plant would not have gone ahead because there was only one company willing to put up any equity to invest in the plant. That was Alberta Natural Gas, and they were only willing to put up that money on a limited-recourse basis.

Using normal rate of return of 15 to 17 percent, we could have interest income or profits of $20 million to $25 million a year being generated by the owners of the plant or going back to the government. That's clearly not the case. All we're experiencing are the continuing costs. I believe that the people in government and in industry thought that there was a reasonable chance that this would be a successful venture. At the time I believe the Alberta government was interested in diversifying the province's economic base. We had seen the collapse in oil prices once in the 1980s and there was a great emphasis on diversification. If this plant had worked, there would have been a lot of secondary industry established in this area. As a result there was great incentive for the province to backstop the plant. But I don't believe that the government should be involved in what is essentially private industry. They should leave these types of investments to private industry, the people with the money that can afford to take the risks and who are in the business of judging the risks.

Since the late 1960s, through the 1970s and into the 1980s, the governments have become more socialistically minded, that big business is bad and that profits are bad. Governments have gradually adopted the attitude that they can take care of society better themselves and they can spend capital moneys more prudently than can industry itself. We have been living, and we continue to live, with a hangover from this period where the governments have invested in capital projects and they have not been successful. To a certain extent some governments are continuing to invest in capital projects of this nature, where industry refuses to put up all of the capital.

Overall there are lots of lessons for all of us. Essentially, no matter how attractive it looks or what the rationale for government involvement, if the private sector is not willing to put up all of the capital for ventures such as this, government should stay away. The government should not be in the business of investing or backstopping economic activities of this nature.

The cost to the taxpayers of Alberta constitutes $102 million in loan repayment plus interest since the loan has been drawn down. Collectively we're talking about $10 million a year since 1990. That will go on for the rest of our lives because the government has had to borrow that money from other people in order to pay the interest and repay the loans. If the money hadn't gone into this project, it would be available for other types of economic activities that the government still needs to fund. For example, we've got a highway a short distance away. The government is paying for that highway with new funds. It could have used the money that was used to pay interest on this loan to build that highway. I think when the politicians made this loan they honestly believed there was a reasonable chance of economic success. But to the best of my knowledge there was very little discussion allowed for the taxpayers of Alberta about this investment in the plant by the province. I think it was a done deal by the time it was made public.

I believe that when the governments use their tax revenues inappropriately in ventures that fail, it hurts all of us because it means they have to take additional revenues from society to replace the funds that have been lost on failed capital projects. And they take funds from society through the tax system that might otherwise be used by people, corporations, private investors in successful ventures.

There is not adequate accountability in politics. Projects such as this can fail, and the politicians and the bureaucrats that are responsible for these types of loans and expenditures continue to be re-elected or continue to enjoy their jobs. It's easier for politicians and people that work for the government to make decisions of this nature because they are not held as accountable as private industry. With private industry, if you bankrupt your company, the company could fail, go out of business and lose all of the shareholders' capital. When the government gets involved in capital projects like this, if they don't work, it may become public knowledge but only the taxpayers lose.

GERARD PROTTI

Alberta: Oil Companies

I want to take you back to 1974 and the first Arab oil embargo. World oil prices jumped up at that time and it looked like prices were going to rise at fairly high rates of change over the next few years. So the Government of Canada made the decision that a number of other governments around the world made, to protect consumers, keep prices low and slowly start the rise in prices to world levels. That resulted in some distortions coming into the economy and it really introduced an era of heavy government intervention in the industry. That culminated in 1980 with the National Energy Program.

By keeping energy prices lower than world levels, as we did in the 1970s, it cost less for people to heat their homes. Meaning it cost industry less. That sounds fine in theory but in practice it causes problems because it's an artificial situation. It's one where you're insulating people from what's really happening out in the world. The longer you do that, the longer you encourage investments that are not consistent with what that real price is out in the rest of the world. So we became relatively more energy inefficient. We didn't change our capital structure, like they did in industries elsewhere in the world, to bring in new energy-efficient technology. If you go on with that type of subsidy and insulation program too long, you're going to run into problems.

In Canada, the way our Constitution is developed, the resource owners are the people of the producing province. The issue that we got into in Canada was one of revenue sharing between the people of Canada, as represented by the national government, and the resource owner, the people of Alberta. As the prices went up, the resource owner captured what is called economic rent, through the royalty system. We got into a fairly divisive time in our history where we had the resource owner, the national government and the industry arguing over who gets what piece of that additional pie.

The key question was, what price should the economy face? Should it face that world price or should it face a made-in-Canada price, an artificially low price? Going with an artificially low price and ignoring the question of who gets the additional revenue is the problem. When you have prices lower than world prices, the impact occurs on both the consumption end and the production end. The impact at the consumption end to a consumer is fairly obvious. If you're paying 20 or 30 or 40 percent less for your gasoline, when you go out to buy your next car — a Volkswagen or the big Buick, loaded — it's going to influence you. If you think gas is going to remain cheap for the foreseeable future, that'll influence that purchasing decision. By having a price signal that's not at world levels, you're not really giving the consumer the right signal as to what the true cost of gasoline is on a global basis.

At the production end, if the company is not realizing a price equivalent to their competitors' on a global basis, a number of things happen. One, you can distort the investment decision and have fewer resources flowing into a certain type of activity in exploration. It can mean that you've got resources that are capable, at world prices, of being developed that aren't developed. Probably worst of all from a supply and industrial side, it doesn't encourage the most energy-efficient technology to be brought to the decision.

Most countries that didn't have their own sources of energy went automatically to world levels because they had no other choice. It would have been a huge cost to their system to subsidize all of their energy imports and consumption. So they immediately had to invest in new technologies and try to develop new approaches. Obviously as well, from their consumer perspective it encouraged the development of energy-efficient technology and energy-saving consumption. In Canada, because we are blessed with bountiful resources of oil and gas, the feeling of the day was, well, we can use that to our competitive advantage for a longer term by keeping those prices low. The problem with that is that you postpone the date at which you bring new technologies into your economy, both from the consumption end as well as the production end.

There are a number of examples of the misallocation of resources, and probably the best example was a decision made by the federal government, through the National Energy Program, to subsidize certain types of activities. Because they thought prices were going to go up, they wanted to encourage the development of a very broad energy base within Canada. They wanted to develop the Beaufort Sea and the Arctic Islands in the north and the East Coast offshore, but they knew that those were high-cost resources compared to the resources in Western Canada and the Western sedimentary basin. Their solution was to subsidize, through grants, the drilling of oil and natural gas prospects and exploration offshore and in the Arctic.

The dollars naturally followed. Because so many of the costs were being offset through grants, they naturally drove people and drove companies and investment decisions to where it was cheapest. So you had lots of artificial activity in the north and off the East Coast. As a result, a lot of dollars were spent that probably would have been more fruitfully spent in the Western sedimentary basin, where we know where the resource is and that it's here in vast quantities.

As a Western oil producer, when you make a decision you take all the factors into account. You look at the price you're going to get for the product, so if it's artificially controlled, that influences your decision. You look at the cost: if you are going to be paid or receive special grants or credits or subsidies to undertake one type of activity versus another, you will incorporate all of that in your planning and in your corporate decision.

The other impact it has is on the financial markets. To do this development you have to bring in new equity — whether it's from Toronto or it's from Boston or it's from London, you have to bring that money in to finance this activity. When financial markets see that degree of distortion and involvement from government in influencing the marketplace, that causes them a lot of concern. So through that time period, even though we were pouring a lot of government subsidy into certain types of activities, financial markets were actually shying away from the industry and saying it's clearly highly regulated, by a highly interventionist government. So we had a double-whammy in terms of a drying up of equity markets and of interest in the industry.

And we all ended up paying for it. We all ended up paying for it as taxpayers, as employees within the industry, as consumers.

Shortly after we deregulated in Canada in 1985, world oil prices fell and we entered a period of very tough times, of low commodity prices and relatively high costs and very low rates of return. As a result, there've been a lot of cutbacks, a lot of mergers, a lot of changes in the industrial structure of the oil and gas industry.

Thankfully this wasn't a long period in Canadian economic history. We're now in a position where we've got a much healthier industry, attracting capital from around the world. The reason is that we've made the changes to be competitive regardless of what the world oil price is or the North American natural gas price. The result is an industry that's leaner, more efficient and able to compete on a global basis. Albertan oil companies now feel like they have control over their own resources. There's always going to be a very high degree of regulation and government involvement in the day-to-day aspects of this industry because the nature of it is that you explore, you develop, and you have to ensure that you definitely have the first-rate environment and health and safety standards. You've got to be able to develop this resource in a way that is going to be in the best interests of Albertans and Canadians. Companies accept that, they know that there's always going to be a large degree of involvement. But in the key areas where they have to make their cost decisions and their investment decisions and the price they receive, they're operating in a free-market environment. They thrive and they respond to that type of environment.

I don't think you can identify any one set of people to lay blame on when you look at the past. We were all there making decisions and everyone was trying to do it in the best interests of Canada, given what they understood the world was going to look like. A lot of the justification for this intrusion, you have to remember, was the belief that the price for oil was going to be $100 a barrel and higher. Natural gas was going to be several times higher than what the price is today. There was a belief that we were going to run out of this resource base and the technology couldn't be developed to bring in new supplies on a competitive cost basis. For all those old assumptions, whoever made them, whether they're politicians or people in industry or consumers, they all failed.

WILF GOBERT
AND RALPH HEDLIN

Alberta: Distorting Oil Markets

Wilf Gobert

You have to understand the economic circumstances at the time. In the 1970s the Western world, North America in particular, was dramatically concerned with security of supply. We had been supposedly cut off in 1973, 1974, by the Arabs. In Canada there was a concern that we were running out of secure oil and gas produced indigenously. So the government was trying to protect the consumer from paying very high prices and trying to harbour the resource for future use by Canadians. So we're talking about the period from 1974, when oil prices quadrupled, through to 1985 when the deregulation started.

There really were two subsidies to the oil industry. One was the consumer was subsidized in terms of the price he was paying for energy. That number has been analyzed to be about $55 billion over the period during which prices were controlled below the world level. So consumers were being subsidized into such things as wasteful consumption. But the government was then using taxation revenues to provide grants to the oil industry to invest that capital in the way that they thought was more productive for future generations.

So we had the absurd example of taxing production in Western Canada, where people were making money, and then using those revenues to drill wells in the Arctic Ocean. Those wells were costing $50 million, $100 million for one well. For that amount of money you could drill 200 wells in Western Canada.

Ralph Hedlin
You're talking about $55 billion, but there's also Petro-Canada, which took over a number of successful operating companies. The leakage of capital was enormous. Would you believe $8 billion?

Gobert
Yes, the government policy was to try and encourage Canadian owner-ship and investing in areas that at the time were uneconomic. As a result we had a national oil company that was an arm of government policy using public money to buy companies away from the private sector.

Hedlin
At extravagant prices.

Gobert
At extravagant prices, and the total value was about $10 billion. When energy prices fell in the late 1980s that $10 billion was worth possibly $3 billion.

Hedlin
Petro-Canada was to be a window on the industry. It was to allow bureaucrats in Ottawa to have somebody they could phone up and find out all about the oil industry. It was just a silly, specious thing and there was no real justification of any kind.

Gobert
But Petro-Canada is a healthy company today. In the 1970s and the first half of the 1980s Petro-Canada was an arm of government policy. Today a significant part of Petro-Canada is owned by shareholders, people who are investing their savings in it, and the company is operating to

generate a profit. So you really have to distinguish between yesterday and today.

Let me give you another example of the evils of subsidy and the cost of it. By subsidizing a company to invest in a government-prescribed manner, you're asking them to do something that is uneconomic. With something called the Lloydminster heavy oil upgrader, the upgrader takes heavy oil and turns it into light oil — it takes low quality and makes it high quality. The oil industry could not finance that project through strictly private investment because it was uneconomic. Because of things like regional economic development, which is a great buzzword, and employment in areas of high unemployment, the governments wanted this project to be built. So they subsidized it into construction and development. Alberta was an investor but they have now sold. They didn't want anything more to do with it. The federal government has realized that it's not their business so they are selling. Billions of dollars have been invested in this project and it is hanging by a hair, in danger of being mothballed.

Gobert

In order to force industry to invest in areas that they felt were uneconomic, the government taxed the revenue of energy production. Then they gave it back to those who were willing to spend the money in the prescribed manner that the government preferred. One of those was in the Beaufort Sea, there was the Arctic Islands, offshore Labrador, the Atlantic Coast. In the Beaufort Sea, for instance, you can only drill for three months of the year because it's ice-infested the rest of the year. So by definition it becomes very high cost. Over the course of this period of subsidy the oil industry probably spent well in excess of $1 billion, possibly as high as $2 billion, drilling something like 15 or 20 wells. Now, these wells found hydrocarbons, they found oil and they found natural gas. It's what the geologists would call a technical success. We proved that it's there.

However, the economic value of it wouldn't be a whole lot different than paying all of us very handsomely to dig a hole in the ground that nobody's going to use. There's no activity taking place now up in the Arctic. We have some glorious $100-million holes that have no value because the science of this is you have to plug them so that no oil or gas will ever leak out of them. So they're never going to be usable.

Hedlin

I think in a nutshell what happened was that the government moved in and replaced the market. We were drilling for oil here, and there were a lot of projections of higher prices and there was activity. They taxed the gross revenues of many of the smaller companies. They encouraged companies like Dome and many others to go into the Arctic with subsidies, your money, and it was never paid back. It's all disappeared, it's sunk in the Beaufort Sea, in the Melville Peninsula, in the Labrador Straits, on the Scotian Shelf, and it's all gone. You or your children get nothing from it. It's all gone. They took it out of an area where the marketplace really dictated people should be, distorted the market by pouring in taxpayers' revenues.

We should also recognize that playing with the oil industry had a very substantial political component. So the money dragged out of Alberta, $55 billion, apart from the other add-ons which are hardly noticeable, just a few billion here and a few billion there, went into central Canada. There was no representation in that government from Western Canada, virtually none.

Gobert

Governments are elected by majority and majority rules. One of the realities in Canada is that when it comes to energy and to some extent when it comes to food production, the large population, the electorate, the consumer is in one sector of the country and the production is in another geographic sector. It's what we call the field-goal posts of economics in Canada and political reality. So there's no vote by popularity of whether or not the oil industry agrees. It's what was best in the minds of the central government.

Hedlin

Had those sediments been in the province of Ontario, with the caucus being what it was, a lot of Ontario and nothing from the West, not one policy would have been initiated. The market would have driven. It was a regional thing, politically. What we witnessed was a raid on the resources of the oil industry in order to enhance the position of the consumers in the major consuming provinces. By holding the price down you got an enormous transfer. It distorted economic development. Had in fact that money been shared in some sensible way, Alberta would have grown more rapidly. There would have been a better population and economic balance in Canada, less damage from the debt, a consequence of subsidy, yes, but also a consequence of tremendously lessening the efficiency of capital use. So it's far reaching. It reaches right through the length of this country.

By lowering the cost of oil you use more energy. When in fact the prices came up, the industrial areas were not adapted to high oil prices. Their competitors south of the border were. So by transferring this money to the consumer of Ontario, for example, they damaged the industrial heartland of Ontario. I wouldn't publicly say this to the government, but seriously, it's shocking.

Gobert
So government taxed oil production in the West, where the cost of drilling a hole was $500,000, in order to spend it in the Arctic Ocean, where the cost was $100 million. They didn't find economic oil in the Arctic.

Hedlin
That is not quite right, but it's close to being right. A couple of shiploads a year!

Gobert
If the money had been spent in Alberta, where we could have drilled 200 holes instead of one, they would have found oil in the West, absolutely. The rate of drilling success in Western Canada averages about 70 percent for both oil and natural gas. When you find oil the wealth of the country for everyone goes up because the investor makes money on having drilled the hole, the provincial government takes a royalty and the oil company makes a profit so the government takes an income tax. In total during this period of subsidy there were maybe as many as 40 or 50 wells drilled. We probably could have drilled 8,000 here, which is about a year's worth of drilling in Western Canada.

So if you take the cost of investment in these government-subsidized areas and look at what the money would have done had it been invested in Western Canada in the conventional oil business, you could have drilled 8,000 wells instead of 50. One well at today's oil prices would generate revenue of about $4 million. Say it's $4 million for one well. At 8,000 wells that's $32 billion. Now, $32 billion is what the cost of buying that oil would be. From that the Alberta government takes a royalty and royalties average maybe 20 percent, so that's $6.5 billion. The Government of Alberta didn't get it because the money was spent in holes that will never produce oil and gas. That's $6.5 billion of government revenues that wouldn't have to come from taxation of the people.

Secondly, the federal government would earn income tax from the profit on the earnings of that oil. That number is, I don't know, maybe 10 or 15 percent. So now there's another $3 billion to $4.5 billion that the government doesn't have to tax the people for. The balance of the money is earned by shareholders who pay income tax on their dividends, people who make money in the stock market and pay capital gains tax.

Hedlin
But it's zero.

Gobert
It's worth nothing.

Now, we're kind of blaming governments here. The oil industry was not totally pure and clean in this process. One of the problems of subsidy is that it does cause private sector companies to do things that they might not otherwise do, but they do them thinking that they are going to get an advantage. A subsidy is the transfer of an advantage. Somebody pays for it. Somebody's going to try and take advantage of it.

What happened in the oil industry was that Canadian-owned companies had an advantage over foreign-controlled companies. So in the early 1980s, right away, some of Canada's best Canadian-owned companies (you might recognize the name Dome Petroleum) borrowed huge amounts of money to buy assets that were in Canada, to buy them away from foreigners. So foreigners were getting such attractive prices from it they thought, "They don't want us, we'll take our money and we'll go elsewhere." Well, the foreigners ended up selling at very high prices and the Canadian companies borrowed huge amounts of money to pay them. Subsequently interest rates went through the roof; in the early 1980s they were about 20 percent. Energy prices subsequently declined and our Canadian companies went bankrupt. The foreigners took their money out of the country and invested elsewhere. Our Canadian companies, along with the shareholder money, investors' money, went down the tube.

At its peak Dome Petroleum was worth several billion dollars, trading at $25 a share, and it went to virtually zero. There was a period of time when everybody thought Dome Petroleum was the best investment you could make. They were the beneficiaries of subsidy but it only worked as long as interest rates didn't skyrocket or if consumers were sheltered from the real price. As soon as everybody had to pay the real price, the distortion started to punish those that were beneficiaries. As a result you have bankruptcy.

The National Energy Program began to be dismantled in 1984, oil prices were deregulated in 1985, natural gas in 1986, and there are virtually no remaining instruments of the National Energy Program in existence. I wouldn't even venture a guess as to how much the Canadian federal debt load is attributable to the National Energy Program. I think you need what they call a Cray computer. It would be a very difficult number and there'd be more assumptions going into that kind of an analysis than would make the exercise worthwhile.

But the legacy of government subsidy, the privilege that it created in some sectors and the costs that it created in other sectors, is that foreigners took money out of the country at a time when Canada needed foreign investors. Consumers were relying on cheap energy that caused wasteful energy use. Oil companies were spending investors' money and the savings of the people of Canada, the taxes of the people of Canada, on inefficient investment, and oil companies went bankrupt when the artificial lift of the privilege transfer from subsidy collapsed in real-world prices.

The lesson of the National Energy Program is an argument you can use on any industry — that governments are not in power to compete with the private sector. Their mandate is not to run companies that make money. They can't run a company that doesn't make money and compete with the private sector that is trying to make money. The national oil company scenario as an arm of government policy competing with a company that's trying to make money for investors doesn't work; you can't have them operating side by side.

We've gone through an interesting cycle where the original intent, at least one of the stated intents of government policy in energy control, was to increase the level of Canadian ownership in the oil industry. So what they tried to do is use a stick to cause that to happen. Canadian control initially went up but it went up through subsidy and through grants and high interest rates, and low oil prices bankrupted those companies.

The result was that the increased Canadian ownership fell backwards because some of the Canadian companies went bankrupt. Once we went into deregulation, free-market prices and profitable use of capital, it created such an attraction of investors that in the development of new oil companies today, the level of Canadian investment in the oil industry has gone back to higher levels than it was at the peak of the government program. And it's largely being done from new companies controlled by Canadians raising money from Canadian savings and investing their money profitably in finding oil and gas that is economic.

Hedlin

I think when the people in government move into the private sector, they're not doing a good job running government. Their objectives are totally different from those of the marketplace because they're responsive not to shareholders but to electors. Government should stay right out of business, other than regulating so that there aren't abuses and the environment is protected and other matters. They simply have no business whatsoever in getting into the combining of land, labour and capital with the objective of making wealth.

These were decisions taken by politicians and bureaucrats in Ottawa, who didn't know a pint of oil from a pint of milk. They took those decisions, and they are the ones that are guilty.

CLOSING THOUGHTS

*Taxation and
the Underground Economy*

CHARLES ADAMS

Taxation in History

Taxes are a very powerful force in the life of people. You yourself get mad about taxes. People get angry about taxes. I had the feeling they were far more important in history than we realize, so that's why I wrote my book. We know taxes started the American Revolution, they started the French Revolution, they started the English Civil War. And rebellion upon rebellion upon rebellion throughout history was based on taxes. So it shows you that within the human being, taxes are a powerful emotional driving force.

The French Revolution is always a great example because we know that they executed the king and their queen, but what most people don't know is they took the whole tax bureau down to the guillotine — they cut off all their heads. One of the real problems that the Republic had, and later Napoleon, is that nobody would run the tax system because they had executed them all. That shows you how mad people get over taxes. I think that when you explore your own feelings about taxes that make you mad, and then you look back at your ancestors, you've a real mild gut. If 300 years ago we'd had life insurance, I don't think a taxman could have got coverage for any price because it was probably one of the most dangerous jobs in society.

Many a taxman went out and disappeared and never returned home. Even back in the Middle Ages. One of the stories I like was about a queen. They wanted to get rid of her rival and so she said the way to get rid of him is to send him out on a tax collection operation because he'll never return, which he didn't. I became fascinated with the role that taxes have played in the lives of people as individuals, how they motivated people. Look at the people that leave the country for taxes. And look at the way it motivates people in so many ways.

There's kind of an iron law in history that when people get mad about taxes, unlike other things, they're going to react in some direction of relief. It may be violence like a revolution or rebellion. It may be tax fraud and evasion, or they may just pack up their bags and leave the country because patriotism is soluble in taxes. As I said, when taxes get too high people will respond for relief in some direction. A good example is this: take the Rolling Stones. Everybody loves the Rolling Stones. In 1971 they said they had to make a decision on whether or not to stay in England. They wondered if they could afford another set of guitar strings or whether they had to leave and hold the band together. Hence they wrote *Exile on Main Street* and they left England because they just couldn't put up with it anymore.

The tragedy of it is that for the country, look at the loss. It wasn't just the Rolling Stones that were lost. Look at all the support industries. Look at all the jobs. Look at all the other financial aspects to the social order, to society, that the Rolling Stones brought to England. But they left. In Canada we had E. P. Taylor, one of the great tycoons. He said he left Canada because of our harsh Canadian winters. He probably really left because of our harsh Canadian taxes. He built Lyford Cay in the Bahamas. What if he'd had that capital and developed a Lyford Cay in Canada, look how many jobs it would have created. Look at how much we lost. So when you drive the wealthy people out of a country, you lose so much more than just their wealth. You lose their enterprise. You lose their spirit. You lose jobs.

So one of the great tragedies is to overtax a society because you have this tendency to react in either violence or flee the country. As I said, patriotism is soluble in taxes. How many great wealthy people have left different countries throughout history because of the tax burdens? The

Rolling Stones are just an example. Take Bjorn Borg, the great tennis player who now lives in Monaco. The great skier from Sweden, he also lives in Monaco. Take Sean Connery, the actor, his home is in Lyford Cay in the Bahamas. This is the great tragedy of excessive taxation. You drive people away. That's an old story, one we read back in early Roman history where a Roman writes and says, "Let us flee to the land of the barbarians where we may live as free men," because freedom was not having your name on the tax roll. So these are studies of human nature.

The average citizen can't leave. That's the problem, so trying to soak the rich is an illusion. You really can't soak the rich because they have the means to avoid taxes, and if they get mad enough they leave the country. The only dependable source of taxation is the middle class. That's another painful law because the wealthy person with tremendous wealth is sort of like a half-starved crow. He's not going to sit around and be shot at. When you tell the rich you're going to soak them, they pack their bags and they go, whereas the average person can't do that. He can't move to Lyford Cay. So he has to put up with the tax system and he reacts in two other ways.

He reacts with violence or he reacts by evading the system. When you see these signs within a society it's a warning that something needs to be corrected, and governments usually miss the point. They think that this requires cracking down on the defiant taxpayer but, really, when you have enough defiant taxpayers it's a warning that maybe the system is wrong and maybe the system needs correcting. They're basically putting government on notice that things are bad and should be corrected. This is one of the great lessons you learn from studying human reaction to taxes, going back through history.

The Bible is full of tax stories. Most people don't know that, but the lost tribes of Israel, how did they get lost? They rebelled against the taxes of the Assyrians. When Nebuchadnezzar came and destroyed Jerusalem he took all the Hebrew people and put them in captivity, called Babylonian captivity. How did that happen? They just decided they weren't going to pay their taxes, so he got mad about it and turned around and flattened them. So if you look back through history you'll see that the reaction of human nature against taxes has a long, dependable and predictable history.

When middle-class people hit that tax wall it's like a warning. I think you can call tax evasion a kind of rebellion. It's not a violent kind, but I think it was Jefferson who said that a nation needed a rebellion every 230 years or so. He said the rebels were pointing out problems that need a correction, that need attention. There will always be some evasion but when you see a large body of responsible and respectable people struggling to get out from under the tax burdens, then maybe you should consider that maybe the burdens are wrong. I think it's a warning. It's letting society and letting government know there is a problem out there. Trying to crack down on them is like trying to pour gasoline on a fire, an analogy I like to use.

I don't think Revenue Canada thinks it's going to go away. I really don't. They have enough intelligence to know that the problem needs correction, but of course they don't have the power. Again, it goes to the legislators to make the correction and they have to do their jobs. At the same time many of them will acknowledge that the tax system is really not good.

To not pay your share of the cost of the country is a sign of a bad citizen. It's the duty of the government to divide up their expenses in some proportionate way so that everyone pays their share. But the tax system breaks down on that. The idea is to make it progressive and soak the rich and let them pick up the whole tab. In fact some of the first tax laws were actually class legislature against the rich, and they exempted the vast majority of people. But that turned out to be wrong and turned out to be proof of a Russian proverb that says when you dig a ditch for somebody to fall in, you fall in yourself. So when you created a tax system that was designed to assault the rich, it turned out in the end that everybody else fell in.

Whenever taxes get excessive you're going to have rebellion. You can't always say where the line is, but once you get excessive taxes you run the risk of having a breakdown on social order. A good example of that is the great sage of the Enlightenment named Montesquieu. His great book did much to inspire the founders of the United States and their constitution. He used the words "excessive taxation," saying it will inevitably result in extraordinary means of oppression. When that happens, he says, the country is ruined. So maybe we like to learn to have respect for the government and respect for the tax system, but if they tax people too much and they have to hammer it on people, then the country is ruined. And maybe we're seeing that unfold to some degree.

It's a give and take between citizens and the government, but it's out of whack because, as we've seen through historical example, all good tax systems tend to go bad. Governments cannot control their spending appetites and this is where our problem lies. It seems that those who manage government are spendaholics. Whenever you take the power to spend and the power to tax and you put them in the same political body, the power to spend will always override the power to tax.

What made Britain great throughout its history, up until recently, was the fact that these two powers were separated. The king could spend but not tax, so it was a natural check. Once you brought those two powers together then the worst came out because you had the power to spend. And so then you became more interested in the tax collector who buttered your bread than in the taxpayer who produced the butter.

The culprit is the spending. That's the culprit. To go back a little bit in history to Gladstone, who was a British prime minister off and on for about 50 years he hated income taxes and was going to get rid of them. Even though he was prime minister and he controlled the government, he never could. He said the culprit, the reason he couldn't get rid of the income tax, was the public expenditure and the abandonment of the spirit of thrift in government. I think that has perpetuated into our century and into our times. Nobody seems to want to work for the government without a fat paycheque. That is what escalates the cost of the things that we enjoy from government.

There was once a time when people served their city unselfishly and without pay — and this is true in ancient history. The Roman magistrates worked for free. The Roman legions, in the days when Rome rode to greatness, the legionnaires worked for free. They even bought their own uniforms and their own swords and their own spears because they loved their city and it was just something you did, to give of yourself for your city. We do that today for the Boy Scouts. We do that for the Brownies. We do that for many social organizations; we'll go out and work for free and if somebody offered to pay us, we'd be offended because it would ruin the experience for us. Yet when it comes to government, everybody wants a fat paycheque and that is what escalates the cost. There's where your public expenditure goes, along with the abandonment of the spirit of thrift in government.

So the taxes are bad because the expenditure side is bad. You may ask the question, "How did we get to be such hogs on the expenditure side?" And that's another story because if you take the Canadian Liberal finance minister 100 years ago, he said the only way you could justify tax was for the essentials of government. Anything other than that, he said, is legalized robbery. Now, that philosophy doesn't fly today, but that's what the founders of this country believed and that created the sense of thrift in government. To take care of us from cradle to grave — we've become seduced by the philosophy of socialism, forgetting that somebody has to pay for it.

Governments have never been thrifty. They've always been wasteful. It's just inevitable. It's just the very nature of government that because they don't have a profit motive, they do waste money. A good example is Adam Smith in his writings in *The Wealth of Nations*. His view was that tax evasion should not be a criminal offence, and not only he believed that — William Blackstone wrote that in his great commentaries on the laws of England, and Montesquieu wrote it in his great book *The Spirit of the Laws*. So here we have three of the greatest thinkers of the Enlightenment all going out of their way in their great books saying tax evasion shouldn't be a crime. That's a crazy idea today, isn't it? But the reason was, if there is suspicion and much waste in government, then the laws to protect the revenue will not be respected. That's human nature. You're going against human nature — you can't expect people to respect waste.

I think that level of suspicion about government waste exists everywhere. Not only in Canada, but it exists throughout most of the world. It's one of the reasons why the government should do less, not more. I don't think it's true at all that Canadians aren't rebellious. It's true that we contrast with the Americans, but you have got to remember we're British and the British were the greatest tax rebels of the last 300 or 400 years. In fact, 300 years ago when an Englishman rode back from Holland, where the taxes were so high, he would say, "Boy, if this was in Britain we'd have rebellion after rebellion." What made Britain great during that period of time, it seems to me, was the rebelliousness of the British people. They were so rebellious the British government couldn't tax them, for every time it pushed them they'd rebel.

There were the tremendous revolts under Robert Walpole, the first prime minister of Britain, around 1730, 1740, when all he tried to do was put an excise tax on tobacco and wine. He had revolts throughout the country. He finally went to the king and the queen and offered his resignation saying, "I will not be minister to collection of taxes by blood." After that they tried to put an excise tax on cider. This was the key to the American Revolution; in 1763, when there were cider revolts all throughout England, that's when the government said we better try and find another source because Walpole said, "We have problems here in London, they're burning down the excise houses, they're burning down the customs houses, they're burning my effigy, hanging me up in the street. So let's try the Americans."

So they had a little meeting and they said, "Well, the Americans wouldn't mind contributing a little bit to help us out with our fiscal problems." And that was their mistake. During the English Civil War when they cut off the head of the King Charles I, that was over taxes. The Magna Carta was over taxes. So if you go back to the British history, you'll find there were rebellions upon rebellions. It just happens that we've got the image that we're softies, but I think in terms of our deeper history we can be just as rebellious as anybody else if we're pushed too far.

The next stage is to correct the system. It's hoped that the governors will catch the message that things have got to be changed and that government has got to be more frugal. They've got to be more responsible and they've got to have taxes that people will tolerate. If they don't then they face any of the three possibilities. The rich will leave. You'll have the wealthy fleeing the country as we see happening today. You'll have more in the underground economy and you might even see some violence at some stage or another. Or you may see some provinces that want to pull out. But certainly people will tend toward the response for relief. That's an iron law of history. Tax too much, you're going to get a reaction.

A good example is in recent American history. George Bush said, "Read my lips." He thought it was just another campaign ploy. Big deal, everybody yelled, but then when he turned around and introduced new taxes after he said no taxes, the people were pretty unhappy with him. Even Ross Perot looked good because maybe this guy would keep his word. So that was a message that you can't fool around with tax promises and not keep them. The voters will forgive you for most promises you don't keep, but don't make a tax promise and bench it. You're in an area of sacred trust, so when you promise no new taxes, as George Bush did, you better deliver. He didn't and they threw him out. I think everybody falls under this rule, Canadians included. It's just basic human nature. When you offer something on the tax level, particularly relief, you had better deliver because people will remember that.

There's an optimum level at which you collect the most tax. If you read back in the Enlightenment period, one of the scholars said if the maximum revenue is the objective, then moderation is the rule. Now, that's true. I think what happens is, well, let's go back to the Rolling Stones and how they were driven out of the country. How many other Englishmen of wealth and of prominence left England? With the Rolling Stones there's a vast exodus.

Perhaps the American example, which interests me, was that in 1916 when they set up the first income tax in America, the top bracket was seven percent. Five years later the top bracket was 77 percent — it went up 1,100 percent and collected no more revenue. About 250 people reported $1 million worth of income in 1916. In 1921 there were only 20. Nine out of 10 would disappear because the tax rate drove them out of the system in some way. They either left the country or they reorganized their finances, but that's what you do. The more you raise, the less and less you get until eventually you get nothing. So you have to have the optimum percentage of tax. On income it's probably around 25 percent. Once you get over that then people will respond by trying to find ways to get out from under the burden.

Here in Canada we're talking about 46 percent, so if history proves right, we're well beyond that critical limit. It would be interesting to see if they had enough courage to reduce the rate to 25 percent. There is a certain stage at which people would tolerate taxes. Once you cross that line people will try to find ways to get out from under the burden. They will try legal ways, all kinds of tax shelters, tax avoidance devices, and the result is that you don't collect as much tax with the higher rate as with the lower rate.

That is called "Reaganomics" but it's as old as history. There's a story in the old Taoist Chinese text in which the Chinese emperor calls in a sage, you know, the respected ancient man, the old, wise man. He says to the sage, "I do not have enough money in the collection of taxes from the Chinese people. What can I do about it?" And the sage says, "Follow the time-honoured tradition of taking 10 percent from the people." And the emperor replies by saying, "Well, I'm taking 20 percent and I'm still not getting enough. How can I get enough at 10 percent?" The sage says, "If you get 10 percent you will increase the prosperity of the people and they will pay more tax." So actually the lower tax, because it rewards people for hard work and for their incentive and enterprise, the result is that the wealth expands, so that the 10 percent then will produce more wealth then the 20 percent. And this is what the ancient sage told the Chinese emperor 2,000 years ago.

I use the marriage analogy. When you get married you take a vow for better or for worse, for richer or for poorer, in sickness and health, and you tolerate a lot of things in the marriage, but there's one thing you don't tolerate, and that is infidelity. You didn't take a vow for that, and I think it's true with the government. There's a sense of infidelity when a government taxes you too much. When it takes too much of your earnings and your wealth and your enterprise, when it gets on your back too much. I think that's a breach of the contract between the people and the state. Sure, we take for better or for worse. Sure, we accept the government for its sins and its follies. But when it comes to taxation we're getting in that area of fidelity and infidelity, and I think governments don't make that distinction. But I think they should.

It's a reason for divorce. For the Rolling Stones it was a reason for their divorce. For Mr. Taylor it was a reason for divorce. People will divorce their country with no remorse because money has no allegiance. Your wealth has no allegiance to a government. So when you find your wealth under assault, when you find your business under assault, when you find you work hard yet can't really keep the fruits of your labour, you'll leave the country. And people do. They've done it, historically. It is said that more people immigrated to the New World to avoid taxes than for any other reason. We saw that happen in Spain and even in the Netherlands. I found in my research a little pamphlet published in Amsterdam in 1630. It was an advertisement for passage on the ship to New Amsterdam, which was New York. The title of the pamphlet in large bold letters is "Freedom," in Dutch. If you read the pamphlet it means freedom from taxes, and that was the pitch. That is one of the main reasons that these people came to the New World — to get out from under Europe's hated taxes.

Another example is a French spy in Madrid around this time, when so many of the Spanish were fleeing Spain for the New World. The French spy wrote back to Paris and he said that 6,000 people went on the galleons this month to the New World because they can no longer live in Spain. He was talking about the tax burdens. So if you go back in history, you find that there comes a time when you drive people out of the country. This is an old story — it's nothing new. And we see it happening today. We see people fleeing not only from this country but also from many other countries because taxes are too high. It's just human nature, you know, let us flee to the land of the barbarians.

Francis LaBrie of the University of Toronto in 1974 said it's our duty to resist. He thought that he had a duty. It's interesting he used the word "duty," he didn't say the "right" to resist as if it's an option. A duty is an obligation. And so here is a professor of tax law at the University of Toronto law school saying that the government's gone too far and we have a duty to resist. It's an obligation to ourselves and to our fellow men to stand up and get the government off the backs of the people when the government's gone too far. It's kind of a revolution, almost like an American concept. The right of insurrection, the right of resisting bad laws, that there is an obligation to resist bad law. Otherwise they don't get changed.

He also predicted that within 10 years there would be a rise in avoidance. I don't know why he selected 10 years. It was going on then, it's going on now and it will always go on when rates are too high. He probably just felt that the resistance against the intrusions and the expansion of the Canadian tax system was such that within 10 years it'd probably reach a melting point.

When taxes are too high, there is the birth of a new industry — tax lawyers and tax accountants. I think this is a symptom of high taxes because if taxes are too high, people will seek relief. Now, what are the choices? They can flee the country. They can join the underground economy. They can hire a sharp accountant, good tax lawyers, and try to do it legally, but they'll try and get relief in some fashion. That's perhaps the first effort, to do it in a lawful way. So you have these big industries that are born, with tax lawyers and chartered accountants, with tax shelters and all kinds of tax gimmicks to reduce the tax burden. And that's unfortunate.

I think one way you could praise Revenue Canada is that they haven't singled out famous people for cheating on their taxes. They haven't used them as public examples to put fear in the hearts of the people. The Americans have Leona Helmsley. She's 71 years old and cheated on less than one percent of her taxes. She paid $55 million in taxes in the year in question — $55 million she paid. She cheated less than one percent and they put her in prison for four years because they wanted to make a public example out of her. It's an abuse of the process because it just means it's very selective, very arbitrary. So if you're a famous person, then you're liable to become a target because everybody knows about you and it really is unfortunate. I think Canada's a little more even-handed about it than Americans.

The history of lynching the taxman goes back a long way. Right after the American Revolution one of the first taxes they created was the whiskey tax. Alexander Hamilton, the secretary of the treasury, was in favour of that. And they had a major whiskey rebellion. The president of the United States, George Washington, led the armies that put down this rebellion, which resulted because they put a tax on whiskey. Even though the whiskey tax was cancelled later on under Jefferson, it came back after the Civil War period very strongly. Throughout the period from the latter part of the 19th century until maybe the First World War, there were an awful lot of lynchings of federal IRS taxmen throughout the South.

North Carolina seems to be the major spot where this lynching took place. I was curious as to whether any studies had been done on that because it seemed to be quite an open season on taxmen, which was sort of reminiscent to me of history. It reminds me of the state of France under Louis XIV, when the chief finance minister told Louis's queen that it was safer for a French soldier to walk through a Spanish village — and this was at the time when Spain and France were at war — than it was for one of his majesty's taxmen to wander through any of the provinces of France. There was really an open season on taxmen historically in the South with respect to the moonshiners and the white lightning and the revenuers.[1] So it was not a very safe job down in the Southern states.

In today's world the taxman has been pretty lucky. The people have not taken out their ire on the taxman, unlike in past history, because the states are more powerful now. People find that assaulting the nearest taxman is really not a very safe way to go. That there are better ways to try and avoid your tax burdens than to lynch the nearest taxman. That maybe you can find something a little more civilized. Perhaps lynching has been replaced by going to the underground economy. They're probably still making white lightning, but maybe the revenuers have kind of backed off, maybe it's not all that important.

In terms of people understanding the relationship between the taxes they give out and the services they receive, I'd say that people are naive. People have to face economic realities. I've often said that there would be an interesting House of Commons if the only people we could elect were individuals who had a five-year track record of balancing the budget, putting aside a little savings and taking care of their family. If they took that same wisdom and they used it to run the government, most of our problems would disappear because you can't spend money you don't have.

There's only so much money to spend, like a housewife with a pay-cheque she has to run her family on, and that's exactly the problem with government. People want all these goodies, all these handouts. They want the new car. They want the recreational vehicle. They want the cottage up north. They want the long vacation in Florida or the Caribbean but they can't afford it. People have got to have it drummed into their heads that if you're going to rebel over taxes, then you're going to have to accept that you're not going to get the entitlements. You're not going to get the public expenditure that is causing the taxes in the first place — worse than that, causing the deficit that is bankrupting the country. So somebody has got to hammer on them. If they have a right to hammer on the government, then somebody's got to hammer on them to get their head screwed on right because that's where the problem is.

In private life people can see the circular relationship between money, in and out, but we can't understand in public life the same sort of relation. We seem to think that the government's funds are inexhaustible. We seem to think that government is kind of a Santa Claus. I remember a statement made by one of the writers of the Enlightenment who said that one of the real dangers is when the people think that government is some wonderful, mysterious thing. It isn't. It's the same principle as the housewife running her household. You can't spend money you don't have. If people want to rebel over taxes, fine, but then you're going to have to accept what there is on the table. Put it like this: we want the government to spend money based on our appetites; really governments should spend money based on our wallets and their wallets. That's really the key to the problem.

This is the second time in history where we've had such a huge social net and the money is divided up and people are rebelling over taxes without an understanding of where the tax is being spent. The first time was in Rome. You might remember free bread for the rabble of Rome, the free entertainment in the Coliseum and the gladiators. So the vast amount of the rabble of Rome got all these handouts from the government, and ultimately they had a welfare state and it broke Rome. We have the same problem. You can't spend money you don't have yet we find out that that isn't true.

Government can spend money it doesn't have because we push this off on our great-grandchildren so they can pick up the tab. All we have to do is pay the interest. Of course, that's outrageously immoral.

It's immoral because we should pay for our own goods and services. We should, and we have no right to push this off on somebody else. What if the housewife, let's use her as an analogy, what if she could go out and borrow money at the bank and she doesn't have to sign the note at the bank, she signs it for and on behalf of my grandchildren who will pick up the tab. Now that's exactly what we're doing. We've discovered a clever way of borrowing money that we don't have to repay. We can just roll it over and roll it over, and then when we die our kids can pick it up. Well that is just outrageous. It's outrageous from a moral point of view because what we should pass on to them is a full treasury, not an empty treasury.

We should pass on to them a debt-free society, not a society burdened with debt. Somewhere along the line we've got to improve our own morality so that we can't spend money that we don't provide. We have no right to burden them with our extravagances. Now, war might be different. If the country's in danger, we have to protect ourselves from a foreign invader. Then we have a right to go in debt and then they can pick up the tab because we're passing on to them a country that's now free from foreign domination. Other than that, we don't have this right. There's a moral issue here that we've lost sight of. And this is a new phenomenon. This ability to pass the debt on to future generations is because of the fiscal go-go whiz kids in Ottawa and in Washington. This ability to create money and not have to repay the debt, this is relatively new.

If we were to be completely happy with our relationship with government, I'm not sure it would be possible to be comfortable with a very high tax. It depends on the way the people feel about it, but we're a pretty highly taxed country as it is. Compared to other countries, we're pretty well near the top of the line. If I compare Canada to countries in Asia like Singapore, Taiwan, Hong Kong, Japan and South Korea, where they don't have the deficits or debts that we do, the governments live on their income, taxes are modest. Well, we could learn from them.

Maybe the answer is in the simple principle of self-reliance. They learn to take care of themselves. What really touches me about Asian countries is the tremendous role that family plays. They take care of their own and we don't.

In Canada when somebody's out of work or there's a problem, the government takes care of him or her. But with Asians the family has a tremendous sense of solid familial responsibility. You'll find that some young people that are successful are actually sending money to their aunts and uncles that they've never even seen before because there's a sense of family duty. You know, there's a breakdown in the sense of self-reliance within the family, within the small community. When people are out of work and the church comes in and takes care of them, maybe pays their rent or finds them a job, they go out and take that job. That's totally different than our unemployment concept where you just get your paycheque and look for a job if you feel like it.

Government has replaced the sense of self-reliance and family responsibility and that's a terrible thing because it wasn't that way in Canada 100 years ago. It has become that and we almost have to relearn certain skills and certain sets of responsibilities. And it is possible for a nation to do that. Anything is possible.

It seems to be so elementary but apparently it isn't. I've heard that people don't want to get rid of their social programs. Well, then they have to put up with the tax system. I think the analogy of the housewife is sound. I think that good government is very simple. You can't spend money you don't have.

A lot of countries believe that. Switzerland is a marvellous example of a country in which the tax system is under control of the people. The people have to vote to approve taxes. The people can redo expenditures if they don't like them. The members of what would be the Swiss congress or legislature all have to work privately. They don't get paid enough money to have full-time jobs. The Swiss also have controlled borrowing because they put a tax on any foreigners that buy Swiss government securities. The result is that only the Swiss people can buy those securities. The Swiss have a very good sense of frugal government and that you have to pay for what you get. Maybe our problem is that if the Canadian people had to get involved in the tax-making process, that might be a great educational factor for them. But if they actually believe that they're entitled to all these goodies from government, and that they don't want to pay taxes, and they believe in Santa Claus or the good fairy, then they're not living in the real world.

The only dependable source of taxation is the middle class — and that's a truism. So if you think you're going to put the burden upon the rich, you're kidding yourself because the rich will disappear. They'll disappear as if by magic. But the middle class, they can't run, they can't hide. They're the ones that will be the driving force for major reform because they're the ones that have to pick up the tab. They're the ones that have to pay the burden and that's where your key to reform is, the key is with the middle class.

Unfortunately most historical parallels are nations going in great decline because they overtaxed their citizens. To be able to break this decline is a rare phenomenon. Good tax systems tend to go bad. Governments become spendaholics. The only way you might break it is to actually separate the power to tax from the power to spend. That seems to be the only key to the solution. It would be a good thing for the Canadian people to take responsibility for their taxes, and then they may be more responsible on their spending. But certainly it's not all that encouraging.

Once there's any kind of uprising government usually tries to crack down. I'm one that believes that the American Revolution was a response to the British effort to crack down on tax evasion. The Boston Tea Party wasn't really that significant, but the British were trying to crack down on tax evasion. Governments do that today but we need a government a little more enlightened than that, one that understands the reasons why people are not paying their taxes. It's because there's something wrong with the system. People just aren't bad when taxes are assessed with a sense of fairness and proportion — then you're going to have obedience to the law. But when they're as arbitrary as our tax systems, then you breed disobedience.

We have the ingredients for decline of government enforcement and I think if we don't reverse the process, there will be a decline. It's happening in social services. It's like buying a home. In my generation you could buy homes. Universities were free. That's gone. Today, instead of a husband being able to support his family, the wife has to work. So we certainly see the taint on the family. Yet with all these so-called services we've seen a great decline in the actual ability to maintain a higher standard of living. The standard of living has really gone down.

The middle class of Canada isn't in the same mood as these people who were lynching tax collectors in the late 1800s in the Southern states. We're not a violent bunch and that's not really a solution. But it would be nice to see the people take a more active role in reforming the revenue system so that they do have a voice in spending, so they do have a voice in taxes. Maybe if they had a voice in it, it would clear their illusion of the role of government as Santa Claus.

NOTES

1. The term "moonshiners" refers to illegal whiskey distillers and "white lightning" to their potent product. "Revenuers" were the IRS taxmen whose mission was to stop this unlawful and *untaxed* activity.

ROD STAMLER

Crime, Punishment and the Underground Economy

People in Canada are protesting tax increases. They're upset with the great burden that taxes bring upon their lives. It's sometimes the straw that breaks the camel's back, when a group of people becomes dissatisfied with the amount of taxes they're paying.

Look at the taxes collectively and across the board over the past few years, with cigarettes and alcohol being highly taxed and income taxes going up. Eventually people get to a point where they are no longer willing to be compliant. And it's at that point, when people really revolt, that the situation becomes most dangerous because our democratic system of government depends on people complying with and believing in the law, and believing in the government. We haven't got enough policemen or tax enforcers in this country to enforce all the laws, all the taxes, all the time, everywhere. So the whole system depends on people believing in the government.

To some extent people have always been involved in cheating, from time to time. But I see a trend in this country. People are coming to a point where they don't want to take it anymore, they don't want to be subjected to laws and penalties, and they simply rise up against them. Or they break the law to get the things they want. It may be alcohol, which is highly taxed. It may mean hiring a plumber or a contractor who doesn't impose the taxes on them. Slowly they're moving into a level of basic law breaking, and it becomes widespread. We certainly saw that with the cigarette situation in Canada, when millions and millions of people were buying contraband cigarettes because they were fed up with the high taxes.

Whenever the public wants something that's illegal, there's usually a lot of profit involved for those people who are willing to break the law on a wholesale basis, in terms of supplying those goods or services. And when that happens an infrastructure emerges, which we often describe as organized crime, but it's really just businesspeople willing to break the law to supply the goods and services that people want. That's the start of organized criminal activity, and that's the way it's been for years and years.

Oftentimes governments unwittingly get involved by trying to make things better for the population at large. They try to collect more taxes for more social programs. They try to stop people from smoking because it's unhealthy. They try to stop people from drinking because it's dangerous. Illicit drugs are basically the same situation. If the public is not willing to participate with the government in that program, whatever it is, then you've got an opportunity for an underground system to evolve.

One package of cigarettes doesn't seem like much to one person, but when you've got millions and millions of people each buying one package of cigarettes every day, an infrastructure evolves that is huge and massive. In Canada the underground market has risen to over $1 billion. That can buy a lot of accountants, lawyers and other supporting staff to put in a system of laundering money, supplying cigarettes and paying people to bring shipments across the border. All of that is possible with money and the basic greed of people who will do anything for it. People are willing to compromise their ethical positions in order to gather huge sums of money. These lawyers and accountants are no different than the people actually involved in supplying that black-market commodity.

Money laundering is necessary whenever money is flowing from illegal sources and is subjected to taxes, the scrutiny of the police and/or the threat of prosecution. It's important to take the money derived from these sales or services and place it beyond the reach of tax people and law enforcement. To do that you have to set up commercial systems that look legitimate to move that money into another jurisdiction, perhaps an offshore tax haven. Then you have to repatriate that money in a way that also looks legitimate. The most common method is to bring the money in and move it to a Grand Cayman or Bermuda account. Then you simply borrow the money, as if from a financial institution, to buy a shopping centre or a house.

You've got a mortgage, and then if someone looks and says, "What has this person got? Well, he's got a big house, but it's mortgaged right to the hilt." It's your own money that's financing that particular mortgage, so it looks legitimate. That style of money laundering makes anyone involved in this activity look not too wealthy, not too rich, but allows them to drive a big car and live in a big house, with everything mortgaged to the hilt, so that people say, "Look, they've got nothing, really."

It's easy for a small entrepreneur to descend into this underground. Go back a year, when cigarette prices in Ontario were quite high, and take the example of a corner store. It's selling legal cigarettes. Then suddenly a store down the road starts selling contraband cigarettes for half the price. All of the customers go from the first person's business to the business down the street. Now that corner-store operator has to make a decision. "How do I stay in business?" It becomes obvious that you have to get involved in the illegal trade of cigarettes if you want to stay in business. So now he puts in a second inventory. And he sells huge quantities of that contraband inventory. He stays in business.

But now the flow from those sales has to be separated from all of the other legal sales. He doesn't want to show that in his books and records. He has to take that money and deal with it differently. He'll think about opening an offshore bank account. So off he goes to do that, maybe through a local money launderer who will provide that facility for him. The services are there on the street for this kind of activity. If the store operator dealt with any legitimate banks or investors, it would leave evidence of the criminality that he was involved in. So it starts small and it grows, in terms of the facilities that one needs.

Now the corner store is in that business, and along comes some new illegal commodity. It's not a very big step to move from illicit cigarettes to that other commodity. He has that offshore bank account and has already made contact with the money launderer, so everything is in place. He can now move into a different world in terms of bringing in funds from unlawful activity. He might even take some of his legitimate money and say, "I'm not going to pay tax on that. I'm going to slide that into the offshore account," because he's now educated in how to do this.

How far will a person go? That's really the issue, and I think it's a question of how easy it is for you to do it, and how likely it is that you'll be detected, or that you're just one of many doing the same thing. The more people that are doing this, the less likely it is that you will be caught. And it's easier then for that person to rationalize why they're doing it: because everybody is doing it. It becomes fashionable to have an offshore bank account. It becomes fashionable not to pay your taxes. A different attitude starts emerging. People want to maintain a standard of living. When they see the possibility of their standard of living going down, they'll often move to another activity that will ensure the kind of cash flow they've grown accustomed to. Across Canada this kind of illegal activity goes up and down depending on opportunities. If we go back in time and look at Chicago and New York in the 1920s, we see street gang criminals like Luciano who were really nobodies in the world, but who profited from an opportunity. The opportunity was the sale of illicit alcohol, and massive profits were obtained.

There are cycles. But if you look at what happened even after Prohibition, in the early 1930s, these people went on to become huge, notorious, international organized criminals involved in controlling unions, waterfront areas and building trades because they had the power. And the power was there because of the money. So once given the opportunity, organized crime can really grow and become a threat in our society and it's very difficult to do away with it once it's in place.

Take again the example of illicit cigarettes; you have people connected with organized crime involved in huge profits and moving contraband goods across the border. If that activity stops tomorrow, they'll have to get into something else. Their connections are worldwide. They have a network of people that they can draw on to do any illegal activity. They can take waste material, for example, and move it the other way, or get into any profitable activity that is unlawful. And it's because it's unlawful that it's profitable to them. By waste material I mean environmental waste. People sometimes find it very difficult to dispose of it.

We have very strict laws in North America in terms of dumping things that destroy any part of our environment, and that's all good. But if you have a barrel of toxic waste that you have to get rid of, you may turn to your local organized criminal, who will come pick up that barrel and dispose of it for a fairly high price, but not as much as it would normally cost you to dispose of it legally. We've had all kinds of situations where waste was shipped to Eastern Europe or dumped out at sea. People who are willing to break the law can do practically anything they want because they have the system in place.

But getting back to the idea of cycles, we're in a profitable mode for organized crime at this particular time. It's heavily involved in the movement of alcohol, drugs and various other commodities. Waste is just another product. It's about moving any commodity in and out of any country.

And we have a great banking system in this country which facilitates the movement of investments into Canada. So we are profitable for organized crime as a place for investment, as a place to do business and as a place to launder out the profits and proceeds of crime.

We also have a long, open, undefended border with the United States. There are many criminal activities in the U.S. that use Canada as a facility to move goods, services and money. So we have a natural threat from the south, and if we have any profitable ventures in this country, you can be sure they're going to be quickly realized and connected. People will move in, in a very sophisticated way, to provide those goods and services.

Incidentally, they're still smuggling cigarettes, but they're doing it from province to province, rather than from abroad or from the United States into Canada. They're also involved in the smuggling of firearms, weapons, drugs and certainly alcohol, which is a big commodity at this particular time. They'll move any product that is profitable to be moved. You need only go to Cornwall. Sit there, talk to people, look at the river and see what people are doing. You can see the criminal activity right in front of you as you stand on the bridge or as you talk to people in that community. They've gone through a situation that is the same scenario as Chicago in the 1930s, with guns going off in the middle of the night, bike gangs coming to town, and Aboriginal people connecting with organized criminals. That's happening today, so it's not something that one can't look at and see.

It came about because of cigarettes. They've been a factor since the mid-1980s, and while there may have been other minor criminal activities, nothing has come along as profitable as cigarettes. There are a number of Aboriginal people who can give their side of the story. Why are they involved in this type of activity? Well, first of all, it's profitable. But also it's their land. They feel that they have a historic right to move from Canada to the United States, and if it's profitable to move a commodity from one part of the reserve to another, they should be able to do it. So they rationalize their position in each of the three states and provinces involved in that area.

The demand comes from the public in Canada — from the same people that are concerned about high taxes. It comes from people who are willing to pay for an illegal package of cigarettes, bottle of booze or gun. These are the people that drive this particular market.

There have been ups and downs in our history, where organized crime has been involved. For example, during the 1930s there was a great deal of activity in Canada, although not necessarily criminal in nature, staging here to supply the United States with illicit alcohol. That brought a lot of interest from U.S. organized crime, and they got established in Canada as a result. We had a fairly flat period through the 1940s and 1950s, and even into the 1960s. Then along came illicit drugs in a big way. They provided huge, huge profits. That may have been a starting point for organized criminal activity profiting from a large venture in Canada. Then along came cigarettes, which were even more profitable, and less risky in terms of being caught or the stigma attached to distributing them. Then came alcohol, gasoline for automobiles and on and on. They were even bringing frozen chickens from the southern United States, bringing them into Canada and selling them at a ridiculously low price. They were able to do it because they had the connections and the facilities in place. They had the trucks that were hauling cigarettes and alcohol.

Now, I'm a forensic accountant. When I was in the RCMP I was in the branch called commercial and economic crime. At that particular time, in the late 1960s, it became necessary to penetrate the business side of organized crime. I became one of the early investigators in that particular unit. For the next 12 years I investigated organized crime and a number of international business crimes. I was personally involved in investigations of massive money-laundering schemes from Southeast

Asia to Canada and back to Southeast Asia. That required a great deal of knowledge of accounting, law, international practices and business. So I became one of the forerunners of this type of investigation.

A forensic accountant looks at both the business records and the people, as opposed to a straight accountant, who may just look at the figures and records, or an investigator, who might only look at the people. We look at both and we put meaning to business transactions and documents. That's what we're really good at. I've been personally involved in quite a number of investigations where funds were hidden away in offshore bank accounts. It becomes a unique type of investigation.

We must remember that with organized criminals, no matter how big, the one thing they always handle personally is the money. So you always follow the money. If you're looking at a drug deal on Yonge Street (in Toronto), the profits from that deal will flow to the top levels of organized crime involved, so you follow the money. And that's where the organized crime connections can be seen at their best, through those transactions.

That's what I've specialized in over the years. There are techniques for finding the money and for investigating this type of activity, and it's probably no more difficult than investigating a traffic offence. If you do it over and over again, eventually you understand and know what you're looking for. We've dealt with people and situations that are real, that are huge, that are live, where you actually see people selling the commodity, delivering it and taking the money. I've seen them move the money into offshore bank accounts. We're watching them do this, and afterwards usually you get to talk to these people. Some of them may not be prosecuted. They may be witnesses close to the centre of the scene, so they provide the background of the people involved: how they do it, why they do it. You get this inside perspective of Canada that you never see when you're doing things on the lawful side.

But policing can't control organized crime in Canada today. It has become very complex. In the era of the 1960s and 1970s, when I was involved in these investigations, life was less complicated for a police officer. Now we have new rules and new laws every day to control law enforcement. And rightly so, all good intentioned, but when I look at law enforcement's capability today, as compared with 10 to 15 years ago, there's no comparison. It took fewer law enforcement officers to do more in the 1960s and 1970s than today. Our world of investigation has become so technical. For example, to get a search warrant you'd need weeks of work and huge bundles of documents because we've developed systems to review searches, and if one is deemed to be improper, if you forgot something, all the evidence that was obtained during the course of that search is thrown out.

Police officers are subjected to a much more rigorous test in developing their cases. That's all well and good, but the other side of that coin is that they need more time and effort put into that case to get the same result. So police today in Canada are much less efficient. And recently budgets have been cut. People are concerned about the size of law enforcement and the amount of money that's expended, so there has been a reduction in the budget. So you've got fewer people involved in law enforcement today. New controls have been imposed by the courts. The Supreme Court of Canada, for example, has made a number of rulings in the past five years that have significantly restricted law enforcement activities and techniques. The use of informants, for example, has been significantly curtailed. A cornerstone of the British law enforcement system was using informants to get information. Now that has become much more technical and difficult. It's hard for a police officer to say that he got information from an informant, and then do something with that, without naming or identifying the informant. These rules have changed law enforcement in Canada forever, and we're following the trends of the United States. It's interesting that the U.S. is probably swinging back, while we're still moving to where they were, on the other side of the spectrum.

One of the reasons for the rise of the underground economy is that when more people get involved in this activity, the less risk there is for individuals to be caught and detected. A good example of that was when I was flying over Cornwall on one occasion, and I could look down and see boats going just steadily back and forth. Cartons of cigarettes and alcohol sat in the boats and were delivered to waiting trucks on the other side. There was a row of trucks to load, and then off they went down the 401. I spoke to the person responsible for enforcement in the Cornwall area. He said that they just can't handle the volume. If they seize three trucks, they have two weeks of work identifying all of the exhibits in those trucks and processing all of the people. It's so complex and heavy in terms of their workload that they just can't handle more. And here you've got between 40 and 100 trucks pulling out of Cornwall and down the 401, going in every direction. It's just sheer volume. It's right there. Fly overhead and you will see for yourself the kind of activity that exists in Cornwall.

They're selling to Canadian people who are fed up with high taxes on whatever products they're buying. They create the demand. That was also true earlier, with respect to the illicit drug problem in this country. If no one buys those drugs, there won't be any supply. If nobody buys illicit cigarettes, there won't be any supply. There won't be an organized crime group behind it. There has to be a person willing to participate before there can be unlawful activity and profits generated from it.

Last summer I had completed a study of tobacco smuggling into the United States, and I toured the southern U.S., talking about what happened in Canada during our problem with illicit tobacco. The one thing that the hosts on the various radio and television stations all identified was that they couldn't believe that Canadians would buy illicit cigarettes on the black market. Everybody thinks we're so honest and upstanding. Perhaps we are, but we're moving from that position to one where people get the straw that breaks the camel's back. It may be a tax on something that is just too much to take. People are not willing to comply anymore.

It may be a new tax imposed tomorrow on some other commodity. It may be in Newfoundland, where they can't fish cod, but they want to and they will, and they'll sell it in spite of the law. It may be a number of factors that cause this attitude toward a government that is well intentioned, laws that are well reasoned, and an application of the law that is supported by all of those people who don't make a livelihood from, but are concerned about, that particular activity. The law is imposed and suddenly it creates an economic impact. It creates hardship on a certain number of people, so they move to the other side and start getting involved in unlawful activity.

And we certainly saw that with the GST when it was applied. We already had the sales tax, and then we got a tax on services. Suddenly this whole business of working at night, whether it's plumbing, electrical work or construction work, was done by individuals who wouldn't charge GST. That whole thing mushroomed because of that one tax.

A lot of people are also upset about how their tax dollars are being used by the government. And I've seen that side of the issue as well. When I was the director of commercial and economic crime, I was responsible for investigating government corruption and wrongdoing with respect to public funds. I got real insight into the activities that occur when public servants suddenly get a lot of money to spend — more money than they ought to have. Or when politicians want to be re-elected in a particular riding, and they want to build a facility there at the taxpayers' expense, and suddenly it's approved; that really is something I've seen from the other side.

In some cases the public can tell that it's happening. When they see that kind of activity with respect to their tax dollars, they get very upset. That's another factor where they would say, "I've had it." That's the straw.

As a forensic accountant going into major corporations on a daily basis to examine fraudulent activity, I see that the companies most susceptible to fraudulent activities are those where there is some corruption at the top. All of the people within that institution know that it is occurring, and everybody tends to look out for themselves, commit their own individual frauds and rationalize them: "Well, look, the boss is doing it." Everybody's putting in false expense accounts, spending money here and there. There are no checks and balances. Everybody's doing it. And that's what happens in a democratic society. That's what's happening in Canada.

There are a number of examples of government officials ripping off the taxpayers. They're so numerous that they're difficult to go through. There are people in Ottawa who have spent a lifetime trying to control public spending, ensuring that public funds are spent properly, in the best interests of the people. And they have expressed concern and will tell you what has happened with a change in government attitude.

In the 1960s the comptroller general of Canada was responsible for budgets. But that office was practically eliminated later, and the spending authority was given to each minister. That changed the attitude of spending in government because prior to that budgets had to be religiously followed. Spending public money was a big issue and had to be justified. You had one person in one office who'd say, "No, you can't spend that. You can't build that facility in that community this year because it wasn't planned for and it's not required." You had an overriding authority.

The position of comptroller general is still there today, but it has been put at a level where it really has no power. We have an auditor general who comes in after the fact and reports to Parliament on spending.

We see in that report all kinds of data on how departments have misspent their budgets and the improprieties.

A series of criminal offences has occurred with respect to the misspending of budgets. You now have the auditor general, who looks at the money after it's spent. But the ability to look at the money before it's spent was given to the politicians at large. If such a politician needs a budget Okayed, he goes to the Treasury Board. The Treasury Board is headed by one of the Cabinet ministers. It's another politician. Therefore the system is circular.

If the Cabinet were to sit down and say, "OK, we need to do this, this and this in order to be re-elected," and that involved putting the facility in the community, then it's obvious that when the other minister goes to the Treasury Board, which is led by one of the ministers that sat in the Cabinet meeting, you're going to get approval for that facility.

Back in the comptroller-general era, that facility would have been planned, budgeted for and approved years in advance of its being built. You have a different set of standards that have come into play now.

In one case that I personally investigated, a director of the Department of Regional Economic Expansion created a contract for a friend. It was a consulting contract. The friend was asked to take a survey of what kinds of pet foods were sold in grocery stores. And for that, in 1972 dollars (because this was investigated in the mid-1970s) he received $30,000, which was within the spending authority of the director involved. So there you have a situation where $30,000 was given to a friend, with no control and no subsequent opportunity to examine it and say, "Was this actually needed?" This case is notorious. It went to the Supreme Court of Canada and the person was convicted.

But that's the kind of thing that can occur. There were probably many contracts granted honestly, honourably and aboveboard, but there was certainly a category of contracts that fell into that questionable area.

There were many other situations which resulted in criminal charges. We had the museum in Hull; a member of Parliament was charged, convicted and sentenced. I can't list them all, but let's go back to the situations that I investigated.

The dredging frauds of the 1970s went to court. Millions and millions of dollars were defrauded because of dredging contracts that may not have been required. The bidding may have been handled improperly. During the course of that investigation we found that just about every contract on the St. Lawrence Seaway was part of a bidding fraud, a fraud against the government, probably with the knowledge of many of the engineers and government officials involved.

I generally found that illegal activity was widespread within the federal government. When I started in 1970 I went to see Mr. Kennedy, who was then a senior legal advisor at the Department of Transport. And he said that the spending in the federal government had become so out of control that fraud was practically everywhere. That statement was borne out in the next four or five years because I went from one case to the next and I recognized a large number of government officials either condoning or involved in fraudulent activities, kickbacks and unreasonable contracts. They were doing it to generate income for themselves, or for corporations which provided benefits back to them. And that extended right up to the highest level of government, the ministerial level.

I must say that there are quite a number of politicians who are not corrupt; very upstanding individuals personally and morally. They're all supposed to be, but they're not.

The other problem that gets things out of control is that most Cabinet ministers have a lot of power and a lot of work, and they have a lot of people around them. And since they don't have the time to look at everything in detail, a lot of that responsibility is given to their executive assistants. In many of the cases that I investigated, I found that the instigator within the department was the minister's executive assistant, who'd used that power improperly.

That's another factor that occurs in our system of government where, as I say, ministers get wrapped up in their overall responsibility of governing. And we must remember that many of these ministers have no previous experience. My belief is that they should all take an extensive course on how to act as a minister, and how to delegate that power and responsibility. They come in not recognizing that fraud is so prevalent and that opportunity is so great.

The other factor is that a politician who runs for office has to spend a lot of money. Many of them are deeply in debt when they hit the office in Ottawa. Then you've got a big pot of gold sitting there that you're responsible for: your discretionary fund. The discretionary fund is something that the ministers and members of Parliament themselves can decide how to spend. So there are often little schemes to try to maximize those funds going back into their pockets. That's all account-ed for, but they often mistake the expenses. They can spend the money, but instead of paying it to A, B or C for services, they put it back into their own pockets.

Let's assume that you're a new member of Parliament and you're not heavily in debt to start with as a result of your election campaign. You're an honest, honourable person in Ottawa trying to change the sys-tem. Let's assume then that you embark upon these honourable first few years of changing things to the benefit of all Canadians. The problem is that you'll get caught up in so much work on a day-to-day basis that you'll delegate some of your power to your subordinates and other people around you. You'll believe that everybody is acting honestly and above-board like you, but they may not be. You may be drawn in by a fellow politician, for example, a powerful minister's executive assistant, who will come and ask for your assistance. You'll become involved, perhaps unwittingly, and the next thing you know, you're supporting a fraudu-lent or otherwise improper activity.

So even though a person is well intentioned, it's the system there that will somehow use you because you'll be an ideal person to hide behind. You're the honourable member of Parliament who would never do anything wrong, and suddenly you have supported a project. And that project happens to be for the benefit of somebody else, but you were asked to give your support because everybody believes that you are honest and straightforward. Eventually you could become corrupted. But usually, because you have so many activities to look after and so much work to do, you'll delegate. In the delegation you'll find people who will benefit in some form.

One of the most difficult tasks for any law enforcement officer in the world is to investigate a politician. And the more powerful the politi-cian, the more difficult they are to investigate.

First of all, it's natural that the person will tell his friends and other powerful ministers that he's innocent of any wrongdoing. And they'll usually believe him because they've worked closely with that person. Secondly, any colleague implicated in criminal activity will bring a black mark against the party as a whole, and may in fact hurt them in the next election. So the general tendency would be to try to prevent this person from bringing this discredit upon the offices of everyone in Ottawa. So you have to overcome that situation. Thirdly, one of the most difficult things that I found when I was carrying out these kinds of investigations was that you had to report on a regular basis to the political level, to people who were perhaps entitled to know, but who had everything to lose if your investigation pointed to fraud or gross misconduct.

That's a big problem in our democratic society, particularly in Canada because of the distribution of powers between the federal government and the provinces with respect to the enforcement of criminal law. It's very important that federal law enforcement officers be permitted to investigate independently any politician believed to be involved in criminal wrongdoing. But the power and responsibility, generally, to investigate criminal matters is local. So, for example, it should be the Hull city police if the crime happened to be in a federal government building across the river from Ottawa. In our legal system it would be their responsibility, theoretically, to investigate that matter.

The prime minister, unlike the president of the United States, cannot appoint a special prosecutor. And the courts have whittled away the power of a royal commission to investigate a criminal offence. So the prime minister, no matter how dedicated he may be to making sure that all criminality is investigated, hasn't even got the power to do that. That belongs to the provinces because of our split in the distribution of power. And it's only by custom that the RCMP has evolved into the role of investigating federal offences.

The requirement to report to the political level evolved out of a royal commission, the McDonald inquiry into the security services of the RCMP. They looked at the reporting arrangements there. A security service works from the top down. It is a function of government, really, to go out there, fact-find and bring back information so that government can politically react to a situation, unlike a police force, which is required to go out and investigate on behalf of the public. The inquiry looked at the security service and put in requirements to report upwards.

The security service was moved out of the RCMP, but the policy of reporting upwards remained. It became a standard practice in every case, including criminal cases, which undermined the very work that the investigators were doing to gather evidence. The first duty of a police officer is to gather the evidence, and that's where the problems arose. In order to gather evidence you have to carry out certain investigative actions, which include getting search warrants and interviewing people.

In these cases the investigation might mean going into Parliament Hill and getting the co-operation of the Speaker or government officials who have documents and records pertaining to the fraudulent activity. And if that's closed down to you as you're walking through the investigation, that's where the problem arises. You can't gather the evidence in order to get the matter to court. And even if you could, there are sometimes additional problems in court. I think that for the most part judges are independent. They pride themselves on that. They're not really corrupt in a general sense, and I think that's true throughout Canada. But in some places there are judges who think that by assisting a high-placed political person they might enhance their career. That's their own personal decision that comes into play there. So it depends on the strength and weakness of the individual member of the judiciary.

For example, there's a justice of the peace by the name of Fliss who has got to have more backbone than anybody I know. Right in the middle of Hamilton he issued search warrant after search warrant against people like John Munro and other very important people in the community, without even batting an eye.[1]

But the next time you'd meet another justice of the peace who just wouldn't do it, who'd refuse. It's the independent person who thinks that they can capitalize by supporting the politician rather than law enforcement.

But for the most part I think judges are straight, honest and honourable, and we've got a good court system in Canada. The turning point for police frustration, with respect to investigating politicians, was not related to the courts. It came when the full measures of the McDonald Commission were implemented. Reporting to the solicitor general became an absolute requirement on any criminal case. That meant that before you could get a search warrant involving a politician you had to report to the solicitor general, who was often in the same party and a close friend of the politician. That evolved through the early 1980s. It's important to note that many solicitors general, and politicians like Prime Minister Trudeau, never interfered in that process. However, I found that was not the case later, when there was in fact an intense interest in determining what was going on. It came not necessarily through the solicitor general, but through the body of executive assistants, chiefs of staff and various other political staff. They became very interested in obtaining information. It undermined our entire investigation. One of the important techniques of law enforcement is to get a search warrant and, with justification and authority, search the offices or the home for books and records pertaining to a particular situation. But if the person is alerted that we're coming with a search warrant, it's not likely that there's going to be much incriminating evidence lying around when we arrive. So that was the potential for undermining. And in some instances we could see that the case just seemed to slip away into nothing as the investigation proceeded.

One of the things that organized crime does very effectively is to have law enforcement officers informing on what's happening inside the police force. If you're constantly involved in a criminal activity, of course you want to know whether anybody is going to be looking at you or is interested in you. So you're going have your "spies" within that system.

But the system in Ottawa was much more direct and controlling, and much less subtle than that of an organized criminal manipulating a police force. In Ottawa there's special status. If a politician wants to exercise the full power of this type of policy, there's no question about it, he has special status. And it's a natural human tendency to do so, given the opportunity. Sometimes it's very self-serving. Again, if a senior member in the political party you're serving is going to create a major embarrassment, you'll try to prevent that. We had a conflict between people doing that and upholding the law. Some people can separate those two issues, but others can't. And that's where the problem lies. The system was wrong. The system is still wrong.

There were a number of cases under investigation that never got anywhere, and those were major cases involving corruption. They're nothing now but files in the offices of the investigators. No prosecutions, no results were ever achieved. So my conclusion is that the situation got much worse.

Where it is now, I can only speculate. But there's one thing I learned in my travels around the world, particularly with the United Nations in developing a convention on money laundering. I found that those countries with the most corruption had the fewest prosecutions with respect to politicians or corrupt practices.

This kind of corruption within our own government leaves the average Canadian disappointed, disillusioned and in the position to say, "Why should I pay my taxes? Why should I pay the high taxes on cigarettes and alcohol? Why should I subject myself to that kind of economic grief when nobody else seems to do it at the top end?" If the example at the top is bad, people are not going to be so inclined to obey the law, pay their taxes and keep their mouth shut, so to speak, or say, "I'm a good, honest Canadian."

It also leaves the police frustrated. And it's true that if today you went to the average fraud squad, a commercial crime unit of a police force, as a victim you would have to wait for months and months to get that matter investigated.

And that again is because of budget cuts and costs. So it is very, very important that the public at large remains honest, honourable and aboveboard, like the people that our southern neighbours think we are.

NOTES

1. Hon. John Munro, former federal Cabinet minister, was charged with fraud and conspiracy. The charges were dismissed after prolonged litigation.

APPENDIX

People Interviewed in This Book

CHARLES ADAMS, a tax historian, author and beekeeper, was an adjunct scholar with the Cato Institute at the time of his interview. His book *For Good and Evil* examines the relationship among governments, people and taxes. His new book, *When in the Course of Human Events*, examines the role of the South in the American Civil War and won the 2000 Paradigm Book Award. He is currently an adjunct scholar with the Ludwig von Mises Institute, an economic think tank at Auburn University in Alabama.

TED ALLEN is president of Agricore United in Winnipeg. (United Grain Growers became Agricore in November 2001.)

MILLER AYRE is a Harvard University graduate and is currently the publisher of *The St. John's Telegram*.

JOE BEWS is a third-generation rancher and farmer who lives in Longview, Alberta.

PAUL BROWN is a professor of public administration at Dalhousie University in Halifax.

ELIZABETH BRUBAKER is the executive director of Environment Probe, a division of Energy Probe in Toronto.

MURRAY COOLICAN is a former vice president of Corporate Communications Ltd. in Halifax and of public affairs at Nova Scotia Power Inc. He was also chairperson of the Halifax Metro United Way and is a former president of the Metropolitan Halifax Chamber of Commerce. He is currently the senior vice president of corporate resources at Maritime Life.

PARZIVAL COPES is professor emeritus at Simon Fraser University in Vancouver. He was the author of *St. John's and Newfoundland — An Economic Survey*, published in 1961.

DEANE CRABBE is the owner of H. J. Crabbe and Sons Mill, the sixth largest sawmill in New Brunswick; 1996 marked the company's 50th year in business.

BRIAN CROWLEY has been president of the Atlantic Provinces Council and a Dalhousie University professor of political science and economics, and is the author of *The Road to Equity*. He is also the founding president of the Atlantic Institute for Market Studies and was on the editorial board of *The Globe and Mail* for two years.

JOHN DUVENAUD operates an information brokerage and management business in Winnipeg. He is an agriculture market analyst and the publisher of *Wild Oats Grain Market Advisory*.

DAVID FRAME was the spokesman for the Council of Ontario Construction Associations in Toronto, Ontario, from 1987 to 1998. He is currently the director of the prevention branch at the Workplace Safety and Insurance Board.

CLAY GILSON, a former member of the U.S.–Canada Joint Commission on Grains, is professor emeritus of agricultural economics at the University of Manitoba.

Wilf Gobert, an oil industry investment analyst, is managing director of research for Peters & Co. Ltd. in Calgary.

Jay Gordon has worked as an investment analyst specializing in the steel industry and was once the president of J. M. Gordon and Associates in Toronto. He is now retired.

John Eldon Green spent 10 years as deputy minister of social services for the Prince Edward Island government and worked on economic development for the island. For the past 20 years he has been a management consultant in Charlottetown. He recently worked on the seminal study which led to the amalgamation of Greater Charlottetown and the Summerside area in P.E.I.

Robert Greenwood is a former director of the Economic Recovery Commission in St. John's, Newfoundland, and adjunct professor with the Faculty of Business Administration at Memorial University. He is currently the vice president of corporate development for the Information Services Corporation of Saskatchewan, a Crown corporation responsible for the on-line administration of land titles and survey legislation.

Jim Harriman was the owner of Palliser Grain at the time of his interview. He is now a mortgage broker in Calgary.

Ralph Hedlin is a veteran journalist and commentator. He is quoted extensively in Peter C. Newman's *Canadian Revolution*, especially in regard to Western discontent in Canada.

Ralph Hindson is a former director general of the materials branch of the federal Department of Industry, Trade and Commerce. He is the author of *The Sydney Steel-Making Study*, released on October 2, 1967. In 1975 he was named the principal advisor on coal, iron, steel and related matters to Nova Scotia premier Gerald Regan.

John Hodge was the senior vice president of Montreal Shipping Inc. in Vancouver, British Columbia at the time of his interview. He has since passed away.

ALLAN JOHNSTON is a grain broker and farmer in Welwyn, Saskatchewan.

GRAHAM KEDGLEY is the president of his own consulting firm, KITAC Enterprises Ltd, in Vancouver, which specializes in international marketing, transportation, intergovernmental relations and finance. In 1970 he was director of marketing and later president of Neptune Bulk Terminals. In the early 1970s he was involved in the Grain Train, a successful bulk-grain transportation experiment to move grain more quickly and efficiently to port.

BRUCE LEGGE, a retired major-general who spent 14 years working with disabled soldiers, was the chairman of the Workers' Compensation Board of Ontario from 1965 to 1973. He now practises law in Toronto.

KEITH LEWIS is a farmer from Wawota, Saskatchewan, who sits on the board of governors of the Winnipeg Commodity Exchange. He is a former president of the Saskatchewan Canola Growers Association.

LES LIVERSIDGE is a management consultant in Toronto who helps guide businesses through the maze of regulations associated with workers' compensation. He is a member of the Employers' Council on Workers' Compensation.

TOM LIVINGSTON is a cattle farmer who lives on his ranch, Three Walking Sticks, on the banks of the Red Deer River near Duchess, Alberta.

MICHAEL MACDONALD, a former vice president of the Atlantic Canada Opportunities Agency (ACOA), was in charge of the G7 summit in Halifax in 1995. He headed Aird Associates, a consulting firm in Halifax specializing in trade and economic development, investment recruitment and public-private partnerships, from 1991 to 1995. In 1995 he founded the Greater Halifax Partnership, where he was president and CEO until 2001. He is currently writing a book about the creation of Canada's "Smart City."

TOM MCMILLAN, from Prince Edward Island, became an MP in 1979 and served as minister of tourism in 1984 and minister of the environment from 1985 to 1988. He was teaching in Boston at the time of interview.

ROBERT NIELSEN, a native of New Brunswick, worked for *The Toronto Star* for 33 years, including a period as acting editor-in-chief. He now lives near Perth-Andover, New Brunswick.

HARRY O'CONNELL worked in government in Prince Edward Island from the late 1970s to 1985. He was the deputy minister for the Department of Community Affairs, whose mandate was the revitalization of more than 30 communities on the island. He now owns his own computer retailing company.

RON OLSON, currently a financial consultant, was the vice president of Citibank Canada in the late 1980s.

JIM PALLISTER's family has been farming in Portage La Prairie, Manitoba, since 1898. A wheat farmer with 4,400 acres, he also grows lentils, navy beans and peas. He is a spokesman for Farmers for Justice, a group battling the Canadian Wheat Board.

ARNIE PATTERSON, a former press secretary to Pierre Trudeau, is a broadcaster and journalist living in Halifax. He has written a number of articles relating to the ongoing situation in Sydney, Nova Scotia.

GERARD PROTTI has held several senior posts with the Alberta Energy and Treasury departments and has worked for the Canadian Energy Research Institute and Ontario Hydro. He is currently the senior vice president of Pan-Canadian Petroleum, in charge of new ventures.

FRED RANDLE is a farmer and rancher in High River, Alberta.

LARRY SOLOMON is the co-founder of Energy Probe Research Foundation in Toronto, an environmental and public policy research institute. He is also an author of numerous books on public utilities, regulation and public-private partnerships. He served as editor-in-chief of *The Next City* magazine before it became a column in the *National Post*. He now writes for the column every second Tuesday.

ROD STAMLER, former head of the white collar crime unit of the RCMP, is a forensic accountant and a specialist on the underground economy. He resigned as assistant commissioner of the RCMP in 1989. He has also written a book, *Above the Law*, about the effectiveness of the Canadian police force in combating corruption.

WILLIAM TERON formerly served as chairman and president of the Canada Mortgage and Housing Corporation, and headed a task force on the practice of a best-buy policy using public funds. He is now chairman of Teron International.

RON WHYNACHT is vice president and general manager of the National Sea Products processing plant in Lunenburg, Nova Scotia.

STAN WILSON was a cattle farmer who lived south of Chain Lakes in Alberta. He passed away in March, 2001.

MOIRA WRIGHT was head of the Saskatchewan Taxpayers Association at the time of her interview. She now lives in Toronto.

INDEX